Circling the Drain

TRUMP'S ASSAULT ON AMERICA

WILLIAM BOARDMAN

YORKLAND PUBLISHING

Y<small>P</small>

Y P
Yorkland Publishing

Published by
Yorkland Publishing
12 Tepee Court
Toronto, Ontario M2J 3A9
Canada
www.yorklandpublishing.com

ISBN 978-1-7390044-6-0

Edited by Ed Shiller
Book Design by Rosemary Shiller
Cover Photo: David Gee/Alamy

Printed and bound by IngramSpark

For my children, Diantha, Ben, and Michael,
and my grandchildren,
Samantha, Nicholas, Walker, and Carter,
and for all those struggling to keep America
from going down the drain of history.

Contents

Foreword

On the End of American Democracy

Senator Claude Malhuret, a physician and lawyer, speaking in the French Senate, Tuesday, March 4, 2025:

> Europe is at a critical turning point in its history. The American shield is crumbling, Ukraine risks being abandoned, Russia strengthened. Washington has become the court of Nero, a fiery emperor, submissive courtiers, and a ketamine-fueled jester in charge of purging the civil service.
>
> This is a tragedy for the free world, but it is first and foremost a tragedy for the United States. Trump's message is that there is no point in being his ally since he will not defend you, he will impose more customs and duties on you than on his enemies, and he will threaten to seize your territories while supporting the dictatorships that invade you….
>
> Never in history has a President of the United States capitulated to the enemy. Never has anyone supported an aggressor against an ally. Never has anyone trampled on the American Constitution, issued so many illegal decrees, dismissed judges who could have prevented him from doing so, dismissed the military general staff in one fell swoop, weakened all checks and

and balances, and taken control of social media. This is the beginning of the confiscation of democracy....

The United States voted at the UN with Russia and North Korea against the Europeans demanding the withdrawal of Russian troops. Two days later, in the Oval Office, the military service shirker was giving war hero Zelensky lessons in morality and strategy before dismissing him like a groom, ordering him to submit or resign. Tonight, he took another step into infamy by stopping the delivery of weapons that had been promised.

What to do in the face of this betrayal? The answer is simple: face it.... Is this the end of the Atlantic Alliance? The risk is great. But in the last few days, the public humiliation of Zelensky and all the crazy decisions taken in the last month have finally made the Americans react.... The Trumpists are no longer in their majesty. They control the executive, the Congress, the Supreme Court, and social networks. But in American history, the freedom fighters have always prevailed. They are beginning to raise their heads.

Introduction

'I Was Saved by God to Make America Great Again.'

— Donald Trump, March 4, 2025

We're well into 2025, with Trump's MAGA brigades flooding the landscape. This is not a flash flood; it is a deliberate deluge. The water is still rising. America, as we once knew it, may be circling the drain. This is a uniquely challenging moment in American history. How long will it – can it – last?

Our constitutional crisis began on day one, January 20, 2025, when Trump asserted that he had the authority to rewrite the Constitution by executive order. This crisis has been expanding ever since in more ways than are easily tracked. As of mid-2025, all three branches of government were controlled by radicals planning a totalitarian America. We have a president who acts like a dictator, a Congress that chooses limp subservience to the president, and a highly suspect Supreme Court whose loyalty to the Constitution is being tested. Only our lower courts have defended the Constitution and the rule of law as best they can. The Democratic Party has been effectively AWOL from any resistance. All across the country, millions of Americans have protested in large numbers, but with little impact. The America we knew in 2024, already battered by decades of prioritizing the desires of the rich, is gone. Now, even that imperfect America is being dismantled, with the apparent goal of turning the U.S. into an authoritarian state in which the rich minority thrives and the majority struggles to survive, not that different from now, but much worse.

Is American Exceptionalism Still Relevant?

We know America may be circling the drain. When the crisis is over, there will still be a country here, but what will that country look like? The possible police state outcome is all too obvious, but it's not a foregone conclusion. Nothing is. We also have the opportunity to restructure America, to conform more closely to its traditional values than ever before, to turn American exceptionalism into something closer to reality. Will we manage to seize this opportunity to make a better America?

The essence of American exceptionalism is enshrined in the Declaration of Independence of 1776: "We hold these truths to be self-evident, that all men are created equal, that they are endowed by their Creator with certain unalienable Rights, that among these are Life, Liberty and the pursuit of Happiness...."

In the midst of the eighteenth-century Enlightenment, we professed to believe that "all men are created equal" – but we weren't going to give up our slaves, or give women rights, and as for Native Americans, what about them?

For more than 200 years, American exceptionalism has been our guide and our excuse. For practical purposes, exceptionalism has been our secular religion. We ritualized our public belief, despite ample evidence to the contrary, that America was a chosen nation, a blessed nation, a nation with a mission to bring liberty and democracy to the world. That was our faith, regardless of our actual behavior. And America has made some progress, such as freeing slaves, promising equal rights to women, and absorbing immigrants from all over the world. During and after World War II, Americans had good reason to be proud of the United States, as it rebuilt much of a shattered world. American exceptionalism seemed to be a real possibility, at least for a while.

MAGA Rejects American Ideals

MAGA – "Make America Great Again" – is the brand for a new, alternative America. But it's only a brand. Trump trademarked MAGA in 2012 and has been promoting it ever since. Shortly before the 2024 election, he told a crowd at Madison Square Garden with characteristic grandiosity:

> We've created the greatest movement in the history, probably of mankind, but certainly within the United States. MAGA – Make America Great Again. There's never been anything like it.… It's the greatest political movement in the history of our country.…

MAGA – "Make America Great Again" – is a slogan, with little history and less meaning. MAGA looks backward without seeing anything. MAGA assumes a "great" past that it can't identify because it never existed. The phrase first entered American politics with Ronald Reagan in 1980, when he campaigned on "Let's make America great again" while at the same time campaigning against government as the enemy. Once in office, he expanded the American government's cruelty, which became a bipartisan effort, destroying the middle-class aspirations of millions of people. Those people are rightly angry now, and the message of MAGA resonates with them. MAGA succeeds in part because it speaks to people's real pain. MAGA draws energy from the bitterness created by the unfulfilled promises of American exceptionalism, even if MAGA believers fail to recognize who's responsible for their suffering.

MAGA is an ad campaign with resonance but no substance. What does MAGA actually mean? It has no definition. It has no context. MAGA is a political Rorschach blot that means whatever the MAGA consumer wants it to mean. MAGA has no articulated meaning. MAGA is an illusion with no historical precedent. For more than four decades, MAGA had been a slowly growing cancer. Now it has metastasized throughout the body politic, and we're frantically searching for a cure, or at the very least, a treatment.

What Does Trump Know, and When Does He Know It?

In March 2025, at Trump's request, the National Archives delivered a copy of the Declaration of Independence for display in the Oval Office.

In an interview with ABC News on April 29, Trump was asked what the Declaration of Independence meant to him. His answer, in its entirety, was: "Well, it means exactly what it says, it's a declaration, a declaration of unity and love and respect, and it means a lot. And it's something very special to our country."

That's all he had to say. MAGA emptiness. There's no record of his ever saying more about our founding document. The interviewer moved on. The clip went viral, receiving special mockery from The Daily Show. If Trump were to read the Declaration of Independence carefully, he might see that it consists mostly of a list of illegal actions taken by the King of England. Many of those actions are the same offenses Trump is currently committing against the United States.

The Fifth Amendment of the Constitution provides that no person shall "be deprived of life, liberty, or property, without due process of law." Trump has given lip service to legal behavior, saying, "We always have to obey the laws." In a May 5 interview on NBC News, when asked about his obligation to follow the Fifth Amendment's requirement for due process for all persons, including immigrants, he hedged:

> I don't know. It seems – it might say that, but if you're talking about that, then we'd have to have a million or 2 million or 3 million trials. We have thousands of people that are – some murderers and some drug dealers and some of the worst people on Earth…. I was elected to get them the hell out of here, and the courts are holding me from doing it….

Asked if he wasn't obliged to uphold the Constitution as president, Trump hedged again: "I don't know. I have to respond by saying, again, I have brilliant lawyers that work for me, and they are going to obviously follow what the Supreme Court said."

Trump is lying about the number of trials; they're not needed. All that's needed is a hearing. But he won't even grant immigrants that much due process. He also lies about the number of criminal immigrants, a lie he's been telling for years. Hardly one in ten immigrants rounded up this year has a serious criminal record. And he's lying about his lawyers following the Supreme Court. Even as he spoke, his administration was defying at least one Supreme Court order in the Abrego Garcia case. The administration was also evading, if not defying, multiple lower court orders. For Trump, the Constitution is optional.

How Much Is Trump's Mental State 'Sanewashed'?

Mary L. Trump is a clinical psychologist and Donald Trump's niece. She has known him for most of her life. In 2020, she published *Too Much and Never Enough: How My Family Created the World's Most Dangerous Man*, which sold over a million copies on the day of its release. On May 13, 2025, Mary Trump published her current assessment of her uncle on Substack:

> Donald has always been easily swayed by whomever or whatever is in front of him, but lately his decline has become even more obvious—whether it's due to some kind of neurological condition or the worsening of his long, undiagnosed and untreated psychiatric disorders or a combination of the two, I don't know. Sometimes it isn't clear if he's oriented as to space, time, and people, and this has been particularly in evidence during some recent press conferences and interviews....

It should be obvious to any objective observer that Donald is losing his cognitive capacities with age. Contributing to the decline, in addition to those untreated psychiatric disorders, are the enormous amounts of stress he continues to be under. He's also well aware of what may be coming for him because his father, Fred, had Alzheimer's.

This might seem like good news for all of us Trumpophobes, but it's not. It suggests two unacceptable scenarios. In one, Trump dodders into dementia but remains in the presidency. In the other, Trump dodders into dementia to the point that Republicans can't ignore it; so, they invoke the Twenty-Fifth Amendment to remove him from office and replace him with J. D. Vance, someone more focused, vicious, and cruel.

MAGA has a tight grip on America as we spiral into the whirlpool, struggling not to drown. But we haven't gone down the drain yet.

Circling The Drain — An Effort to Stay Afloat

It's still a long way to the mid-term elections of 2026, the first real opportunity to check the MAGA onslaught. Democrats can reclaim one or both Houses of Congress. Not that having generally spineless Democrats in charge will be any panacea, but it would at least be a check on the carnage. We need more serious people in Congress who are willing to push back against MAGA with more than failed centrist clichés. For that to happen, what happens from now on is crucial.

Circling the Drain is my attempt to support the search for fundamental change in a flawed state, one so broken it could elect someone like Trump.

During the late days of June 2025, as this manuscript approached the production stage, flood waters kept rising, as they likely will for the foreseeable future. Trump is testing and challenging the will and stamina of the American people.

At the June 24-25 summit, NATO allies made a concerted effort to flatter and praise Trump, and the meeting remained calm. Bowing to Trump's wishes, our NATO allies agreed to increase their military spending to 5% of GDP by 2035, when Trump will presumably be out of office. A third of that spending would be allowed to be non-military. This allowed Trump to claim victory without actually winning anything. But it did little to strengthen the U.S. commitment to NATO.

At the end of the summit, NATO General Secretary Mark Rutte reached a peak fawning moment when he said, referring to a Trump outburst about Israel and Iran: "And then Daddy has to sometimes use strong language." The moment exploded on social media. Rutte tried to walk it back, without success. The Trump White House posted a video announcing: "America's back. Daddy's home." And within a day, Trump interests were selling "Daddy" and "Daddy's Home" T-shirts for $27 each.

On June 24, Zohran Mamdani declared victory with 43% of the ranked-choice vote in the multi-candidate Democratic Party primary for Mayor of New York City (his final total was 56%). Mamdani is a 33-year-old Muslim and self-declared Democratic Socialist who campaigned to make New York affordable for all its residents. He was opposed by Andrew Cuomo, the former New York Governor who resigned amidst multiple sexual abuse scandals, but was supported by establishment Democrats, including Bill Clinton, Jim Clyburn, and Mike Bloomberg. After the primary, establishment

Democrats rejected Mamdani and shifted their support to the current, corrupt mayor Eric Adams, amidst racist attacks on Mamdani.

In the Senate, Republicans managed to pass their 900-plus-page, so-called "One Big Beautiful Bill Act" by one vote (cast by the vice president to break a 50-50 tie). It passed the House by two votes. The bill is an almost unmitigated attack on most Americans. It amounts to a legislative coup d'etat. Among the bill's features are a multi-trillion-dollar tax cut for the rich, a much smaller tax reduction (more than offset by cuts in government services and benefits) for lower-income people, and an estimated $4 trillion increase to the national debt.

The bill would deprive some 16 million people of Medicaid, significantly reduce Medicare, cut food payments for poor families, and eliminate tax credits for electric vehicles and other "green" energy initiatives. The bill cuts funding for rural hospitals, nursing homes, and schools. It sells off millions of acres of public lands and raises the budget debt ceiling to make room for the tax cuts for billionaires. No one knows what the bill's overall impact will be, but only liars and oligarchs pretend it will be good for the rest of America.

Perhaps the worst outcome of the big brutal bill is that a democracy (by a margin of only three votes) has chosen to finance its own fascist police state. The current annual budget for ICE is $8 billion, enough to fund the current level of ICE raid terror across the country. This bill explodes spending for ICE raids and detention centers to $175 billion over five years. The estimated annual ICE budget of $28 billion is more than most nations' militaries (almost as large as Canada's military budget). The $28 billion annual budget is more than the combined budgets of the FBI, DEA, BATF, and U.S. Marshall Service combined. How many cruel and dehumanizing concentration camps will that buy? And how many innocent migrant citizens and non-citizens will be arrested to fill them? How much more will this racist policy tear the country apart? Trump signed the brutal bill into law on July 4. Happy Fascist Police State Day.

Just Because It's Unconstitutional, You Can't Rule Against It

On June 28, the Supreme Court dealt another blow to the rule of law with its blatantly hypocritical and dishonest ruling in *Trump v. CASA* (No. 24A884), which drastically restricted the ability of lower federal courts to issue national injunctions. The case revolves around Trump's unilateral attempt to rewrite the Constitution to abolish birthright citizenship, despite the clear language of the Fourteenth Amendment: "All persons born or naturalized in the United States, and subject to the jurisdiction thereof, are citizens of the United States and of the State wherein they reside." According to Trump, this is no longer accurate based solely on his authority, though the Constitution states otherwise. The Supreme Court ignored this fundamental issue. Cowardly, they voted 6-3 to restrict the use of national injunctions to prevent this constitutional overreach. The court left clearly unconstitutional presidential actions to be addressed another day. Maybe.

Justice Sonia Sotomayor wrote a long, stinging dissent, joined by Justices Elena Kagan and Ketanji Brown Jackson. Sotomayor wrote, in part:

> Children born in the United States and subject to its laws are United States citizens. That has been the legal rule since the founding, and it was the English rule well before then. This Court once attempted to repudiate it, holding in *Dred Scott v. Sandford* (1857), that the children of enslaved black Americans were not citizens. To remedy that grievous error, the States passed in 1866 and Congress ratified in 1868 the Fourteenth Amendment's Citizenship Clause, which enshrined birthright citizenship in the Constitution. There it has remained, accepted and respected by Congress, by the Executive, and by this Court. Until today.
>
> It is now the President who attempts, in an Executive Order, to repudiate birthright citizenship. Every court to evaluate the Order has deemed it patently unconstitutional and, for that reason, has enjoined the Federal Government from enforcing it. Undeterred, the Government now asks this Court to grant emergency relief, insisting it will suffer irreparable harm unless it can deprive at least some children born in the United States of citizenship....
>
> The rule of law is not a given in this Nation, nor any other.

It is a precept of our democracy that will endure only if those brave enough in every branch fight for its survival. Today, the Court abdicates its vital role in that effort. With the stroke of a pen, the President has made a "solemn mockery" of our Constitution. Rather than stand firm, the Court gives way. Because such complicity should know no place in our system of law, I dissent.

Justice Jackson wrote in her concurring dissent: "The Court's decision to permit the Executive to violate the Constitution with respect to anyone who has not yet sued is an existential threat to the rule of law."

Epstein Threatens Trump from Beyond the Grave

On July 16, Trump posted defensively on Truth Social, attacking his own MAGA followers:

Scams and Hoaxes are all the Democrats are good at.... Their new SCAM is what we will forever call the Jeffrey Epstein Hoax, and my PAST supporters have bought into this "bullshit," hook, line, and sinker. They haven't learned their lesson, and probably never will.... I don't want their support anymore! Thank you for your attention to this matter. MAKE AMERICA GREAT AGAIN!

Jeffrey Epstein, the convicted pedophile and longtime Trump chum, was found dead in his cell in 2019. He came back to life as an issue in 2025, driven by MAGA demands for release of the evidence of customers for his sex trafficking of minors. Attorney General Bondi said she had the "list" on her desk. Months later, she denied there was any list. Or any other relevant evidence. MAGA voices raised in protest. The Wall Street Journal published a slimy letter purporting to be from Trump on Epstein's 50th birthday. Trump sued the Wall Street Journal. Where this ends, nobody knows.

There's a feel about it akin to Shakespeare's Macbeth, when a banquet for his courtiers is interrupted by the appearance of Banquo's ghost. Macbeth has had Banquo murdered. No one else in the room can see the ghost. But Macbeth knows he is guilty and that the secret of his guilt is insecure. Trump's response to the ghost of Epstein raised by MAGA echoes Macbeth's denial in the face of Banquo's ghost:

> Avaunt, and quit my sight! Let the earth hide thee.
> Thy bones are marrowless; thy blood is cold;
> Thou hast no speculation in those eyes
> Which thou dost glare with.

Checklist of Disasters

Since January 20, 2025, Trump has unleashed wave after wave of lawlessness, cruelty, and greed on a scale designed to overwhelm the population and destroy our system of constitutional checks and balances. While admittedly incomplete, the following list conveys the scale of our shared catastrophe:

- **Flooding the zone:** Overwhelming the population, the opposition, the media, and the courts with hundreds of executive orders and other actions that were mostly illegal, more than any person or system could effectively cope with. In his first 100 days, Trump signed only five pieces of legislation. The rest was deliberate executive turmoil. As of July, Just Security's "Litigation Tracker: Legal Challenges to Trump Administration Actions" was following 330 federal cases challenging Trump.

- **Illegally creating the Department of Government Efficiency** (DOGE) and allowing Elon Musk, an unelected bureaucrat, to run it. On May 27, federal judge Tanya Chutkan ruled that a lawsuit brought by 14 states challenging the legality of actions by Musk and DOGE may proceed. She dismissed Trump as a defendant. Previously, the judge had denied a restraining order after the lawsuit was filed in February.

- **Looting government data for private gain.** In an unprecedented assault on personal privacy and government information security, Elon Musk has used DOGE to access private citizen data and official government data from numerous agencies, including, at a minimum:

Department of the Treasury (USDT)
Internal Revenue Service (IRS)
Veterans Administration (VA)
Social Security Administration (SSA)
Department of Education (DoEd)
Energy Information Administration (EIA)
Department of Housing and Urban Development (HUD)
Department of Homeland Security (DHS)
United States Agency for International Development (USAID)
Department of Agriculture (USDA)
Department of Health and Human Services (HHS)

■ **Illegally firing thousands of government workers** selected by DOGE and the Office of Management and Budget (OMB) for no articulated reason and with no plan, thus undermining government functions at dozens of agencies, which sometimes needed to hire workers back. In a May 8 press release, Public Citizen, an advocacy group, reported that Elon Musk has a business interest in more than 70% of the agencies affected by DOGE cuts. These agencies include:

Consumer Financial Protection Bureau (CFPB)
Department of Agriculture (USDA
Department of Commerce (DOC)
Department of Defense (DoD)
Department of Energy (DOE)
Department of Health and Human Services (HHS)
Department of Homeland Security (DHS)
Department of the Interior (DOI)
Department of Justice (DOJ)
Department of State (DOS)
Department of Transportation (DOT)
Department of the Treasury (USDT)
Department of Veterans Affairs (VA)
Environmental Protection Agency (EPA)
Equal Opportunity Employment Commission (EOEC)

    Federal Communications Commission (FCC)
    Federal Trade Commission (FTC)
    Food and Drug Administration (FDA)
    General Services Administration (GSA)
    National Aeronautics and Space Administration (NASA)
    National Labor Relations Board (NLRB)
    National Science Foundation (NSF)
    Securities and Exchange Commission (SEC)

DOGE workforce reductions have negatively impacted public services, among them: disaster response, veterans' healthcare, environmental protection, public health initiatives, and park services. Federal judges have temporarily blocked some of these cuts while legal cases progress in the courts. On May 22, Judge Susan Illston of the District Court for the Northern District of California issued a restraining order that froze most federal workforce reductions, ruling that Trump likely acted outside his legal and constitutional authority. The judge stated that the president required Congressional authorization for any large-scale reorganization of federal agencies. (For additional details about DOGE's activities, go to en.wikipedia.org and search "US federal agencies targeted by DOGE.")

■ **Appointing cabinet members who oppose the legal responsibilities of their agencies.** Education Secretary Linda McMahon aims to dismantle the agency, while Attorney General Pam Bondi and FBI Director Kash Patel are seen as weaponizing their respective agencies. Health and Human Services Secretary Robert Kennedy Jr. is on record as opposed to basic science. Director of the Internal Revenue Service Billy Long, who, as a congressman, sponsored legislation to abolish the IRS.

■ **Endangering the environmental health of all Americans** by appointing attorney Lee Zeldin head of the Environmental Protection Agency (EPA), a post for which he had little qualification and significant hostility to its mission. He has attempted to cut the budget by 65%, fire more than a thousand scientists, and dissolve the EPA's Office of Research and Development. In March, the EPA relaxed standards on coal- and oil-burning power plants. In May, the EPA relaxed standards on toxic forever chemicals in drinking water nationwide.

■ **Illegally impounding funds allocated by Congress.** This unlawful action has led to numerous lawsuits and restraining orders. It has also left agencies understaffed and, in some cases, unable to function efficiently. The Constitution grants Congress the power of the purse. The 1974 Impoundment Control Act prohibits presidents from withholding enacted funding. In 1975, a unanimous Supreme Court upheld this provision. Examples of improper impoundments during Trump's administration include:

•**Infrastructure Aid:** The Government Accountability Office (GAO) found that the administration improperly withheld funds intended for state infrastructure.

•**Foreign Assistance Funding:** An executive order froze all foreign assistance funding for 90 days and mandated a review of U.S. development work abroad. This effectively shut down USAID, leading to tens of thousands of deaths worldwide.

•**Inflation Reduction Act and Infrastructure Investment and Jobs Act Funding:** Another executive order paused the release of funding from these two acts.

•Sanctuary City Funding: An executive order froze federal funding for sanctuary cities.

•Federal Grants, Loans, and Other Financial Assistance: A memo from the Office of Management and Budget (OMB) instructed executive branch agencies to pause grant, loan, and other financial assistance programs.

•**Specific Programs and Initiatives:** Funding cuts or pauses have been reported for various programs, among them:

Teacher-preparation grants.

Mental health services in schools.

Pandemic relief funds.

Climate change research.

Education programs.

Infrastructure.

> FEMA preparedness.
> Substance use disorders.
> Environmental protection.
> Refugee assistance.
> Housing enforcement.
> Heating assistance.
> Community services.
> Rental assistance.
> Workforce programs.

While some of Trump's actions have been blocked by federal judges, compliance with these rulings has varied.

- Enforcing censorship across the government by preventing agencies from considering such public policy issues as climate change, gender, race, and diversity, equity, and inclusion.
- **Denying climate science.** In addition to banning the mention of climate change and related words in government communications, the Trump administration cancelled National Science Foundation grants for more than 100 climate studies, whether already approved or in progress. This is a crime against future generations.
- **Banning books** in Pentagon schools and other government libraries, public school libraries, public libraries, and wherever MAGA individuals deem a book "woke."
  The Department of Education's Office of Civil Rights dismissed all of its pending cases opposing book banning. The Department of Defense implemented bans on books throughout its library system, including a picture book about the late Supreme Court Justice Ruth Bader Ginsburg.
- **Erasing the entire public report library** of the U.S. Trade and Development Agency on January 31, with no public notice. The public affairs director called it "an abundance of caution" to avoid problems from mentioning Trump-banned subjects such as women, race, climate,

gender identity, civil rights, etc. According to the website
Just Security, more than 8,000 government websites
and datasets have been scrubbed for the sake of the new
political correctness. According to Dissent in Bloom, the
FDA removed drug safety reports, the CDC removed over
3,000 pages of health data, and the Census Bureau deleted
thousands of research pages.

- **Attempting to take over the Library of Congress**,
  the largest library in the world, which is not part of the
  executive branch. For the first time in history, Trump fired
  the head of the Library of Congress, as well as the head of
  the U.S. Copyright Office, a separate department of the
  library. Library officials locked the intruders out, and even
  some Republicans in Congress expressed their objections. As
  of July 2025, the issue was unresolved.

- **Attacking civil rights for minorities** by upending the
  traditional purpose of the Equal Employment Opportunity
  Commission (EEOC). The EEOC removed safeguards
  against discrimination based on sexual orientation and
  gender identity (defying the Supreme Court ruling Bostock
  v. Clayton County). The EEOC sent letters to more than
  20 big law firms, warning them against continuing DEI
  programs and stating that white males are a "protected
  class" against whom discrimination is illegal.

- **Banning the teaching of critical race theory**, thereby
  denying the history of slavery and racism in America.
  Trump sought to ban its teaching in K-12 education, where
  it's not currently taught.

- **Honoring Confederate traitors** by restoring their
  names on U.S. military bases and restoring Confederate
  monuments.

- **Intimidating news media** by using lawsuits, regulations,
  and public attacks to coerce them into providing passive
  news coverage or worse. Trump has successfully pressured

outlets such as The Washington Post and The Los Angeles Times, both of which are owned by billionaires. ABC News settled a potentially winnable lawsuit, giving Trump $15 million. Paramount's Shari Redstone protected a planned merger requiring Trump's approval by settling a lawsuit against Paramount-owned CBS News over the editing of a news story, giving Trump $16 million. Additionally, Trump has attempted to defund PBS and NPR and has restricted Associated Press reporters from accessing White House news facilities, while exerting control over who can be part of the White House press pool. The Pentagon press office barred ABC News, CNN, The Washington Post, and The New York Times.

- **Intimidating law firms.** According to the Cato Institute, Trump has issued executive orders that threaten specific law firms in violation of the Constitution. He primarily targeted firms involved in prosecuting crimes for which he had been indicted. As a result, nine firms quickly agreed to deals with the White House, committing to provide a billion dollars in free services. Other firms chose to fight back in court. Currently, more than 180 court cases are ongoing, but the resistance is growing. The law firms that complied with Trump's demands have lost both attorneys and clients. However, the prevailing climate of fear has made law firms hesitate to engage in pro bono work for causes opposed by Trump. Four law firms that challenged Trump in court have successfully obtained restraining orders.
- **Intimidating universities.** Trump withdrew government funding from various universities. Columbia University caved, while Harvard was the first to challenge Trump by taking him to court. As a result, Trump cancelled over $2.2 billion in Harvard funding. Although Harvard won a restraining order, the case continues to unfold. [See a more detailed account of Harvard's response to Trump's attacks

on page 233.]

• **Attacking programs on diversity, equity, and inclusion (DEI).** The Trump administration banned more than a hundred words from government use, including "women." His policies promote traditional American bigotries against women, Black individuals, LGBTQ+ people, ethnic minorities, and immigrants, essentially targeting everyone but white men. This makes bigotry official policy.

• **Illegally detaining and deporting documented and undocumented immigrants** – sometimes even citizens – by heavily-armed, masked agents without warrants, identification, or due process. Trump has lied for years about deporting "the worst of the worst." In his first five months, there was little evidence to support this claim. Almost all of the individuals deported had no criminal record other than immigration violations. Trump carried out most deportations unlawfully, with no due process of law. Courts issued orders to block these actions, but he often ignored court orders, leading to widespread public resistance across the country. Many Americans oppose the deportation of their peaceful, hard-working neighbors, including children, some of whom are citizens, and some suffering serious illnesses, such as cancer. [See detailed account of the Abrego Garcia case on page 258.]

• **Eroding women's reproductive rights.** Within hours of taking office, the Trump administration began removing information on reproductive health and rights from government websites. Trump effectively ceased enforcing the 1994 Freedom of Access to Clinic Entrances (FACE) Act, which protects healthcare providers and patients from violence. He pardoned 23 people convicted of violations of the FACE Act, including violent offenders. Additionally, Trump has refused to enforce the federal laws that require hospitals to provide stabilizing treatment to all patients in emergencies, including life-saving abortion care.

- **Discrimination against the LGBTQ+ community**
and other vulnerable groups by illegally denying their
constitutional right to equal protection under the law.
Trump's administration has issued three executive orders
(14151, 14168, and 14173) that deny the existence of
transgender people and eliminate grants for the LGBTQ+
community. On February 20, Lambda Legal filed a lawsuit,
San Francisco AIDS Foundation v. Trump, challenging
these executive actions, which marked their fourth lawsuit
against Trump. On June 9, the federal court issued a
preliminary injunction blocking all three executive orders.

- **Pardons for criminal supporters and others.** On his
first day in office, Trump pardoned approximately 1,500
convicted criminals, rioters who stormed the Capitol on
January 6, 2021, in their attempt to overturn the 2020
presidential election. This was an insurrection. Trump
enabled it, then was slow to counter it. About 650 of those
pardoned had been convicted of violence against Capitol
police. Despite calls from the public, Republicans in
Congress have refused to honor the Capitol police with a
plaque in the Capitol. The pardons erased nearly $3 million
in restitution owed by those convicts, whose actions resulted
in approximately $2.7 billion in damages to the Capitol.
While these pardons are legally permissible, they are widely
viewed as unconscionable. For example, Idaho resident
Pamela Hemphill, 72, served two months in jail for her
involvement at the Capitol, and subsequently rejected her
pardon, calling it "a slap in the face to the Capitol police
officers and to our rule of law." Some of Trump's pardons
may also appear illegal, as they give the impression of being
granted in exchange for bribes, such as Paul Walczak, who
received a pardon after his mother donated $1 million to a
Trump fundraiser. What a coincidence!

- **Illegally imposing tariffs** on almost every country in an erratic and unpredictable manner that disrupted global trade. This pattern continued throughout the first six months of the Trump administration. By one count, Trump has issued over 50 changes in tariffs. The Constitution grants tariff powers to Congress, which has shown little interest in exercising its Constitutional authority. On May 28, the U.S. Court of International Trade froze most of the tariffs imposed by Trump on April 2, on almost every country in the world (except Russia, Belarus, and North Korea). The court ruled that Trump had illegally declared an "emergency" under the 1977 International Emergency Powers Act. Federal Judge Rudolph Contreras in Washington, D.C., also ruled that Trump's tariffs were illegal but stayed his order. On May 29, the U.S. Court of Appeals in Washington, D.C., issued a stay on the decision by the Court of International Trade.
- **Attacking the sovereignty of Canada.** Trump's efforts to make Canada the 51st state of the U.S. are borderline illegal under international law. He has refused to unequivocally rule out the use of force against Canada, which clearly violates international law. His actions have aggravated one of America's oldest and closest allies, further exacerbated by the thuggish behavior of U.S. border officials along the Canadian border, harming the tourism industry as a result.
- **Attacking the sovereignty of Panama.** Trump's demands for control over the Panama Canal constitute illegal interference in its sovereignty. Secretary of State Marco Rubio reinforced this interference when he visited Panama in February and demanded that Panama run the canal the way the U.S. wanted, alleging Chinese interference. Panama's president, Jose Raul Mulino, responded that, "The sovereignty of Panama is not up for debate."
- **Attacking the sovereignty of NATO ally Denmark** by

seeking to take over Greenland, which is illegal under international law. Greenland is a self-governing territory within the Kingdom of Denmark and a NATO ally of the US. Trump has hinted at using force, another violation of international law as well as the NATO treaty.

• **Undermining the NATO alliance** by siding with Russia against Ukraine. This may not be illegal, but it may not be sane, either. NATO countries have been reliable U.S. allies for decades, even joining the U.S. in its illegal invasion of Afghanistan (the only time NATO's mutual defense article has been invoked). Trump has this thing for Putin that makes no obvious sense. He refuses to hear NATO members' advice about Russia. And he criticizes Germany for not coddling neo-Nazis.

• **Undermining Ukraine.** Trump even claimed that Ukraine started the war that began with a Russian invasion. He betrayed Ukraine by waffling on U.S. support. He betrayed NATO allies by undermining Ukraine. He undermined decades of U.S. foreign policy by promoting the talking points of Putin and other dictators. Trump's campaign promise was to end the war in a day. His efforts over six months have only seen the war grow more bloody and destructive.

• **Violating international law.** By supporting Israel's genocide of Palestinians in Gaza, Trump maintains a longstanding, bipartisan American policy that commits war crimes and crimes against humanity.

Part 1

Bringing Peace to Ukraine – Or How Not to Conduct Foreign Policy

O n February 28, President Trump met with Ukraine's president, Volodymyr Zelensky, in the Oval Office. The stated intention of the meeting was to sign a deal between the two countries, under which the United States would take part in developing Ukraine's rare earth metals, a substantial portion of which are currently in Russian-occupied territory.

Seated in the semi-circle facing the two presidents were members of Trump's cabinet: Vice President Vance, Secretary of State Rubio, Secretary of Defense Hegseth, and Secretary of the Treasury Bessent. Five Ukrainian officials were left to sit or stand outside the circle. The Oval Office was also filled with reporters.

The meeting would last about 50 minutes. What follows is a partial transcript with commentary.

> **TRUMP:** Well, thank you very much. It's an honor to have President Zelensky of Ukraine, and we've been working very hard, very close. So, we've actually known each other for a long time. We've been dealing with each other for a long time and very well.

Trump falsely represents his past dealings with Zelensky.

Trump was president in April 2019 when Zelensky was first elected president of Ukraine, winning 73% of the vote in a run-off election. Trump called to congratulate him. In mid-July, unbeknownst to Zelensky, Trump put a hold on $391 million in U.S. security assistance to Ukraine. The White House withheld details of the hold from Congress for two months.

On July 25, 2019, Trump called Zelensky again, this time to leverage a deal. He wanted Zelensky to gather dirt on former Vice President Biden, his son Hunter Biden, and the energy firm Burisma, which paid Hunter millions to sit on its board. Despite the threat of losing $391 million, Zelensky played it straight, allowing the legal process to proceed in Ukraine. In August, news trickled out that Trump had withheld aid to Ukraine and attempted to use it to extort Zelensky. On September 11, the aid was released. But the affair served as part of the basis for Trump's first impeachment (acquitted in the Senate).

Two and a half years later, on February 24, 2022, Russia invaded Ukraine. In March 2023, then-candidate Trump promised, "Before I even arrive at the Oval Office, I will have the disastrous war between Russia and Ukraine settled. And it will take me no longer than one day."

He did not achieve this. The war entered its fourth year in 2025. Russia has occupied about a fifth of Ukraine. Throughout his 2024 campaign, Trump repeatedly expressed skepticism about continued U.S. support for Ukraine.

In September 2024, Zelensky appeared with Kamala Harris at a campaign event, though he says he's neutral. He later met with Trump. He told the New Yorker magazine at the time, "My feeling is that Trump doesn't really know how to stop the war, even if he might think he knows how. With this war, oftentimes, the deeper you look at it, the less you understand. I've seen many leaders who were convinced they knew how to end it tomorrow, and as they waded deeper into it, they realized it's not that simple."

After meeting with Zelensky, Trump falsely commented: "Every time Zelensky comes to the United States, he walks away with $100 billion. I think he's the greatest salesman on Earth. But we're stuck in that war unless I'm president."

Vance Favors Sacrifices — By Ukraine

Vice President J. D. Vance has questioned aid to Ukraine for years, arguing that Ukraine must give up territory. Zelensky responded:

> His message seems to be that Ukraine must make a sacrifice. This brings us back to the question of the cost and who shoulders it. The idea that the world should end this war at Ukraine's expense is unacceptable. But I do not consider this concept of his a plan, in any formal sense. It would be an awful idea, if a person were actually going to carry it out, to make Ukraine shoulder the costs of stopping the war by giving up its territories. But there's certainly no way this could ever happen. This kind of scenario would have no basis in international norms, in UN statute, or in justice. And it wouldn't necessarily end the war, either. It's just sloganeering.

Ukraine and the United States Are Allies, Right?

In the weeks leading up to the February 28 Oval Office meeting, things got increasingly gnarly.

On January 22, Trump posted on Truth Social, seeming to threaten Putin:

> Settle now, and STOP this ridiculous War! IT'S ONLY GOING TO GET WORSE. If we don't make a "deal," and soon, I have no other choice but to put high levels of Taxes, Tariffs, and Sanctions on anything being sold by Russia to the United States, and various other participating countries.... Let's get this war, which never would have started if I were President, over with! We can do it the easy way, or the hard way - and the easy way is always better. It's time to 'MAKE A DEAL'. NO MORE LIVES SHOULD BE LOST!!!

The next day, Trump told the World Economic Forum that Zelensky "wants to make a deal," but Putin "might not."

Around January 30, Defense Secretary Pete Hegseth halted 11 flights of U.S. arms shipments to Ukraine, apparently unbeknownst to Trump. By February 2, European and Ukrainian officials were querying the pause in shipments. They resumed on February 5. This story broke on May 6. A source familiar with the incident described it as a "misunderstanding of the President's orders" by Hegseth, forcing other administration officials to "cover" for the Pentagon chief and hastily renew the $2.2 million in aid shipments. The debacle cost the U.S. an estimated $1.6 million. The report invites renewed scrutiny of Hegseth, a Trump loyalist who has found himself at the heart of scandals over the use of the messaging app Signal to discuss U.S. military strikes on Houthi rebels in Yemen.

In mid-February, Zelensky wrote that he had begun working with Trump's team, adding: "The world is looking up to America as the power that has the ability to not only stop the war but also help ensure the reliability of peace afterward." At the Munich Security Conference, Trump officials tried to get Zelensky to sign a version of the deal for Ukraine's rare earth minerals. Zelensky refused.

Let's Try Peace Talks With Only One Side, See How That Works

On February 18, the U.S. and Russia held bilateral talks in Saudi Arabia about ending the war in Ukraine. Ukraine was excluded. Trump did not call on Putin to withdraw his troops from Ukraine. The talks produced no progress. Zelensky took offense that they took place "behind Ukraine's back," adding: "Once again, decisions about Ukraine are being made without Ukraine."

Trump said he was "disappointed" in Zelensky's reaction. He told reporters:

> I hear that they're upset about not having a seat. Well, they've had a seat for three years and a long time before that. This could have been settled very easily…. You should have never started it. You could have made a deal. I could have made a deal for Ukraine. That would have given them almost all of the land, everything, almost all of the land, and no people would have been killed, and no city would have been demolished.

Besides proposing to concede Ukrainian territory to an invader, Trump also called Zelensky "a dictator without elections" who has "done a terrible job." Zelensky responded the next day, "With all due respect to President

Donald Trump as a leader... he is living in this disinformation space." Zelensky also said he wasn't offended by Trump calling him a dictator: "If I were a dictator, I'd be offended. But I take it. Well, okay, good."

On February 19, on Truth Social, Trump attacked Zelensky in a post riddled with lies:

> Think of it, a modestly successful comedian, Volodymyr Zelensky, talked the United States of America into spending $350 billion [LIE], to go into a War [LIE] that couldn't be won, that never had to start, but a War that he, without the U.S. and "Trump," will never be able to settle. The United States has spent $200 billion more than Europe [LIE], and Europe's money is guaranteed [LIE], while the United States will get nothing back. Why didn't Sleepy Joe Biden demand Equalization, in that this War is far more important to Europe than it is to us – We have a big, beautiful Ocean as separation. On top of this, Zelensky admits that half of the money we sent him is "MISSING." [LIE] He refuses to have Elections [LIE], is very low in Ukrainian Polls [LIE], and the only thing he was good at was playing Biden "like a fiddle." A Dictator [LIE] without Elections, Zelensky better move fast, or he is not going to have a Country left. In the meantime, we are successfully negotiating an end to the War with Russia [LIE], something all admit only "Trump," and the Trump Administration, can do [LIE]. Biden never tried, Europe has failed to bring Peace, and Zelensky probably wants to keep the "gravy train" going. I love Ukraine, but Zelensky has done a terrible job, his Country is shattered, and MILLIONS have unnecessarily died – And so it continues....

Trump Lies Endlessly About U.S. Support for Ukraine

Who, exactly, are Trump's allies here?

On February 24, Trump lied again about the U.S. contribution to aid Ukraine: "The United States has put up far more aid for Ukraine than any other nation, hundreds of billions of dollars. We've spent more than $300 billion, and Europe has spent about $100 billion. That's a big difference.... We're in there for about $350 billion. I think that's a pretty big contribution." It would be, if it were true.

An ABC News fact check shows the U.S. has delivered $119 billion in aid to Ukraine, much of it spent in the U.S. on American-made weapons; Europe has delivered $138 billion. One motive for Trump inflating the figure was to use it as a fraudulent claim against Ukraine, to be paid back through access to Ukraine's rare earth metals.

As Fox News reported, the February 28 Oval Office meeting took place after "roughly a month of growing tensions between the Trump administration and Zelensky, who had frustrated White House officials with some of his rhetoric and actions."

> **TRUMP**: We had little negotiations spat, but that worked out great. I think for both countries, I think for the world actually, beyond both countries. And we have something that is a very fair deal, and we look forward to getting in and digging, digging, digging, digging and working and getting some of the rare earth. But it means we're going to be inside, and it's a big commitment from the United States, and we appreciate working with you very much, and we will continue to do that.

Trump reinforces his oft-stated negotiating position that having U.S. workers working in Ukraine will be a sufficient security guarantee. He knows Zelensky wants more security than that.

> **TRUMP**: We have had some very good discussions with Russia. I spoke with President Putin, and we're going to try and bring this to a close. It's something that you want and that he wants. We'll have to negotiate a deal, but we've started the confines of a deal, and I think something can happen.
>
> The big thing is the number of soldiers, mostly at this point, but soldiers being killed. You're losing thousands of soldiers. So, on both sides we're losing a lot of soldiers, and we want to see it stop, and we want to see the money get put to different kinds of use, like rebuilding, the rebuilding. And we're going to be working very hard. But we've had a lot of very good conversations.

Claims of happy talk with Putin notwithstanding, there was no sign of progress toward peace in Ukraine on February 28. In the months since then, the prospect has waxed and waned, growing more remote as Russia has intensified the war.

Russian forces are bolstered by troops from Eastern Europe, Syria, and North Korea. According to Zelensky, on April 9, at least 155 Chinese nationals were fighting with the Russians in Ukraine. Ukraine has no official troop support from other nations but has estimated as many as 20,000 volunteer fighters in the International Legion for the Defense of Ukraine (Ukrainian Foreign Legion) from as many as 52 countries (including Russia, Belarus, Poland, Georgia, Chechnya, Germany, the U.S., the UK, Canada, Australia, Venezuela, Colombia, Argentina, Ecuador, Armenia, and Moldova).

As of March 2025, according to the BBC:

> The true number of Russian military deaths could range from 146,194 to 211,169. If one adds estimated losses from DPR (Donbas People's Republic) and LPR (Luhansk People's Republic) forces, the total number of Russian-aligned fatalities may range from 167,194 to 234,669.... The website Ukraine Losses, which compiles casualty data from open sources, currently lists more than 70,400 surnames of Ukrainian soldiers. Our verification of a random sample of 400 of them found the database to be reliable.

A quarter of a million military deaths, or likely more, as well as civilian casualties (dead or wounded) on both sides, estimated at well over a million! And the war goes on.

TRUMP: I will say until we came along, the Biden administration didn't speak to Russia whatsoever. They didn't speak to anybody. They just allowed this to continue. And I will say that... I'll say in front of you, you've heard me say it a thousand times, if I were president, this war would've never happened. We would've had a deal negotiated for you without having to go through what you've gone through.

But your soldiers have been unbelievably brave. We've given

them great equipment, but they... somebody has to use the equipment; they've been unbelievably brave, and we give them great credit. This was supposed to be over very quickly, and here we are three years later.

So, I give tremendous credit to your generals and your soldiers and yourself in the sense that it's been very hard fighting, very tough fighting. They're great fighters, and you have to be very proud of them from that standpoint.

ZELENSKY: I'm very proud.

That's all Zelensky said at that point. One supposes he could read the room. He was encircled by Trump administration officials, several of them on the record as pro-Russian. Somehow, he needed to get more aid in the near future and security in the long term. None of that seemed to be a high priority for his host, who was playing to the cameras.

TRUMP: But now we want to get it over with. It's enough, right, if we want to get it over with? So, it's an honor to have you here. Thank you very much for coming. We're going to sign the agreement at the conference in the East Room in a little while, right after lunch.

And we'll be having lunch together. We're also discussing some other things, and we appreciate everybody being here. It's somewhat of an exciting moment, but the really exciting moment is where we get to... when they stop the shooting and we end up with the deal. And I think we're fairly close to getting that, and an honor to have you. And please, like to say something.

ZELENSKY: Yeah, thank you so much, Mr. President. Thank you for invitation. And really, I hope that this document, first document, will be first step to real security guarantees for Ukraine. Our people, our children, really count on it. And of course, we count that America will not stop support. Really, for us, it's very important to support and to continue it.

I want to discuss it with details for them during our conversation. And of course, the infrastructure or security guarantees.

Because for today, I understand what Europe is ready to do. And of course, I want to discuss with you what United States will be ready to do.

And I really count on your strong position to stop Putin. And you said that enough with the war. I think that is very important, then, to say these words to Putin at the very beginning, at the very beginning war, because he's a killer and terrorist. But I hope that together we can stop him.

But for us, it's very important to save our country, our values, our freedom, and democracy. And of course, no compromises with the killer about our territories, but it'll be later. And of course, what I wanted....

Zelensky begins by saying thank you twice. This will be important later. More importantly, he emphasizes two points fundamental to Ukraine. He needs security guarantees, which no one is yet promising. And he needs to insist on Russian culpability, that Putin is "a killer and a terrorist," a characterization Trump would never make. Even though it's true. Even though Trump's "spiritual advisor," Pastor Mark Burna, has said, "Putin is pure evil."

ZELENSKY: We spoke about it by phone with you about the drones' production. We have very good drones production, I think the best one in the world for today, because of the war. Yes. And of course, we need very much the air defense. You have the best air defense in the world, and really, you helped us under attacks of Russians.

And I want to speak how we can exchange the licenses. We're open to share the licenses of all our drones with you, of course, with the United States. And we need licenses for quick production of air defense. Even after the war, we need our nation to be calm, that we are secure. That's why we need this air shield.

And of course, about this, I want to speak about the contingents. I think that France and UK already spoke to you, and we know that Europe is ready, but without United States, they will not be ready to be as strong as we need.

And the last point, last but not least, about exchange, about our people and children. And you know that this crazy Russian, that they've stolen 20,000 of children, Ukrainian children. They changed their names, they changed their families, relatives, and now they're in Russia. We want to bring them back. And really, it's a big, big dream task and goal for me and end our wars.

Trump has no response to this clear articulation of Ukraine's position in the face of Russian aggression. Zelensky changes his approach to show Trump pictures of some of the horrors of the war.

ZELENSKY: By the way, Mr. President, we brought, we exchanged, we, yes, released more than 4,000 warriors from Russian prison, but there are thousands more in the prison. I wanted to share with you some images. How... Can I now?

TRUMP: Yeah. Please. Please.

ZELENSKY (showing images): Some minute, one minute, one minute. I just you to understand in what circumstances, in what situation they are, and what the attitude of Russia to our prisons. That guys, just you.... Before and after. And you see before and after, just you to understand. Now, thousands of such guys, ladies, and men there, and that... So, they don't eat. They beat them, and they do a lot of bad things.

Even during the war, there are rules. Everybody knows there are rules during the war. These guys, they don't have any rules. You see that 50, 60 kilograms left and a lot of such things. And I didn't want to show you what the changes with images of children because I will just share with you. And I mean, it's looking tragic.

TRUMP: Yeah, that's tough stuff.

ZELENSKY: Yeah. I wanted very much to give you, and you see?

TRUMP: Yeah.

ZELENSKY: This is Pastor, by the way. They've stolen pastors because it's not Russian church. They've stolen pastors and moved pastors to the prison. At the end of last year, we brought three pastors, and we could exchange them. This is pastor, you see?

TRUMP: Yeah. It's tough.

ZELENSKY: Yeah. So, I mean this. I wanted to show you and this... So, thank you very much.

TRUMP: We want to get that ended, right?

ZELENSKY: Yeah, yeah, of course. Of course, we will.

TRUMP: And I think we will. I think we will. And-

ZELENSKY: We have to, of course.

TRUMP (to the press): Do you have any questions, please?

Breathtaking. Faced with vivid depictions of the war, a war he abhors rhetorically, Trump has no empathetic reaction. Twice, he manages to say it's "tough." But that's all. And then he gets back to the deal and sidesteps the issue of Russia's conduct by soliciting questions from the media.

REPORTER: Thank you, Mr. President. How much money is the U.S. going to put into the fund that is being created today, and how does this provide long-term security for Ukraine?

TRUMP: Well, we don't know exactly how much because we're going to be putting some money in a fund that we're going to get from the raw [rare] earth that we're going to be taking and sharing in terms of revenue. So, it's going to be a lot of money, will be made from the sale and from the use of raw [rare] earth. And as you know, our country doesn't have much raw [rare] earth. We have a lot of oil and gas, but we don't have a lot of the raw [rare] earth. And what we do have is protected by the environmentalists, but that could be unprotected. But still, it's not very much.

They have among the best in the world in terms of raw [rare] earth. So, we're going to be using that, taking it, using it for all of the things we do in including AI and including weapons and the military. And it's really going to very much satisfy our needs. So, it was something that just worked out really well.

We have a lot of oil, and we have a lot of gas. We have a lot, but we don't have raw [rare] earth. So, this has just about every component of the raw [rare] earth that we need for computers, for all of the things we do....

REPORTER: And on long-term security for Ukraine, how does this provide us?

TRUMP: I think they're going to have great luck. I think once we make the agreement, that's going to be 95% of it; they're not going to go back to fighting. I've spoken with President Putin, and I think... I feel very strong....

I've known him for a long time, and I feel very strongly that they're very serious about it, and we'll make a deal. And when the deal is made, I don't think.... We talk about security. Everyone's talking about the other day; all they talked about was security. I said, "Let me make the deal first."

I have to make the deal first. I don't worry about security right now, we have to have a deal because right now, last week, 2,000 soldiers died on both sides – 2,000. And they're losing a thousand, 2,000, 3,000 a week.

So, as we sit here and we talk, people are getting shot and dying on the battlefield. And they're not American soldiers, but they're Russian soldiers and they're Ukrainian soldiers. And we want to be able to stop it....

Trump avoids the question of security, so important to Zelensky. Instead, Trump focuses on the deal, which lopsidedly benefits the U.S. The deal has nothing to do with Russia. As for security, Trump essentially says, "Trust me." Oh, and trust the guy who invaded your country. Some comfort.

TRUMP: ... also to spend money on other things. We don't want to.... This is a tremendous amount of money. And what the Biden administration did was terrible. They were giving money, but he had no security on the money. Europe, as you know, gave much less money, but they had security. It was in the form of a loan. They get their money back. And we didn't.

Little of this is true. The money from both the U.S. and Europe came in grants, not loans. Europe gave more than the U.S. Europe didn't get its money back.

> **TRUMP**: And now, at least we're protected because the American taxpayer has to be protected, too. But this is an incredible agreement for Ukraine because we have a big investment in their country now, and what they have, very few people have. And we're able to really go forward with very, very high-tech things and many other things, including weaponry, weaponry that we're going to use in many locations, but that we need for our country....

Trump doesn't say it in so many words, but what he describes as "protecting the American taxpayer" is extorting Ukraine. He wants to force a deal on a disadvantaged country at war, a country desperate for help, a country he thinks he can leverage, a country that the U.S. once considered an ally. Trump wants to force a deal that allows the U.S. to exploit Ukraine's mineral resources in exchange for next to nothing. Ukraine gets to share profits on what it already owns, with no security guarantees at all. Russia isn't even a party. This is rationally unacceptable. But Zelensky tries to put a good face on it.

> **ZELENSKY**: If I can just.... Yes. In the document, there is one of the very important points if we speak about business and investment. We never had LNG terminals in Ukraine. This document will open... I mean, the next document.... But anyway, here we see in the framework, we see a really good will for this. LNG terminals for us is very important and I think for security of European continent. We have the biggest storage, gas storage. We have the biggest in Europe, yes. Yes, and we can use it. Use it for LNG, use it for LNG and we will do it.
>
> And really, we can help Europe because Europe really helped. President Trump said that they made less support, but they're our friends and they are our very supportive partners. They really gave a lot, Mr. President.

Zelensky has quietly challenged Trump with a reality check.

> **TRUMP**: Oh –

ZELENSKY: Really, they did.

TRUMP: I gave a lot, but they gave much less.

ZELENSKY: No.

TRUMP: Much less.

ZELENSKY: No, no.

TRUMP: Okay.

ZELENSKY: Okay.

So far, about 12 minutes into the meeting, Zelensky has held his ground against Trump on a matter of fact. In the Oval Office. In front of the media. Awkward.

A reporter interjects a softball question.

REPORTER: Mr. President Trump, you have repeatedly called the deal with Ukraine as a historical one, and as a President of the United States, you make historical decision in other issues which affect America and other world. So, what place in the world history do you want to take, and do you associate yourself with any famous historical figures?

TRUMP: Yeah, I'd say George Washington, Abraham Lincoln. I would say I'm far superior to George Washington and Abraham Lincoln. Now, you know I'm only kidding, right? Because when I say that the fake news is going to go wild. They're going to say he considers himself to be better than Washington. But you never know....

REPORTER: And a question to President Zelenskyy. Do you feel like the U.S. is on your side, that President Trump is on your side at this moment?

Washington!? Lincoln!? Whiplash. Back to the real world. Fair question. What evidence is there that Trump is on Ukraine's side? How can Zelensky answer that honestly without giving offense?

TRUMP: Go ahead.

ZELENSKY: What do you think?

TRUMP: He wants to know do you think that.... It's sort of a stupid question because I guess we wouldn't be here if I wasn't.

ZELENSKY: I think that United States on our side from the very beginning of occupation, and I think that President Trump on our side, and of course [inaudible 00:14:54] I'm sure that United States President will not stop support. This is crucial for us. It's important for us. And president speaks about the people and the soldiers which are dying, but they came to our territory. They came to our land, they began this war, and they have to stop.

And I think this is the question with ... really, the most important question. Can President Trump, I hope yes, with some other allies to stop Putin, withdraw these troops from our land? And I think that you asked about the history, about [inaudible 00:15:32]. I think that if President or when he will stop Putin, if President Trump will bring peace to our country, I think he will be on this wall, I think.

TRUMP: We've had very, very good talks.

REPORTER: Mr. President, President Zelenskyy just said that there'll be no compromises with Vladimir Putin. I just wanted to ask both of you, firstly, are there compromises that you think that President Zelensky is going to have to make, and President Zelensky, is there anything that you might think you may be able to offer or bring to the table, for example, elections? Thank you.

What a dishonest question! Zelensky did not say "no compromises" or anything like that. Why is this reporter asking Trump about compromises Zelensky might have to make? Why is the reporter posing a question that panders to Trump? Why would any reporter think it's reasonable to ask about compromises amid ongoing negotiations that have shown little or no progress? Is this reporter a plant? Why put Zelensky in that kind of squeeze? And why would any competent reporter ask about elections, when he should know the Ukrainian constitution allows for the suspension of elections when the country is at war? Any reasonable person would give this question short shrift. But...

TRUMP: I think you're going to have to always make compromises. You can't do any deals without compromises. So, certainly, he's going to have to make some compromises, but hopefully they won't be as big as some people think you're going to have to make. That's all. That's all we can do.

I'm here as an arbitrator, as a mediator to a certain extent between two parties that have been very hostile, to put it mildly, they've been very hostile. This has been a vicious war. It's been a vicious war. It's a very level battlefield, and those bullets go out, and as I've said many times, many times, the only thing stopping those bullets is a human body. And in the case we're talking about, generally, young human bodies are stopping a lot of bullets.

It's dead level. That's why it's great farmland, it's great land, it's great farmland, but there's very little protection against the bullets and other things that are being shot. So, all I can do is see if I can get everybody at the table and get an agreement, and I think we're going to end up with an agreement. Otherwise, I wouldn't probably be even here today.

Trump gives the game away. He says, "I'm here as an arbitrator, as a mediator...." When Trump took office in January, the U.S. was an ally of Ukraine, supporting its defense against a Russian invasion, not an intermediary. Now, Trump officials are blaming the invasion on Ukraine. Trump is playing games with aid to Ukraine. And Trump is positioning himself as a mediator between the invader and the victim! That's an abandonment of international law. Surely the media would like to know if it is Trump's policy to reward countries for invading their neighbors and committing war crimes.

> **REPORTER**: Mr. President, I've got two questions for you. You think ultimately your legacy will be the peacemaker and not the president that led this country into another war and ended foreign wars? And I've got a question –
>
> **TRUMP** (interrupting): I hope it will. I mean, I hope I'm going to be remembered as a peacemaker. This would be a great thing if we could do this. I'm doing this to save lives more than anything else. Second is to save a lot of money, but I considered

that to be far less important.

Thank you, Brian, for that question. It was a nice question. I hope I'll be known and recognized as a peacemaker. This would be a great thing to solve. This is a very dangerous situation. This could lead to a third world war. This was headed in the wrong direction. If this election were lost, if we didn't win this election, and by the way, we won it by a lot, that was a mandate. We won every swing state. We won the popular vote by millions and millions of votes. We won everything. The districts, you look at the areas of red, take a look at a map. This was a big mandate, and this was one of the things, I said, "We're going to get this thing settled." If we didn't win, I think this could've very well ended up in a third world war and that would not have been a good situation.

What was your second question?

The reporter strokes Trump's ego, and Trump purrs. Then he goes off-topic with his canned claim of having a mandate, even though no mandate exists. Still, nothing specific about how peace can be achieved. Like Russia withdrawing from Ukrainian territory. Or the U.S. providing more meaningful military support. Well, maybe Brian's second question will go deeper.

REPORTER: My second question is for President Zelensky. Why don't you wear a suit? Why don't you wear a suit? You're the highest level in this country's office and you refuse to wear a suit. Do you own a suit?

Why don't you wear a suit?!?!?!

Earlier in the day, when Zelensky arrived at the White House, Trump had mocked his attire, saying, "You're all dressed up today." Zelensky was wearing his usual attire, a military-style black pullover, adorned with the Ukrainian crest, and black slacks. If Brian had done any homework, he'd know that Zelensky has worn military-style clothes since the invasion in 2022, to show solidarity with Ukrainian troops fighting the Russian invaders. Complaints about Zelensky's appearance have been a chronic thread in the rightwing blogosphere. How is the question anything but a deliberate insult in a setting akin to an ambush?

ZELENSKY: You have problems?

REPORTER: Yeah, a lot of Americans have problems with you not respecting the dignity of office.

ZELENSKY: Really? Perhaps I will wear a costume after this war will finish. Yes, maybe something like yours.

REPORTER: Maybe something like this? Yes, sir. That be great.

ZELENSKY: Maybe something better. I don't know. We will see. Maybe something cheaper than, yeah....

The exchange dribbles off. Another reporter asks a question with actual relevance.

REPORTER: Mr. President, are you going to send more arms to Ukraine in case there's no peace?

TRUMP: Yeah, we're going to have arms to Ukraine. Yeah, sure. Hopefully, I won't have to send very much because hopefully we're going to have it finished. We're looking forward to finishing this quickly. We're not looking forward to sending a lot of arms. We're looking forward to getting the war finished so we can do other things. But we very much appreciate the agreement because we needed what they had, and our country is now treated fairly.... But sure, the answer is yes, but hopefully we won't have to send much because I'm looking forward to getting it done quickly. Very quickly.

REPORTER: Does that mean you'll provide security guarantees, Mr. President?

TRUMP: I don't want to talk about security yet because I want to get the deal done. You fall into the same trap like everybody else a million times. You said over and over. I want to get the deal done. Security is so easy. That's about 2% of the problem. I'm not worried about security. I'm worried about getting the deal done. The security is the easy part. Security is very nice. Everybody stops shooting.

And now will Europe put people there? I know France is going to, I know the UK is going to, I know other countries are going to, and they happen to be right next door. We haven't committed, but we could conceivably. We have security in a different form. We'll have workers there digging, digging, digging, taking the raw [rare] earth so that we can create a lot of great product in this country. So, in that sense, you have something, but we haven't determined that yet.

I will say in speaking to France, and they were here as you know last week, and just the other day, they have committed to a lot of security. I don't think you're going to need much security. I think once this deal gets done, it's over. Russia is not going to want to go back and nobody's going to want to go back.

ZELENSKY is shaking his head [inaudible 00:21:20].

TRUMP: When this deal ends. I really believe this deal is going to be over.

ZELENSKY: [inaudible 00:21:24] Yeah, thank you. Thank you so much [inaudible 00:21:25].

Trump all but says there will be no security guarantee for Ukraine's future. Trump pretends that some number of American workers in Ukraine for a limited time is all the security guarantee Ukraine needs for the indefinite future. This is preposterous. Zelensky is at a loss for words.

The meeting has gone off the rails for the moment, until another ego stroke for Trump.

REPORTER: Part of that involved, though, re-engaging Russia in diplomatic relations, something that previous leaders lacked the conviction to do. So, what gave you the moral courage and conviction to step forward and lead that?

TRUMP: Well, I love this guy. Who are you with?

REPORTER: One American News, sir.

TRUMP: Well, that's why I like him. One American News does a great job. I like the question. I think it's a very good question. It's a pathway to peace. It's a pathway to getting something solved. And I feel that as the head of this country, I have an obligation to do that. Plus, we're very much involved. We got involved. It's too bad we got involved, because there should have been no involvement, because there should have been no war.

And there shouldn't have been October 7 [in Israel]. That would've never happened. As you know, Iran was broke, they had no money to give to Hezbollah, they had no money to give to Hamas. They were stone-cold broke, and then under Biden they became rich as hell. They went from no money to $300 billion in a period of four years, and they gave a lot of that money away. And you see what happened. And that's a real mess also, that we hope to be able to solve. But no, I appreciate your question very much. It's just I feel I have an obligation to try and do something to stop the death.

His ego properly stroked, Trump runs on, and on, off-topic, offering nothing about how to engage with Russia. Zelensky interjects.

ZELENSKY: If I can answer. Yes, if I can answer. Sorry.

TRUMP: Please, go ahead.

ZELENSKY: Please, please.

TRUMP: And I do like your clothing, by the way.

ZELENSKY: Really?

TRUMP: I think he's a great guy, by the way. But I don't know if you two like each other, but you know what? I think he's dressed beautifully. I think he's dressed beautifully.

ZELENSKY: No, no, I like this guy. I don't know him. So, I have more serious things than answer on side question.

TRUMP: [inaudible 00:23:20].

ZELENSKY: I will answer on more serious questions if I can.

TRUMP: That's [inaudible 00:23:21].

ZELENSKY: Yeah. So, please about security guarantees and about the ceasefire. We can't just speak about ceasefire and speak and speak. It will not work. Just ceasefire will never work because I'm like the president. I have this experience and not only me, Ukraine, before my presidency from the 2014 Putin broken 25 times. Twenty-five times. He broken his own signature 25 times, he broken ceasefire, it was [inaudible 00:23:53].

TRUMP: But he never broke to me. He never broke to me....

ZELENSKY: In 2016, you been the president, Mr. President. You've been the president. But he had, of course, not with you, but he had during those period, he had conversations with our side, and we had Normandy format, the France, Germany, Ukraine, and Russia. And he broken 25 times.

That's why we will never accept just ceasefire. It will not work without security guarantees. Security guarantees, maybe president is right about this document and other, but this document is not enough. Strong army is enough because his soldiers afraid. Putin's soldiers afraid of our soldiers when we strong enough. If we are not strong enough, we are empty; if our storage is empty, we can't defend our land. Today, all the world knows that we have meeting, yes? Why he's using ballistic? Putin today using ballistic on our hospitals, schools, and et cetera. Ballistic.

So, he knows that we are here and that President Trump really have good goodwill to stop this war. And you hear now the President, so why he's using? So, he doesn't want to stop. He doesn't want. But I hope that we will do it, really, we'll do it. Security. When we speak about security guarantees, when the Europeans are ready for contingents, they need USA backstop.

If they will not be United States, we will not never have any strong contingents from the Europeans because they don't want to divide alliance connection between the United States, the main and strongest ally, and Europeans. This is crucial. This is supportive. That what we want to speak about very much. This is very important and air defense. So, air defense, really, we have big deficit with all the systems, and we need to provide this. We need it very much. Otherwise, Putin will never stop and will go further and further. It doesn't work. He hate us.

It's not about me, he hate Ukrainians. He thinks that we are not a nation. He thinks and he shared his thoughts, I think maybe with your team also? I don't know. But with all the Europeans, in media, official, and not, he always said that there is no such country, such nation, such language, and such life, like Ukrainian. No, he really doesn't respect all the Ukrainians, and he wants destroy us.

And you are right, Mr. President, that's [inaudible 00:26:33]. This document, maybe other documents, it's very good start, very good, but it will not enough to stop this person.

Despite the broken English, this is about as real as it gets. It's about survival. It's not about minerals. It's about harsh realities in the real world. It's about having your country invaded. It's about Ukraine surviving. It's about defending international law. It's about justice. Trump has nothing to say.

REPORTER: Should Russia pay to rebuild Ukraine?

ZELENSKY: They have to pay. This is the rule. This is rule of the war. This is the rule of the war. During all the centuries, all the history, this is the rule of the war. Who began, those pay.

REPORTER: Do you agree, President Trump?

The question is addressed to Trump. He doesn't answer.

ZELENSKY: This is the rule. Putin began this war. He has to pay all money for invasion. He has to pay. Of course, some Russian assets, what we have in Europe, about 300 billion. We can use them. We can use for invasion and buy military support from the United States also. We can do it, but it's not enough. It's not.

REPORTER: Do you envision the trilateral [inaudible 00:27:27] wouldn't end President Zelensky?

TRUMP: Wait one second.

REPORTER: I ask this question that you didn't flag because I wanted to know if you want to position yourself in the middle between Russia and Ukraine....

TRUMP: No, I'm in the middle. I want to solve this thing. I'm for both. I want to get it solved, and it's wonderful to speak badly about somebody else, but I want to get it solved. If we can solve it, great. If we can't solve it, they're going to have to fight it out, and who knows what's going to happen, but I want to see it get solved.

REPORTER: May I follow up? One more question about U.S. troops in Europe. After Russian invasion of Ukraine, your predecessor sent additional troops to Eastern Europe, including Poland, my country. Are you committed to keeping these troops on the eastern flank of NATO in the future?

TRUMP: I'm very committed to Poland. I think Poland has really stepped up and done a great job for NATO. As you know, they paid more than they had to. They are one of the finest groups of people I've ever known. I'm very committed to Poland....

With Poland, as is typical of Trump, it's mostly about the money. Trump ignores the question about keeping U.S. troops in Eastern Europe to deter Russia. The conversation has shifted away from Ukraine's security.

TRUMP: The Baltics, they got a lot of, it's a tough neighborhood too, but we're committed. We're going to be very committed, and we're committed to NATO, but NATO has to step up, and the Europeans have to step up more than they have, and I want to see them equalize because they are in for far less than we're in, and they should be at least equal. You understand that? Why is the United States, we have an ocean in between, why is the United States in for so much more money and other things as Europe? With that being said, and as you said, they've also been obviously very helpful, but we have put in far more than they have and I think they should equalize....

REPORTER: Mr. President, what and how do you envision a trilateral summit with President Zelensky and Putin under these circumstances?

TRUMP: I don't know. Well, they don't like each other. I can tell you that they do not like each other. This is not a love match, and it's unfortunate.

That's why you're in this situation. The United States should not have allowed this to happen. Okay? The United States run by a man that didn't know much. I'm going to be very nice. Run by an incompetent person. Very incompetent person.

Should never have allowed this to happen. I've stopped wars, I've stopped many wars. My people will tell you I stopped wars that nobody ever heard about. I stopped wars before they ever started. You can look at some of, some of… I could give you a lot of nations that would tell you right now they were probably going to war. I could tell you right now there's a nation thinking about going to war on something that nobody in this room has ever even heard about. Two smaller nations, but big still. Still big. And I think I've stopped it, but this should have never happened….

In response to Trump's self-puffery, Zelensky tries to bring the discussion back to the actual war in Ukraine.

ZELENSKY: [inaudible 00:30:53] Sorry, just a second. About any negotiations… First of all, I want really to tell you, and I think that everybody understand that Ukraine, more than Ukrainians, nobody wants to stop this war, but the future, any negotiations, it's understandable that two sides of the war, not Russia and the United States because this is not the war between Russia and the United States. This is war of Russia against Ukraine and Ukrainian people. So, these two sides will be, any way will be at the negotiation and negotiation table.

Then of course, United States like the strongest partner of the Ukraine and of course Europe. I think Europe is very important. I want to speak about it with the President. Yes. Europe is very important for us because we really defend Europe for today, all Europeans are really recognized that we are defending the line, and they have real life and our people are dying. That's why they helped us. And also, it's about the need. Yes, between….

Like the President said, you have big, nice ocean. Yes, between us, but if we will not stay, Russia will go further to Baltics and to Poland by the way. But first to the Baltics. It's understandable for them because they've been in the USSR, one of the republics of the USSR, and Putin wants to bring them back to his empire. It's a fact. And when he will go there, if will not stay, you'll fight your American soldiers. It doesn't matter do you have ocean or not. Your soldiers will fight.

Zelensky is pushing hard, essentially challenging Trump's affinity for Putin, his support for Russian perspectives. A reporter asks another deflecting question.

REPORTER: Mr. President, would you be willing to visit Ukraine? Maybe Kiev or Odessa, which is known to be a 30-year [inaudible 00:32:46].

ZELENSKY: It was my question.

TRUMP: I'm sorry. I don't want to talk about Odessa now. Let's not talk about Odessa. I want to talk about making a deal, getting peace. We don't have to talk about Odessa, but a lot of cities have been destroyed. A lot of cities that are not recognizable. There's not a building standing.

Trump seems off balance. Zelensky presses on.

ZELENSKY: Oh, no. You have to come Mr. President. You have to come and to look. No, no, no. We have very good cities. Yes, a lot of things have been destroyed, but mostly cities alive and people work, and children go to school. Sometimes it's very difficult, sometimes closer to the front line. Children have to go to underground schools or online. But we live, Ukraine is fighting, and Ukraine lives. This is very important, and maybe it's Putin who sharing this information that he destroyed us. He lost 700,000 people, 700,000 soldiers. He lost everything. Yes....

Trump has no response. A reporter throws a lifeline.

REPORTER: When did you last speak with President Putin, and what did he say that...?

TRUMP: A couple of days ago.

REPORTER: And what did he tell you that gave you the assurance that he wanted peace?

TRUMP: Well, that's what I do. My whole life is deals, I know pretty good. And I really, I've known him for a long time. I've dealt with him for a long time. He had to suffer through the Russia hoax. You know, Russia, Russia, Russia was a hoax. It was all Biden. It was nothing to do with him. So, he had to suffer through that, and he was able to do that.

I think that he wants to make a deal, and he like to see it end. That's all I do, that's what I do. My whole life, that's what I do is make deals. I'm in the middle of a mess because this is a real mess. It's a very dangerous one. If this doesn't get solved now, it's not going to get solved for a long time. So, I hope we're going to get it solved. In the back please.

This is a complete non-answer answer. What assurances did Putin give that he wants peace? Trump offers none. Whether Putin wants peace or just wants to play the situation for what it's worth remains an open question. (In the weeks that follow, Putin will offer no persuasive assurance that he wants peace as he escalates the war.)

The conversation about free speech in Europe meanders for the next few minutes. Trump officials have accused Europeans of suppressing the free speech of neo-Nazis online. Earlier in February, Secretary of State Rubio and Vice President Vance commented on free speech in Europe, agreeing that Americans should be able to speak their minds online without interference from European governments. Both officials expressed support for the right-wing German party Alternative for Germany (AfD) shortly before the German election in which the party finished second.

On May 2, Germany's Federal Office for the Protection of the Constitution (BfV) issued a 1,100-page confidential report classifying the Alternative for Germany (AfD) party as a "right-wing extremist" entity, subjecting it to increased state monitoring. The report highlighted the party's use of hateful rhetoric and incitement to undermine democratic institutions. It also found the AfD to be a racist and anti-Muslim organization, a designation that allows the security services to recruit informants and intercept party communications, and which has revived calls for the party's ban. Other organizations classified as extremist in Germany are neo-Nazi groups such as the National Democratic Party (NDP), Islamist groups including Islamic State, and far-left ones such as the Marxist-Leninist Party of Germany.

U.S. Secretary of State Marco Rubio promptly misrepresented the decision on X: "Germany just gave its spy agency new powers to surveil the opposition. That's not democracy – it's tyranny in disguise." The German Foreign Ministry replied: "This is democracy. The decision is the result of a thorough and independent investigation to protect our constitution.... We have learnt from our history that right-wing extremism needs to be stopped."

In response to further questions, Trump says the U.S. doesn't have much interest in Ukrainian LNG (liquid natural gas).

Then there's a question relevant to the subject at hand, and it gets interesting as Trump struggles to come up with a credible answer.

> REPORTER: On the minerals deal, Mr. President. Some of those minerals are in the east of Ukraine, not far from the front lines, and in areas that Russia has occupied. Will you direct President Putin to withdraw his forces from those areas if there's U.S. interest?
>
> TRUMP: Well, we'll take a look at the time. We have a lot of area. It's a very big area we're talking about, so we'll take a look. I'll study that and I'll see.
>
> REPORTER: And who would protect those minerals if they are U.S. interests? Would that be Ukrainian forces? European forces?
>
> TRUMP: They will be protected. The agreement will protect them.
>
> REPORTER: U.S. forces?
>
> TRUMP: The agreement. Yeah, we're signing an agreement.
>
> REPORTER: Right, but what if Russia tries to invade or there's Russian [inaudible 00:37:56]?
>
> TRUMP: I just told you I don't think that's going to happen. And if that were going to happen, I wouldn't make a deal. If I thought that was going to happen, I wouldn't make a deal.
>
> REPORTER: Some people may wonder why...
>
> TRUMP: You know, they ought to focus on CNN, on survival, not asking me these ridiculous questions.

REPORTER: Why do you have the confidence that…

TRUMP: Focus on surviving cause CNN's got such low ratings. I don't think they're going to survive. Let's go. Please go ahead.

REPORTER: I already mentioned Poland, that Poland was under Russian control for decades after the Second World War. When I was a kid, I looked at the United States not only as a most powerful country, richest country in the world, the country that has great music, great movies, great muscle cars, but also as a force for good. And now I'm talking with my friends in Poland, and they are worried that you align yourself too much with Putin. What's your message for them?

TRUMP: Well, if I didn't align myself with both of them, you'd never have a deal. You want me to say really terrible things about Putin, and then say, "Hi, Vladimir, how are we doing on the deal?" That doesn't work that way. I'm not aligned with Putin. I'm not aligned with anybody. I'm aligned with the United States of America, and for the good of the world. I'm aligned with the world, and I want to get this thing over with.

You see the hatred he's got for Putin. It's very tough for me to make a deal with that kind of hatred. He's got tremendous hatred. And I understand that, but I can tell you, the other side isn't exactly in love with him either. So, it's not a question of alignment. I'm aligned with the world. I'm aligned with Europe. I want to see if we can get this thing done. You want me to be tough? I can be tougher than any human being you've ever seen. I'd be so tough. But you're never going to get a deal that way. So that's the way it goes. All right, one more question.

The question that goes unasked: Why have you called Zelensky a dictator and not called Putin a dictator?

And why have you accused Ukraine of invading Russia, but not said anything about Russia invading Ukraine?

REPORTER: [inaudible 00:39:54]

VANCE: I will respond to this. So, look. For four years in the

United States of America, we had a president who stood up at press conferences and talked tough about Vladimir Putin, and then Putin invaded Ukraine and destroyed a significant chunk of the country. The path to peace and the path to prosperity is maybe engaging in diplomacy. We tried the pathway of Joe Biden, of thumping our chest and pretending that the President of the United States' words mattered more than the President of the United States' actions. What makes America a good country is America engaging in diplomacy. That's what President Trump is doing.

ZELENSKY: Can I ask you?

VANCE: Sure....

ZELENSKY: Okay. So, he occupied it, our parts. Big parts of Ukraine, parts of East and Crimea. He occupied it on 2014. During a lot of years, I'm not speaking about just Biden, but those time was Obama, then President Obama, then President Trump, then President Biden, now President Trump, and God bless, now President Trump will stop him. But during 2014, nobody stopped him. He just occupied and took. He killed people, you know. What the contact line –

TRUMP: 2015.

ZELENSKY: 2014.

VANCE: 2014 to 2015.

TRUMP: 2014. I was not here.

VANCE: That's exactly right.

ZELENSKY: Yes, but during 2014 till 2022 was the situation the same? People are been dying on the contact line. Nobody stopped him. You know that we had conversations with him. A lot of conversation. My bilateral conversation, and we signed with him. Me. Like a new president in 2019, I signed with him the deal. I signed with him, Macron, and Merkel.

We signed ceasefire. Ceasefire. All of them told me that he will never go. We signed him gas contract. Gas contract. Yes, but after that, he broken this ceasefire. He killed our people,

and he didn't exchange prisoners. We signed the exchange of
prisoners, but he didn't do it. What kind of diplomacy, JD, you
are speaking about? What do you mean?

VANCE: I'm talking about the kind of diplomacy that's going
to end the destruction of your country.

Only a few days earlier, Vance had publicly called for Ukraine to end the
war by giving up territory. How is that not the destruction of the country?

ZELENSKY: Yes, but if you do not stop –

VANCE: Mr. President. Mr. President, with respect, I think
it's disrespectful for you to come into the Oval Office and try
to litigate this in front of the American media. Right now, you
guys are going around and forcing conscripts to the front lines
because you have manpower problems. You should be thanking
the president for trying to bring it into this conflict.

This is the trap Zelensky now finds himself in. It's a set-up. Trump
brought in the media for no useful purpose. Typically, the media come in
after a deal has been signed. Trump has been litigating the agreement since
the meeting began. And now Vance strikes, first by gratuitously insulting
Zelensky, then berating him for the weakness of his situation as the result
of having been invaded by Russia. This is pure thuggery. Zelensky seems
taken aback.

ZELENSKY: Have you ever been to Ukraine that you say what
problems we have?

VANCE: I have been to –

ZELENSKY: Come once.

VANCE: I've actually watched and seen the stories, and I know
that what happens is you bring people. You bring them on a
propaganda tour, Mr. President. Do you disagree that you've
had problems bringing people into your military?

ZELENSKY: Do we have problems? I will answer it. I will answer it.

VANCE: And do you think that it's respectful to come to the
Oval Office of the United States of America and attack the administration that is trying to prevent the destruction of your

country?

ZELENSKY: A lot of questions. Let's start from the beginning.

VANCE: Sure.

ZELENSKY: First of all, during the war, everybody has problems. Even you, but you have nice ocean and don't feel now. But you will feel it in the future. God bless you will not have a war. True enough, but this sets Trump off, almost shouting. Trump berates Zelensky. Zelensky remains calm, but tries to respond.

TRUMP: You don't know that. You don't know that. Don't tell us what we're going to feel. We're trying to solve a problem. Don't tell us what we're going to feel.

ZELENSKY: I'm not telling you. I'm answering on this question.

TRUMP: Because you're in no position to dictate that.

ZELENSKY: That's exactly what you're doing.

TRUMP: You're in no position to dictate what we're going to feel.

ZELENSKY: You will. You will feel influence.

TRUMP: We're going to feel very good. We're going to feel very good and very strong.

ZELENSKY: I'm telling you, you will feel influence.

TRUMP: You're right now not in a very good position. You've allowed yourself to be in a very bad position, and he happens to be right about it.

ZELENSKY: From the very beginning of the war, I was – -

TRUMP You're not in a good position. You don't have the cards right now. With us, you start having cards. But right now, you don't –

ZELENSKY: We're not playing cards. I'm very serious, Mr. President. I'm very serious.

TRUMP: You're playing cards. You're playing cards. You're gambling with the lives of millions of people.

ZELENSKY: I'm the president in a war.

TRUMP: You're gambling with World War III. You're gambling with World War III.

ZELENSKY: What do you [inaudible 00:44:04]

TRUMP: And what you're doing is very disrespectful to the country, this country, that's backed you far more than a lot of people said they should have.

ZELENSKY: I'm with all respect to your country. I'm with all respect.

VANCE: Have you said thank you once this entire meeting?

ZELENSKY: A lot of times.

VANCE: No. In this entire meeting, you said thank you today?

ZELENSKY: Even today. Even today.

Vance is just wrong on the "thank you" thing; maybe he knows it. Now he throws in the kitchen sink, which has the feel of a grudge.

VANCE: You went to Pennsylvania and campaigned for the opposition in October.

ZELENSKY: What? What are you speaking about?

VANCE: Offer some words of appreciation for the United States of America and the president who's trying to save your country.

ZELENSKY: Please. You think that if you will speak very loudly about the war, you can –

TRUMP: He's not speaking loudly. He's not speaking loudly. Your country's in big trouble.

ZELENSKY: Can I answer him? Can I answer –

TRUMP: Wait a minute. No, no, you've done a lot of talking. Your country is in big trouble.

ZELENSKY: I know. I know.

TRUMP: You're not winning. You're not winning this. You have a damn good chance of coming out okay because of us.

ZELENSKY: Mr. President, we are staying in our country, staying strong. From the very beginning of the war, we've been alone. And we are thankful. I said thanks in this cabinet, and not only in this cabinet. I said thank you.

TRUMP: We gave you through this stupid president, $350

billion …. We gave you military equipment, and your men are brave, but they had to use our military…. If you didn't have our military equipment, this war would have been over in two weeks.

ZELENSKY: In three days. I heard it from Putin, in three days. This is something –

TRUMP: Maybe less.

ZELENSKY: In two weeks. Of course, yes.

TRUMP: It's going to be a very hard thing to do business like this, let me tell you.

VANCE: Just say thank you.

ZELENSKY: I said a lot of times thank you to American people.

VANCE: Accept that there are disagreements, and let's go litigate those disagreements rather than trying to fight it out in the American media when you're wrong. We know that you're wrong.

TRUMP: But you see, I think it's good for the American people to see what's going on.

VANCE: I understand, sir. I understand.

TRUMP: I think it's very important. That's why I kept this going so long. You have to be thankful. You don't have the cards.

ZELENSKY: I'm thankful.

TRUMP You're buried there, your people are dying.

ZELENSKY: I can tell you … I know. Don't, please, Mr. President –

TRUMP: You're running low on soldiers. Listen. You're running low on soldiers. It would be a good thing –

ZELENSKY: Mr. President –

TRUMP: Then you tell us, "I don't want a ceasefire. I don't want a ceasefire. I want to go, and I want this." Look. If you could get a ceasefire right now, I tell you you'd take it, so the bullets stopped flying and your men stop getting killed.

ZELENSKY: Of course. Of course, we want to stop the war.

But I said –

TRUMP: But you're saying you don't want a ceasefire. I want a ceasefire.

ZELENSKY: But I said to you with guarantees.

TRUMP: Because you'll get a ceasefire faster than an agreement.

ZELENSKY: Ask our people about ceasefire, what they think. It doesn't matter for you what [inaudible 00:46:27]

TRUMP: That wasn't with me. That wasn't with me. That was with a guy named Biden, who was not a smart person. That was with Obama.

ZELENSKY: But this is your president. It was your president.

TRUMP: Excuse me. That was with Obama, who gave you sheets, and I gave you Javelins [shoulder-fired anti-armor rocket system].

ZELENSKY: Yes.

TRUMP: I gave you the Javelins to take out all those tanks. Obama gave you sheets. In fact, the statement is, Obama gave sheets and Trump gave Javelins. You got to be more thankful, because let me tell you, you don't have the cards. With us, you have the cards, but without us, you don't have any cards.

REPORTER: One more question to Mr. Vice President. I'm sorry, here.

TRUMP: It's going to be a tough deal to make, because the attitudes have to change.

REPORTER: What if Russia breaks ceasefire? What if Russia breaks these talks? What do they do then? I understand that it's a heated conversation, right? [inaudible 00:47:19]

The reporter raises a serious contingency, especially in light of Russia's breaking previous agreements.

TRUMP: What are you saying?

VANCE: She's asking, what if Russia breaks the ceasefire?

TRUMP: What if anything? What if a bomb drops on your head right now?

REPORTER: But they have [inaudible 00:47:29]

TRUMP: Okay. What if they break it? I don't know. They broke it with Biden, because Biden, they didn't respect him. They didn't respect Obama. They respect me.

REPORTER: But [inaudible 00:47:38]

Whatever this question was, it triggers Trump to launch into a familiar, irrelevant litany of self-pity.

The truth is that Russia did interfere in the 2016 election to help Trump and to hurt Clinton. The evidence is overwhelming. What is unknown for certain is whether Russia coordinated any of its activities with Trump agents.

TRUMP: Let me tell you, Putin went through a hell of a lot with me. He went through a phony witch hunt where they used him and Russia ... "Russia, Russia, Russia." You ever hear of that deal? That was a phony Hunter Biden, Joe Biden scam. Hillary Clinton, shifty Adam Schiff. It was a Democrat scam.

And he had to go through that, and he did go through it. We didn't end up in a war, and he went through it. He was accused of all that stuff. He had nothing to do with it. It came out of Hunter Biden's bathroom. It came out of Hunter Biden's bedroom. It was disgusting. And then they said, "Oh. Oh. The laptop from hell was made by Russia." The 51 agents. The whole thing was a scam, and he had to put up with that. He was being accused of all that stuff.

All I can say is this. He might have broken deals with Obama and Bush, and he might have broken them with Biden. He did, maybe. Maybe he didn't, I don't know what happened. But he didn't break them with me. He wants to make a deal. I don't know if you can make a deal. The problem is, I've empowered you to be a tough guy, and I don't think you'd be a tough guy without the United States. And your people are very brave.

ZELENSKY: Thank you.

TRUMP: But you're either going to make a deal or we're out, and if we're out, you'll fight it out. I don't think it's going to be pretty, but you'll fight it out. But you don't have the cards. But once we sign that deal, you're in a much better position. But you're not acting at all thankful, and that's not a nice thing. I'll be honest, that's not a nice thing. All right, I think we've seen enough. What do you think? Yeah.

REPORTER: What's this negotiation [inaudible 00:49:17]

TRUMP: This is going to be great television; I will say that. All right. We'll see what we can do about putting it together. Thank you.

REPORTER: [inaudible 00:49:31]

TRUMP: We'll see, I don't know.

VANCE: [inaudible 00:49:43]

STAFF: Guys, come on. Let's move, please. If we could bring down this tripod, please. Got to keep moving.

Thanks for Nothing?

Although Zelensky's final words had been, "Thank you," Trump responded with insults and denigration: "You're not acting at all thankful, and that's not a nice thing. I'll be honest, that's not a nice thing." And without further diplomatic niceties, Trump abruptly ended the meeting.

Ushered into a separate room, the Ukrainians asked for the talks to continue. But Trump refused, telling aides he felt disrespected. Then he cancelled the planned joint press conference about the minerals agreement. Then he cancelled lunch. And then he ordered Zelensky and his advisors to leave the White House, out of sight of reporters.

Insofar as the White House had staged this event to celebrate getting its hands on Ukraine's rare earth minerals, it might as well have closed out of town. This production showcased the art of blowing the deal.

What went wrong? Trump's assumptions about Zelensky, whatever they were, were wrong. Zelensky was not prepared to sell out his country for a minerals deal alone. Zelensky remained committed to his country's long-term survival, with its occupied areas returned to Ukrainian control. This spirit of national integrity has been obvious for years. Could Trump not see it, not understand it, not think it worth considering? Did Trump think it was just a negotiating position? Did Trump not understand the idea of quid pro quo? Did he really think he could make a deal in which Zelensky provided the quid (minerals) while Trump provided only the illusion of a quo (non-security and an unreliable promise of a ceasefire)? Did Trump truly believe he had Zelensky at such a disadvantage, with Russia occupying a fifth of Ukraine, that Zelensky would accept any offer of help, no matter how illusory? Is that what Putin had told him?

Zelensky left with his dignity intact. He told the truth, he had remained calm, and he insulted no one (except Putin and those insulted by the truth). He expressed gratitude appropriate to past U.S. aid but stopped short of fawning over an ally who was openly leaning toward his country's aggressor. How much sense would it make for him to rely on an ally who was openly unreliable?

Allies Appalled, Russia Pleased

Shortly after the globally televised meeting ended, Russia weighed in publicly. Dmitry Medvedev, deputy chairman of Russia's security council, posted on X (aka Twitter): "The insolent pig finally got a proper slap down in the Oval Office. And @realDonaldTrump is right: the Kiev regime is 'gambling with WWIII.'" So said the only combatant with nuclear weapons.

French President Emmanuel Macron also weighed in on X: "There is an aggressor: Russia. There is a victim: Ukraine. We were right to help Ukraine and sanction Russia three years ago – and to keep doing so."

Secretary of State Marco Rubio posted fawningly on X: "Thank you @ POTUS for standing up for America in a way that no President has ever had the courage to do before. Thank you for putting America First. America is with you!" Rubio made no reference to Washington, Lincoln, or anyone else.

The same day, former representative Liz Cheney (R-WY) posted:

> Generations of American patriots, from our revolution onward, have fought for the principles Zelenskyy is risking his life to defend. But today, Donald Trump and JD Vance attacked Zelenskyy and pressured him to surrender the freedom of his people to the KGB war criminal who invaded Ukraine. History will remember this day – when an American President and Vice President abandoned all we stand for.

Later that day, Trump posted a dishonest, distorted summary of the meeting on Truth Social:

We had a very meaningful meeting in the White House today. Much was learned that could never be understood without conversation under such fire and pressure. It's amazing what comes out through emotion, and I have determined that President Zelenskyy is not ready for Peace if America is involved, because he feels our involvement gives him a big advantage in negotiations. I don't want advantage, I want PEACE. He disrespected the United States of America in its cherished Oval Office. He can come back when he is ready for Peace.

What does Trump mean by "Peace"? He never says with any specificity. Based on his comments and those from his administration, peace seems to include: a ceasefire, Russian retention of a fifth of Ukraine, and U.S. access to Ukraine's mineral wealth. What else? Nothing about withdrawing Russian troops. Nothing about rebuilding Ukraine. Nothing about assuring future stability.

Trump Punishes Ukraine for Peace

On March 1, the day after the Oval Office ambush, the U.S. officially halted military aid for Ukraine and also cut off Kyiv's access to American-derived intelligence.

Without U.S. intelligence, Ukraine's ability to conduct long-range strikes within Russian territory was severely impaired, as these operations relied heavily on real-time data provided by U.S. satellites and intelligence assets. Additionally, the pause in military aid has disrupted the delivery of critical weaponry, including artillery ammunition, howitzers, armored vehicles, and advanced missile systems like HIMARS and ATACMS. American and European leaders criticized the Trump administration for the action that not only helped Russia but also cost Ukrainian lives.

On March 3, Trump expressed fresh outrage over Zelensky saying that the end of the war could be "very, very far away." Trump posted a link to an Associated Press story outlining Zelensky's comments and said:

This is the worst statement that could have been made by Zelensky, and America will not put up with it for much longer! It is what I was saying, this guy doesn't want there to be peace as long as he has America's backing, and, Europe, in the meeting they had with Zelensky, stated flatly that they cannot do the job without the U.S. Probably not a great statement to have been made in terms of a show of strength against Russia. What are they thinking?

Trump also said Zelensky "won't be around very long" unless he succumbed to pressure and made a deal on U.S. terms. The Trump administration was also reported to be drawing up a plan to restore ties with Russia and lift sanctions on the Kremlin.

On March 4, the Guardian reported:

The Trump administration suspended delivery of all U.S. military aid to Ukraine, blocking billions in crucial shipments, as the White House piles pressure on Kyiv to sue for peace with Vladimir Putin. The decision affects deliveries of ammunition, vehicles, and other equipment. Ukraine's prime minister, Denys Shmyhal, said that Kyiv still had the means to supply its frontline forces but warned thousands of lives were at risk and vital U.S.-provided air defense systems could be affected.

"We will continue to work with the U.S. through all available channels in a calm manner," Shmyhal told a press conference. "We only have one plan – to win and to survive."

Moscow celebrated the decision, with the Kremlin spokesperson Dmitry Peskov saying the U.S. had been "the main supplier of this war so far." European and NATO allies were not informed in advance, a Polish foreign ministry spokesperson said.

"This is a very important decision, and the situation is very serious," Paweł Wroński told reporters. "This sentence may sound banal, but it has great political significance – it [the decision] was made without any information, or consultation, neither with NATO allies, nor with the Ramstein group," he said. The Ramstein group is an alliance of 57 countries that has coordinated aid to Ukraine during the war.

Governments in Europe, fearful of an emboldened Russia during a U.S. administration that resents a cold war-era pact to support its allies against aggression, have rushed to boost their own military spending.

The U.S. has provided $65.9 billion in military support to Ukraine since Russia's 2022 invasion, but further contributions hang in the balance after Donald Trump ordered a pause on aid to Kyiv. U.S. assistance to Ukraine includes military aid, budgetary assistance largely delivered through a World Bank trust fund, and other funds that have been delivered through the U.S. Agency for International Development, which has been throttled by the Trump White House. Some of the money sent by the U.S. to Ukraine helps the country pay the salaries of teachers and doctors and keeps the government running.

Trump Pushes 'Peace' Through Capitulation?

Oleksandr Merezhko, the chair of Ukraine's parliamentary foreign affairs committee, said Trump appeared to be pushing Ukraine towards capitulation. "To stop aid now means to help Putin," Merezhko told Reuters. "On the surface, this looks really bad. It looks like he is pushing us towards capitulation, meaning [accepting] Russia's demands."

Razom for Ukraine, a Ukrainian advocacy group, said: "By abruptly halting military assistance to Ukraine, President Trump is hanging Ukrainians out to dry and giving Russia the green light to continue marching west. Razom for Ukraine urges the White House to immediately reverse course, resume military aid, and pressure Putin to end his horrific invasion."

The announcement pertains mainly to aid that had been previously approved but not yet disbursed. Trump has not approved any new aid under his own presidential authority since taking office, and a new congressional aid package appears unlikely, at least in the near term.

U.S. Democrats said the aid pause was dangerous. Brendan Boyle, a congressman in Pennsylvania who is a co-chair of the congressional EU caucus, said it was "reckless, indefensible, and a direct threat to our national security."

On March 11, 2025, the U.S. agreed to resume military aid and intelligence sharing with Ukraine.

Weeks With No Progress in Ending the War

Zelensky's efforts to mollify Trump had little effect. Trump read Zelensky's letter during his March 4 speech but showed no sign of softening his attitude. Putin made no peace initiatives. On the contrary, he increased the intensity of the war.

In mid-March, the U.S. and Ukraine proposed a 30-day full ceasefire. Putin rejected it.

On March 30, Trump told NBC News he was "very angry" and "pissed off" at Putin for criticizing Zelensky's leadership, saying the comments were "not going in the right direction." Then he threatened Putin:

> If Russia and I are unable to make a deal on stopping the bloodshed in Ukraine, and if I think it was Russia's fault - which it might not be – but if I think it was Russia's fault, I am going to put secondary tariffs on oil, on all oil coming out of Russia. That would be that if you buy oil from Russia, you can't do business in the United States. There will be a 25% tariff on all oil, a 25- to 50-point tariff on all oil."

On April 15, Trump posted on Truth Social:

> The War between Russia and Ukraine is Biden's war, not mine. I just got here, and for four years during my term, had no problem in preventing it from happening. President Putin, and everyone else, respected your President! I HAD NOTHING TO DO WITH THIS WAR, BUT AM WORKING DILIGENTLY TO GET THE DEATH AND DESTRUCTION TO STOP. If the 2020 Presidential Election was not RIGGED, and it was, in so many ways, that horrible War would never have happened," Trump continued. "President Zelensky and Crooked Joe Biden did an absolutely horrible job in allowing this travesty to begin. There were so many ways of preventing it from ever starting. But that is the past. Now we have to get it to STOP, AND FAST. SO SAD!"

On the same day, the Washington Post reported that Trump had proposed to end U.S. funding for NATO, as well as for the United Nations and other international organizations. The proposal calls for cuts of roughly 90% in 2025. It would also cut the budget for the State Department by almost half, to $28.4 billion.

The proposal also calls for a complete cessation of funding for international peacekeeping missions, citing "recent mission failures" without providing further details.

The Post wrote:

> The U.S.'s funding of NATO is crucial in the face of Russia's threats to Ukraine, the EU, and other global security challenges. Its support helps deter Russian aggression by ensuring NATO remains a credible and unified military alliance, capable of responding to any hostile actions. This funding is also vital for supporting Ukraine, as NATO has pledged billions in security assistance to help Ukraine defend itself and maintain regional stability.

Also on April 15, Reuters reported that North Korea was supplying up to 100% of Russian artillery shells used in Ukraine.

Talks – apparently not really negotiations with the primary parties at the table –continued in various venues with no demonstrable progress. U.S. envoy Steve Witkoff, a billionaire real estate developer and lawyer, met several times with Putin and expressed a fondness for him. Witkoff suggested at one point that a peace deal would depend on what would happen with the Ukrainian territories occupied by Russia, implying that Ukraine would have to give up some territory. Witkoff claimed that Russia's invasion of Ukraine "was provoked."

Zelensky was not amused, telling a Kyiv press conference:

> I think that Mr. Witkoff has taken the strategy of the Russian side. I think it's really dangerous, because consciously or unconsciously, I don't know, he is spreading Russian narratives. I don't see him as having a mandate to discuss Ukrainian territories, because our territories belong to our people, not only to us, but to future Ukrainians. So, I don't understand what he is talking about at all.

Trump Prepared to Accept Sacrifice – By Ukraine

On April 18, Newsweek reported that the Trump administration was prepared to concede Crimea to the Russians, who occupied it in 2014. The only nations that currently recognize Crimea as Russian are North Korea, Belarus, Nicaragua, and Venezuela. Zelensky maintained his position that Ukraine will not give up any territory.

On the same day, Trump expressed impatience with the time it was taking to reach a peace deal that he had predicted he could accomplish in one day. Trump told reporters, "If for some reason, one of the two parties makes it very difficult, we're just going to say, 'you're foolish, you're fools, you're horrible people,' and we're going to just take a pass. But hopefully we won't have to do that."

In Paris, Rubio echoed the president's sentiment:

If we're so far apart, this won't happen, then the president is ready to move on.... We're not going to continue to fly all over the world and do meeting after meeting after meeting if no progress is being made. We're going to move on to other topics that are equally, if not more important in some ways, to the United States.

Does Putin care? Why would he?

Apparently, from limited mainstream media reporting, Ukraine is left to twist slowly, slowly in the wind, while the Western alliance spins in impotence.

In contrast, on April 18, British special services veteran Robin Horsfall had a different view in a Substack post:

Trump Has Inadvertently Dealt a Death Blow to Russia.

Despite his best efforts to prevent a Ukrainian victory, Trump has inadvertently dealt a death blow to Russia with his arbitrary tariffs on multiple nations. The slowdown in industrial activity has reduced the demand for oil. This, combined with increased output from Norway, the USA, and Saudi Arabia, has caused crude prices to drop, reducing Russian income to levels that threaten its ability to maintain its war economy....

While this is bad news for the world economy, it can only be good news for Ukraine. Russia depends on hydrocarbons for more than 60% of its income. Russia has lost 70% of its gas sales since Europe found new suppliers. International sanctions have prevented most international sales of oil, and even India and China have reduced demand under the threat of secondary sanctions.

Russia has already used almost three-quarters of its National Wealth Fund to continue the war. The final tranche will disappear faster as Russia's income drops even further. With current trends, Russia will soon have to decide whether it wants to maintain its national economy or its war with Ukraine.

On the war front, Russian weakness continues to show. Russia has lost an estimated 70% of its prewar military stock in armor, artillery, and ammunition, 50% of its fast jets have been destroyed, and its Black Sea fleet is unable to leave port. Russia's only resource on the battlefield are hordes of forced conscripts who are being killed or wounded at an average rate of 1,200 per day for no return.

F16s and Mirage 2000 fast jets, combined with overwhelming superiority in drone numbers and technology, have given Ukraine air superiority for the first time in three years. Ukrainian missiles and long-range fast drones can now fly 1,500 kilometers into Russia. With the end of the fake ceasefire agreement on energy infrastructure imposed on Ukraine by the Trump "'negotiators'," Ukraine can look forward to adding more pain to the Russian oil industry by destroying more refineries in the coming weeks. The supposed 'ceasefire' simply allowed Russia to restore some of the 45 facilities that had been damaged.

Ukraine now produces more than 40% of its own ammunition requirements. It produces its own drones and missile systems. With the continued support of the West, Ukraine is proving once again that it can defeat Russia. After Trump's repeated claims of Ukraine freeloading on USA money, President Zelensky offered $50 billion to purchase more Patriot missiles. The offer was immediately declined by Trump, showing once again that he intends to extort a minerals deal from Ukraine in return for any assistance.

The summer months are approaching; dry weather will increase the mobility of the armed forces on both sides. However, Russia has been reduced to using civilian cars and motorcycles to mount assaults, has used donkeys to transport ammunition, instructed men not to carry first aid kits into battle, 'because no one will recover you.' Russia is running out of money and time; the only hope that keeps them firmly in the war is the Trump negotiating team....

Putin and Trump are facing similar issues: no money, no friends, and no future. Europe, on the other hand, could benefit from their integrity and firm resolve regarding Ukraine.

Russia Declares Unilateral Easter Ceasefire

On April 19, Putin declared a 30-hour Easter "ceasefire." It got plenty of media coverage, for what it was worth. Zelensky accused Russia of violating "Putin's ceasefire more than 2,000 times" and proposed a 30-day cessation of long-range missile and drone strikes on civilian targets: "We are ready to move toward peace and a full, unconditional, and honest ceasefire that could last for at least 30 days –- but there has been no response from Russia on that so far."

Zelensky posted on X: "Either Putin does not have full control over his army, or the situation proves that in Russia, they have no intention of making a genuine move toward ending the war, and are only interested in favorable PR coverage."

On Easter – also Hitler's birthday – Trump had little to say about Ukraine, posting on Truth Social:

> Happy Easter to all, including the Radical Left Lunatics who are fighting and scheming so hard to bring Murderers, Drug Lords, Dangerous Prisoners, the Mentally Insane, and well-known MS-13 Gang Members and Wife Beaters, back into our Country.
>
> Happy Easter also to the WEAK and INEFFECTIVE Judges and Law Enforcement Officials who are allowing this

sinister attack on our Nation to continue, an attack so violent that it will never be forgotten! Sleepy Joe Biden purposefully allowed Millions of CRIMINALS to enter our Country, totally unvetted and unchecked, through an Open Borders Policy that will go down in history as the single most calamitous act ever perpetrated upon America. He was, by far, our WORST and most Incompetent President, a man who had absolutely no idea what he was doing -- But to him, and to the person that ran and manipulated the Auto Pen (perhaps our REAL President!), and to all of the people who CHEATED in the 2020 Presidential Election in order to get this highly destructive Moron Elected, I wish you, with great love, sincerity, and affection, a very Happy Easter!!!

Later, Trump posted: "Hopefully Russia and Ukraine will make a deal this week. Both will then start to do big business with the United States of America, which is thriving, and make a fortune!"

Also on Easter, former National Security Council (NSC) official Alexander Vindman, who was born in Ukraine, posted an assessment of Trump's progress on Ukraine on Substack:

Having run on the promise to end the war in Ukraine on "day one" after taking office, Donald Trump has failed to secure any meaningful progress towards a diplomatic settlement to the conflict. What we have seen over the past three months has been the needless extortion of our besieged ally, the rapid decline in relations between Europe and the United States, and the bizarre parroting of Russian talking points by senior members of the administration. Even the brazen attack on Palm Sunday church services in Sumy last week wasn't enough to convince the administration to change course with regards to Russia....

This administration is a disaster, and the inability to secure a ceasefire is just one of a thousand failures from Donald Trump and his team. What I am especially bothered by, however, is the inability of administration figures like Rubio and Witkoff to realize how much of a fool's errand it is trying to make peace with Putin. So far, we've burned bridges with friends and threw Ukraine under the bus, trying to meet the Russians half-way, and all we've been met with is more maximalist demands and more strikes against civilian targets.

The inability to secure a ceasefire isn't just a failure by Trump - it's also a failure by everyone in the administration who continues to enable him and give legitimacy to this fruitless endeavor. In the process of looking for a quick diplomatic win, Trump has completely fumbled the initial prospects for peace and shown himself to be unable to handle a drawn-out negotiation process. Peace doesn't come from surrender to Russia; it comes from pressuring Russia while continuing to support Ukraine. The United States must make the futility of Putin's war clear before Moscow will come to the negotiating table.

U.S. Undermines Peace Talks, Helps Moscow

On April 23, London-based multilateral "peace" talks collapsed, as U.S. "negotiators" Rubio and Witkoff declined to take part. Other countries promised to carry on, but no one seemed clear what was being negotiated.

The U.S. proposed a "final offer" calling for Ukraine to give up all the territory Russia has occupied, including Crimea, and to give up any future membership in NATO. These are the essential terms Putin has been demanding for almost a year. Russia would also benefit from eased economic sanctions and increased trade with the U.S. All Ukraine would get in exchange would be a cessation of hostilities (at least for a while), with no future security assurances. In other words, U.S. policy is for Ukraine to surrender and get it over with. This is a complete reversal of longstanding U.S. policy (the Welles doctrine), which refuses to concede territory to an invading army.

The U.S. blamed Ukraine for the collapse of the talks after Zelensky refused to relinquish his country's claim on Crimea and other Russian-occupied territories. He told a news conference: "There is nothing to talk about. This violates our Constitution. This is our territory, the territory of the people of Ukraine." Trump responded on Truth Social:

This statement is very harmful to the Peace Negotiations with Russia in that Crimea was lost years ago under the auspices of President Barack Hussein Obama, and is not even a point of discussion. Nobody is asking Zelensky to recognize Crimea as Russian Territory, but, if he wants Crimea, why didn't they fight for it eleven years ago when it was handed over to Russia without a shot being fired? [Zelensky was not president in 2014.] The area also houses, for many years before "the Obama handover," major Russian submarine bases.

It's inflammatory statements like Zelensky's that makes it so difficult to settle this War. He has nothing to boast about! The situation for Ukraine is dire. He can have Peace, or he can fight for another three years before losing the whole Country. I have nothing to do with Russia, but have much to do with wanting to save, on average, five thousand Russian and Ukrainian soldiers a week, who are dying for no reason whatsoever. The statement made by Zelensky today will do nothing but prolong the "killing field," and nobody wants that! We are very close to a Deal, but the man with "no cards to play'" should now, finally, GET IT DONE. I look forward to being able to help Ukraine and Russia, get out of this Complete and Total MESS, that would have never started if I were President!

On April 30, America and Ukraine signed a deal that grants America access to Ukraine's valuable minerals in the shape of a new reconstruction investment fund that the two countries will jointly manage.

Trump's promise to end the war within 24 hours of his inauguration went unfulfilled a hundred days later and counting. Trump courted Putin while relentlessly bullying Zelensky, who may still have cards to play. Ukraine is stronger now than it was three years ago, although perhaps not strong enough, without significantly increased support from Europe. American popular support for Ukraine has reached its highest level in months. Ukraine has become the world's largest arms importer.

In a May 7 interview with the BBC, former President Biden described U.S. pressure on Ukraine to give up territory to Russia as "modern-day appeasement," without mentioning Trump. According to Biden, "Anybody that thinks he (Putin) is going to stop if some territory is conceded as part of a peace deal is just foolish. I just don't understand how people think that if we allow a dictator (Putin), a thug, to decide he's going to take significant portions of land that aren't his, that that's going to satisfy him. I don't quite understand."

Aspects of the New American Foreign Policy

The highlights of Trump's first 100 days of foreign policy have featured, as we have seen, the disruption of decades of traditional international norms, leaving allies (and probably enemies) wondering if there is any plan for some unspoken new world order. Or is chaos the point?

Meanwhile, other expressions of the American worldview have included:

- Unquestioning support of the Israeli genocide of Palestinians in Gaza, combined with repressive police tactics in the U.S. against anyone who opposes genocide.
- Establishing foreign concentration camps in places like El Salvador (a dictatorship) and Libya (the part that's not even a state but a warlord-controlled territory). These overseas gulags are supported by utterly lawless domestic disregard for due process of law by masked ICE agents who seize people on the street with no warrant, no identification, and no lawful authority.
- Alienating pretty much the whole world with an erratic imposition of tariffs with no rational justification, creating uncertainty and disruption in world supply chains and markets. Trump's April 2 "Day of Liberation" included tariffs on almost every country, including one with no people. One exception was Russia (although other sanctions remain in place).
- Targeting Greenland for increased surveillance, part of Trump's plan to acquire Greenland, an autonomous Danish territory, one way or another. Denmark was not amused and summoned the U.S. Ambassador for consultations.
- Declaring that the United States had no significant interest in the conflict between India and Pakistan, which broke out (again) on April 22, with a terrorist attack that killed 26 people in Kashmir. India blamed

Pakistan. Pakistan denied responsibility. Pakistan also violated the 2003 ceasefire agreement for 12 consecutive nights. On May 6-7, India launched airstrikes against nine locations in Pakistan. Fighting continued for several days. India has nuclear weapons. Pakistan has nuclear weapons. Any nuclear war would have global consequences, including a possible nuclear winter. On May 8, while other administration officials quietly called for India and Pakistan to de-escalate (without U.S. involvement), Vice President JD Vance told Fox News: "What we can do is try to encourage these folks to de-escalate a little bit, but we're not going to get involved in the middle of war that's fundamentally none of our business...."

American Foreign Policy in 2025: Nuclear War Is None of Our Business

After a few days, with 36 nations engaged in negotiations, India and Pakistan worked out a ceasefire. Trump took credit for the ceasefire. India said Trump was not involved, that the ceasefire was a bilateral agreement. On June 21, Pakistan announced it was nominating Trump for the Nobel Peace Prize for his role in the ceasefire, whatever it was.

Peace Still Doesn't Break Out in Ukraine

More than 30 years ago, in 1994, Ukraine had more nuclear weapons than any country in the world other than the U.S. and Russia. Ukraine surrendered those weapons in exchange for assurances of territorial integrity from the U.S, the UK, and Russia. That lasted until 2014, when Russia seized Crimea. Little wonder that Zelensky feels the need for powerful security commitments to keep his country safe.

On June 1, 2025, Ukraine surprised Russia and pretty much the rest of the world by simultaneously attacking five air bases deep inside Russia, thousands of miles apart. Ukrainian President Zelensky said 117 drones, separately piloted, were used in operation Spider's Web. SBU (Ukrainian Security Service) claimed the drones struck 34% of Russia's strategic cruise missile-carrying bombers. The claim was that 13 bombers were destroyed and others were damaged). The operation took 18 months to carry out, infiltrating drone-laden trucks into Russia that could be remotely activated and self-destroyed. According to Zelensky, everyone involved in Spider's

Web was safely evacuated before the attacks, which took place the day before scheduled peace talks in Istanbul.

Zelensky did not alert Trump ahead of the attacks. In the aftermath, Trump called Putin and reportedly spoke for 75 minutes. Trump did not call his putative ally, Zelensky. According to Trump, Putin said he would "have to respond to the recent attack on the airfields." In recent months, Russia has launched more than 1,000 drones per week at military and civilian targets in Ukraine, including more than 355 drones and at least 9 missiles on May 26 (leading to Trump calling Putin "absolutely CRAZY" on Truth Social). Trump has not approved any new military aid to Ukraine in 2025 and has not spent the $3.85 billion already authorized by Congress for Ukraine. The peace talks on June 2 produced little, if any, progress. Russia responded to Ukraine's surprise attack with some of the heaviest bombing of the war.

Trump Maintains Lack of Pressure on Russia

Since returning to office, Trump has issued no new sanctions on Russia despite Russia's continuing aggression against Ukraine that prompted sanctions in 2022. This has helped the Russian war effort. Trump has lifted sanctions on Russia imposed in 2015 in relation to Syria. Trump has eased sanctions on Russian banks critical to Putin. And according to The New York Times, "the administration has eased restrictions. And without new ones, analysts say, existing measures lose their force. The result has created an opening for new dummy companies to funnel funds and critical components to Russia, including computer chips and military equipment." Any serious response designed to repel Russian aggression would at least tighten sanctions as well as impose new ones.

On July 1, Robin Horsfall wrote on Substack: "The Putin/Trump plan to discredit President Zelensky failed miserably. The world openly admires Zelensky." Horsfall went on to assess Ukraine:

> In Ukraine, the war has progressed in a positive manner for
> Ukraine. Ukraine continues to deplete Russian air defences.
> Air defence numbers in Donbas are so low missiles were moved
> from Crimea to fill gaps. This left gaps in Crimean defences that

Ukrainian drones penetrated and struck even more air defences, fuel storage centres and oil refineries. Russia's response was to once again attack Ukrainian civilian centres....

Russia still attempts to use its mass of infantry in an attempt to overwhelm Ukrainian defences. In the past year, these tactics have made small incremental gains at enormous cost in men and materiel. Now, the cracks are appearing in Russian forces.... Russia is on the edge of defeat, but we would never know it to hear their representatives. Their economy is failing, inflation is climbing fast, the ruble is worthless on the international markets.

The only hope for Putin is Trump. Trump intends to unilaterally halt sanctions on Russian banks, enabling Putin to trade more easily and earn more income to keep his war going. Trump wants, or needs to save Putin from defeat; his recent actions show this very clearly. Without Trump, Putin would be looking for peace.

Also on July 1, NBC News reported more evidence that Trump was increasingly a Russian ally. According to NBC, the Pentagon stopped shipping missiles and ammunition to Ukraine "amid concern about the U.S. military's stockpiles, according to two defense officials, two congressional officials, and two sources with knowledge of the decision." That suggests that it requires six anonymous sources to carry off an incredibly bogus argument. To believe that, you'd have to believe the Pentagon wasn't paying attention to its supplies for years. The U.S. was withholding air defense weapons when Russia had launched a record 5,438 drones during June alone. NBC reported that the weapons Ukraine isn't getting are among the weapons it needs the most:

> ...dozens of Patriot interceptors that can defend against incoming Russian missiles, thousands of 155 mm high explosive Howitzer munitions, more than 100 Hellfire missiles, more than 250 precision-guided missile systems known as GMLRS and dozens each of Stinger surface-to-air missiles, AIM air-to-air missiles and grenade launchers.

Ukraine has repeatedly appealed for additional U.S. and European air defense weaponry as Russia has stepped up its air raids in recent months. Over the weekend, Ukraine's Defense Ministry said Russia had launched the largest aerial attack on the country since Moscow's full-scale invasion in 2022, firing 60 missiles and 477 drones.

According to the BBC, when Trump and Zelensky met during the NATO summit on June 25, Trump told reporters the U.S. was going to try to make more Patriot missiles available to Ukraine. The BBC also wrote: "The Kremlin, for its part, welcomed news of the reduction in weapons shipments, saying reducing the flow of weapons to Kyiv will help end the conflict faster." On July 9, Trump announced he was reversing his July 1 decision to halt military aid to Ukraine. He did not indicate the scale of the resumed aid, commenting to reporters: "We're going to send some more weapons. We have to [so that Ukrainians] have to be able to defend themselves."

The next day, Trump had some harsh but empty words for Putin, unaccompanied by new sanctions: "We get a lot of bullshit thrown at us by Putin, if you want to know the truth. He's very nice all the time, but it turns out to be meaningless."

Part 2

The Golden Age of America – Or What You Need to Believe to Make It So

On March 4, 2025, after 43 days in office, President Trump spoke to a joint session of Congress at the Capitol in a virtual State of the Union address. His speech lasted about a hundred minutes, perhaps a record. The transcript of the speech, edited for length and relevance with appropriate ellipses, is punctuated by commentary to clarify, correct, and rebut the president's words.

The Golden Age of America

> **TRUMP**: Six weeks ago, I stood beneath the dome of this Capitol and proclaimed the dawn of the golden age of America. From that moment on, it has been nothing but swift and unrelenting action to usher in the greatest and most successful era in the history of our country. We have accomplished more in 43 days than most administrations accomplish in four years or eight years – and we are just getting started. Thank you.

Golden Age? Who doesn't want a Golden Age? What is the evidence of a Golden Age after 43 days? What is the evidence of a Golden

Age by the time you're reading this?

Trump certainly delivered "swift and unrelenting action" during his first six weeks and ever since. He issued at least 143 executive orders, at least 56 of which mirror the plans outlined in Project 2025, which seeks to transform the American government from its traditional form into an authoritarian state with power concentrated in the presidency and government agencies staffed with loyalists. Among the other stated goals of Project 2025 (922 pages) published by the Heritage Foundation (irony unintended) are:

Eliminate checks and balances;

Eliminate due process of law;

Reduce taxes on corporations and rich people;

Cut funding for Medicaid and Medicare;

Eliminate environmental regulations, promote fossil fuels;

Restrict immigration and deport millions of immigrants;

Eliminate rights for LGBTQ people and other minorities;

Weaken unions, reduce worker safety regulations;

Abolish the Department of Education, cut education aid to states;

Eliminate reproductive rights for women;

Allow child labor;

Rewrite American history in government, museums, and schools;

Suppress the vote.

With his co-president of sorts, Elon Musk, appearing to run the illegal DOGE (Department of Government Efficiency), Trump moved quickly to disrupt wide swaths of American government and culture. Most of his actions were unexplained, unjustified, disruptive, or destructive. And many of them were promptly blocked by the federal courts, which have consistently ruled against Trump in the overwhelming majority of some 300 or more lawsuits, most of which are still in litigation [thrown in doubt on June 27 by the Supreme Court's ruling in *Trump v. CASA*, which strictly limited federal judges' ability to issue nationwide injunctions.

As for Trump's boast that this is "the greatest and most successful era in the history of our country," there is no credible basis for the claim. Certainly not after 43 days. Or after 160 days. Or now. Presumably, the boast is false.

But when he says, "We are just getting started," you've been warned.

> **TRUMP**: I return to this chamber tonight to report that America's momentum is back. Our spirit is back. Our pride is back. Our confidence is back. And the American dream is surging bigger and better than ever before. The American dream is unstoppable, and our country is on the verge of a comeback the likes of which the world has never witnessed, and perhaps will never witness again. Never been anything like it.

Momentum? Pride? Spirit? Confidence? These are tropes of American exceptionalism that Trump preposterously invokes over and over again. Never seen anything like it.

But what does the "comeback" actually look like? Thousands of fired federal employees. Dozens of alienated allies. Threat after threat to the social safety net. Hundreds of lawsuits, mostly upheld by judges. The Orwellian obliteration of America's history across almost all government websites. Untold amounts of personal information were compromised by Elon Musk's trolls in the sham Department of Government Efficiency (DOGE). This is the "unstoppable" American dream? We need to wake up.

This is the MAGA version of American exceptionalism in a distorting mirror, pretending to reclaim a past that never was by projecting a future that will never be.

The early months of the second Trump administration are surely something "the likes of which the world has never witnessed." But it will take luck – and serious mass resistance – to have any assurance that it will not be carnage we "will never witness again."

The Election Was a Mandate?

> **TRUMP**: The presidential election of November 5 was a mandate like has not been seen in many decades. We won all 7 swing states, giving us an Electoral College victory of 312 votes. We won the popular vote by big numbers....

Here, Trump sandwiches one fact between two lies. He won the electoral college with a middling 312 votes, but the electoral college distorts the popular vote.

The 2024 presidential election delivered no clear mandate. Trump won 49.8% of the popular vote, enough to win, but only a plurality, not a majority. He won the popular vote by a margin of 1.5%. More people voted for someone else than voted for Trump. Trump's 77 million votes were fewer than Joe Biden's 81 million votes in 2020. Biden won a majority of the votes, 51.3% of the total, but even so, only a scant mandate.

During this part of the speech, U.S. Rep. Al Green, D-TX, interrupted to shout: "You have no mandate to cut Medicaid." Trump did not respond. House Speaker Mike Johnson had Rep. Green thrown out. He went willingly. His shameless fellow Democrats offered no support.

> **TRUMP**: Over the past six weeks, I have signed nearly 100 executive orders and taken more than 400 executive actions, a record to restore common sense, safety, optimism, and wealth all across our wonderful land. The people elected me to do the job, and I'm doing it. In fact, it has been stated by many that the first month of our presidency – it's our presidency – is the most successful in the history of our nation. By many. And what makes it even more impressive is that do you know who No. 2 is? George Washington. How about that? How about that? I don't know about that list, but. But we'll take it.

The claim that "many" have stated that "the first month of our presidency – it's our presidency – is the most successful in the history of our nation" is not easily supported by evidence. There's no useful definition of what constitutes a "successful" first month.

No wonder he says "it's our presidency," using the royal "we." The rest of you 340 million Americans just get to watch. And submit. Until we lock you up. There's no basis for saying it's the most successful first month of any presidency. How is that even measured? Over 100 executive orders may be a record. So is the number that have been taken to court. So is the number that have been blocked. Where's the "success"?

The January 20 executive order #14156, in which Trump, on his own authority, rewrote the Fourteenth Amendment to the Constitution, is patently unconstitutional. And it's in court. This created a constitutional crisis on Trump's first day in office. Courts in four states issued nationwide preliminary injunctions blocking enforcement, deeming the order to be unconstitutional. The order has been challenged in at least 10 different lawsuits. The Trump administration had appealed, without success, until it reached the Supreme Court. On June 27, that court issued a stunningly dishonest and cowardly ruling in the case, *Trump v. CASA*. The court's ruling sharply reduced federal judges' authority to issue nationwide injunctions, grossly expanding Trump's power. But the corrupt majority in the 6-3 decision lacked the honesty or the courage to rule on the fundamental issue of birthright citizenship, leaving the Constitution wounded and its attacker on the loose. The Supreme Court order allowed lower courts to issue national injunctions by way of class action suits.

On July 10, New Hampshire Federal District Court Judge Joseph N. Laplante certified a lawsuit before him as a class action, effectively blocking (for the moment) Trump's executive order that rewrote the Constitution on birthright citizenship. When it comes to measuring a president's early term, if creating confusion and chaos, legal and illegal, isn't a measure of success, it's a warning.

National Emergency on Our Southern Border?

TRUMP: Within hours of taking the oath of office, I declared a national emergency on our southern border. And I deployed the U.S. military and Border Patrol to repel the invasion of our country. And what a job they've done. As a result, illegal border crossings last month were by far the lowest ever recorded ever. They heard my words, and they chose not to come. Much easier that way.

The "emergency" and the "invasion" are useful figments of Trump's imagination, allowing him to assert unjustified authority. But there appears to be some truth to his claim about border crossings. It is also the continuation of a trend that began a year earlier, when President Biden issued an executive order shutting down asylum requests. The decrease in illegal border crossings is also the result of increased efforts by Mexico in recent years. Reliable statistics are hard to come by.

Trump's claim of an "invasion of our country" is false. It doesn't matter how many times he repeats it. No other country is invading us. On March 15, Trump invoked the Alien Enemies Act of 1798, claiming that a Venezuelan gang was invading the U.S. He used that false claim to justify the deportation of hundreds of immigrants with no due process of law.

On May 1, in the case of J.A.V. et al. vs Donald Trump, Texas federal judge Fernando Rodriguez, Jr., a Trump appointee, ruled that the U.S. was not being invaded in any way contemplated by the 1798 law. The ruling also held that the government must allow the migrant plaintiffs to exercise their habeas corpus rights to due process of law.

> **TRUMP:** In comparison, under Joe Biden, the worst president in American history, there were hundreds of thousands of illegal crossings a month, and virtually all of them, including murderers, drug dealers, gang members, and people from mental institutions and insane asylums, were released into our country. Who would want to do that?

Trump has been repeating some version of this lie for years, if not decades. Unfortunately, there is a grain of truth embedded in the lie – some very bad people have been released, but their number is minuscule overall. Trump uses the lie because it works. It creates fear among people who have no reliable way of knowing what's true. It's pure demagoguery. And it serves to justify the creation of a police state.

The attack on Biden is gratuitous and unjustified, unsupported by any evidence. Biden's successful border policy made any success for Trump's border policy possible.

In the first weeks of the Trump administration, border enforcement has been rounding up people, but they're having a hard time finding anyone who has committed any crime other than entering the country illegally, which is a misdemeanor equivalent to trespassing. Sometimes the border agents don't even try: they just deport people with tattoos. Or they target legal immigrants who oppose the Israeli genocide in Gaza. The American police state is growing bolder, acting without warrants, without identification, without due process of law required by the Constitution.

'I Imposed an Immediate Freeze on Hiring'

TRUMP: Upon taking office, I imposed an immediate freeze on all federal hiring, a freeze on all new federal regulations, and a freeze on all foreign aid.

None of this is thought out or supported by rational analysis. Instead, it's like doing surgery with a chainsaw. The hiring freeze was followed by waves of firings so random, for example, that they had to hire some people back to protect nuclear weapons. The freeze on foreign aid is incredibly mindless. The virtual destruction of USAID is causing disease and death in countries around the world. Thousands, if not millions of people, are suffering needlessly as a result. This is not rational policy at work; it is irrational ideology.

In January, Elon Musk, running DOGE, said of USAID, "It's time for it to die." In May, Bill Gates, himself once the world's richest man, said of Musk: "The picture of the world's richest man killing the world's poorest children is not a pretty one."

In February, approximately 24,500 probationary federal employees were terminated without prior notification to states and local governments. Agencies affected included the Department of Health and Human Services (HHS), which planned to cut about 10,000 employees, and the Department of Agriculture (USDA), which laid off approximately 5,700 workers. These mass firings were challenged in court and subsequently blocked by U.S. District Judge James Bredar, who ruled that the dismissals violated necessary procedures for mass layoffs [they were illegal]. This ruling led to the reinstatement of the terminated employees in the 19 Democratic-led states and Washington, D.C.

U.S District Court Judge William H. Alsup for the Northern District of California also ruled that the firings were illegal, stating: "It is sad, a sad day when our government would fire some good employee and say it was based on performance when they know good and well that's a lie."

In addition to the probationary employee terminations, other significant layoffs occurred:

■ Department of Energy (DOE): Approximately 1,200 to 2,000 employees were laid off, affecting critical areas such as the National Nuclear Security Administration (NNSA).

- Department of Veterans Affairs (VA): Over 1,000 probationary employees were dismissed, including researchers focused on mental health, cancer treatments, addiction recovery, prosthetics, and burn pit exposure.
- Department of the Treasury: The Internal Revenue Service (IRS) fired about 6,000 to 7,000 probationary employees during the peak tax-filing season, raising concerns about potential delays in tax return processing and reduced customer service.

Firings by the thousands continued across government agencies in March and April, as have court challenges to their legality. By May, the total workforce cuts had reached 130,000, with another 150,000 anticipated, with impacts felt across the government.

> **TRUMP:** I terminated the ridiculous "green new scam." I withdrew from the unfair Paris climate accord, which was costing us trillions of dollars that other countries were not paying.

Trump's denial of the human causes and impacts of climate change is longstanding. He's just wrong. He doesn't care about the science. He doesn't care about the causes. He doesn't care about the human impacts. And he lies about the cost.

His claim about the Paris accord is another lie. It has not cost the U.S. "trillions." The U.S. has pledged $3 billion but has paid only $2 billion. The U.S. joined the Paris accord in 2016 under Obama, withdrew in 2017 under Trump, rejoined in 2021 under Biden, and withdrew in 2025 under Trump.

Trump's climate policy is to increase warming – "Drill, baby, drill." He may as well have said, "Burn, baby, burn."

I Withdrew From WHO

> **TRUMP:** I withdrew from the corrupt World Health Organization. And I also withdrew from the anti-American U.N. Human Rights Council.

Trump quit the World Health Organization (WHO) in 2017, Biden rejoined in 2021, and now the U.S. is out again. The U.S. support for the WHO was about $1.3 billion last year. Trump's executive order of January 20, 2025, justifies the U.S. withdrawal based on "inappropriate political influence of WHO member states" (no further detail), and its demand for "unfairly onerous payment" from the U.S. WHO has had its scandals, notably in 2022 when the head of the Syria office was placed on leave amidst allegations of corruption. WHO has also made efforts to address its problems.

Somewhat hilariously, Trump also blames WHO for its 2020 "mishandling of the COVID-19 pandemic." The blame rightfully falls on Trump, whose administration's disastrous response to the same pandemic caused more than 450,000 unnecessary American deaths, according to The Lancet, a highly reputable medical journal.

In a letter to the editor published in the Financial Times on February 12, 2025, Ahmed Uzair Khatri from the Shaheed Zulfikar Ali Bhutto Institute of Science and Technology (SZABIST) at the University of Karachi, Pakistan, wrote:

> The funding of the World Health Organization is more than just a financial commitment; it's a reflection of global priorities. As a student of international relations, I see the WHO's financial instability as a geopolitical power play that leaves billions of people vulnerable. The U.S. decision to withdraw funding was not just a moment of political grandstanding; it revealed a troubling trend, where nations use financial influence as leverage, often at the cost of global well-being.

Trump quit the UN Human Rights Council (UNHRC) in 2018. This year, he quit three UN organizations based primarily on unsupported charges, in defense of Israel, stating in his executive order of February 4:

> Three UN organizations that deserve renewed scrutiny are the UNHRC, the UN Educational, Scientific, and Cultural Organization (UNESCO), and the UN Relief and Works Agency for Palestine Refugees in the Near East (UNRWA).

UNRWA has reportedly been infiltrated by members of groups long designated by the Secretary of State (Secretary) as foreign terrorist organizations, and UNRWA employees were involved in the October 7, 2023, Hamas attack on Israel. UNHRC has protected human rights abusers by allowing them to use the organization to shield themselves from scrutiny, while UNESCO has demonstrated failure to reform itself, has continually demonstrated anti-Israel sentiment over the past decade, and has failed to address concerns over mounting arrears.

These are longstanding Israeli complaints against organizations that oppose Israel's war crimes, such as illegally seizing Palestinian land or committing genocide in Gaza. These are war crimes and crimes against humanity that Trump supports, as have his predecessors. For all practical purposes, U.S. policy is that the only good Palestinian is a dead Palestinian – an indefensible continuation of U.S. policy toward Native Americans for more than three centuries.

> **TRUMP**: We ended all of Biden's environmental restrictions that were making our country far less safe and totally unaffordable. And importantly, we ended the last administration's insane electric vehicle mandate, saving our auto workers and companies from economic destruction….

He also makes unsupported claims about eliminating unspecified regulations and threatens federal workers with losing their jobs if they don't come into the office to work, ending remote work.

The lie here is that "environmental restrictions" make the country unsafe or unaffordable. Trump is in denial about climate change. He has been for years. But it's climate change that is making our country unsafe and unaffordable. As for the "insane electric vehicle mandate," he offers no rationale. He ignores the impact on his "co-president's" Tesla Inc., an automobile and clean energy company. He has no cogent analysis of climate change and pretends the damage it causes has nothing to do with science. Then he sets about to fire scientists and suppress the science. Trump doesn't know what's real, and he doesn't want to know what's real.

'We've Ended Weaponized Government'

> **TRUMP**: And we've ended weaponized government where, as an example, a sitting president is allowed to viciously prosecute his political opponent, like me. How did that work out? Not too good. Not too good.

Not too good, indeed. America elected its first convicted felon (34 counts) to the presidency. Also, the first adjudged finger-rapist president. And the first multi-bankruptcy president. But not the first draft-dodger.

The American justice system, with the collusion of the Supreme Court, failed to hold Trump accountable for most of the serious charges against him in multiple other cases. Justice was delayed. Justice was denied. It didn't matter how strong the cases against him were. There was no reckoning. It was a constitutional failure of staggering proportions.

Now we have our first presidential convicted felon and finger-rapist. And he's seeking revenge on all those involved in the failed effort to hold him accountable before the law. Not too good.

TRUMP: And I've stopped all government censorship and brought back free speech in America. It's back.

This is a preposterous lie. The opposite is true. Trump has imposed censorship and issued executive orders banning free speech.

Under Trump, government censorship is unprecedented. Trump has ordered a purge of anything "woke," which is undefined. Government agencies have banned the use of hundreds of words, including: accessible, activism, advocate, barrier, bias, Black, DEI, disabilities, discrimination, diverse, environmental quality, equitable, ethnicity, female, gender, hate speech, historically, immigrants, inclusive, inequality, injustice, LGBTQ+, marginalize, mental health, minority, MSM, Native American, oppression, polarization, political, pollution, pregnant people, prejudice, privilege, pronoun, prostitute, race, sex, social justice, stereotype, systemic, they/them, transgender,, trauma, unconscious bias, underserved, undervalued, victim, and women.

There has never been anything like this. The Pentagon attempted to erase the official memory of Jackie Robinson, Colin Powell, Navajo code talkers, Tuskegee airmen, and non-white Medal of Honor winners – this is overtly racist.

Censorship at other agencies – including Health and Human Services, the National Park Service, and the Arlington National Cemetery – has been equally bigoted, targeting Black people, gays, women, and anything considered "DEI" (diversity, equity, and inclusion) related. This is an Orwellian perversion of language.

In the real world, bigotry is clear. If you're against diversity, you're a bigot. If you're against equality, you're a bigot. If you're against inclusion, you're a bigot.

Trump's world is all, blatantly intellectually corrupt. It consigns the majority of Americans to the status of un-persons, un-citizens, unworthy of the concern their government owes them.

The Trump administration is committed to this new bigotry, even trying to force private European companies and others to drop DEI efforts.

> **TRUMP:** And two days ago, I signed an order making English the official language of the United States of America. I renamed the Gulf of Mexico the Gulf of America. And likewise, I renamed, for a great president, William McKinley, Mount McKinley again. Beautiful Alaska, we love Alaska. We love Alaska.

These are all executive orders without the force of law. Most of the world rejects "Gulf of America." The Associated Press (AP) refuses to use it, and in response, Trump bans AP reporters from the White House. Alaska rejects Mount McKinley, retaining the traditional Mount Denali.

We've Ended Diversity, Equity, Inclusion

> **TRUMP:** We've ended the tyranny of so-called diversity, equity, and inclusion policies all across the entire federal government. And indeed, the private sector and our military. And our country will be woke no longer. We believe that whether you are a doctor, an accountant, a lawyer, or an air traffic controller, you should be hired and promoted based on skill and competence, not race or gender. Very important. You should be hired based on merit. And the Supreme Court, in a brave and very powerful decision, has allowed us to do so. Thank you. Thank you very much. Thank you.

He might as well have announced: we've made American bigotry great again.

Trump's argument is based on a false premise that unqualified people are hired under DEI policies. The reality is that, for most of American history, women and minorities of all sorts would not be hired, just because of who they were, regardless of their ability or qualifications. DEI policies were designed to address this by hiring qualified people other than cis white males.

There has been no showing that DEI hires are anything but qualified.

Invoking the toxic rightwing trope of "wokeness," Trump orders that bigotry be reestablished as official policy. "Woke" remains undefined by the right, but is always used pejoratively. The Urban Dictionary defines "woke" as "being aware of social injustice and racism in the community." Being anti-woke, then, is to be pro-injustice, pro-racist. Trump is reinstating discrimination based on prejudice.

As a Reddit post put it: "Actually, old white dudes asking a friend to hire their idiot nephew or buying their lazy grandson's admission into their legacy school got more unqualified people into places than DEI."

As for the Supreme Court, Clarence Thomas is a DEI hire.

> **TRUMP**: We have removed the poison of critical race theory from our public schools, and I signed an order making it the official policy of the United States government that there are only two genders: male and female. I also signed an executive order to ban men from playing in women's sports….

Trump lies about critical race theory. Public schools K-12, do not teach critical race theory. This is another false rightwing trope. There is no showing to the contrary. Some colleges and graduate programs may teach about critical race theory, but there's no evidence anyone teaches it as a mandatory ideology. That would be because it frames an approach to history that is rooted in factual reality: the American immersion in slavery and bigotry since 1619.

Pretending that there are only two genders is just silly and does not change reality. The pretense is without scientific basis. But it will do real harm to those whose actual biology fails to conform to the arbitrary demands of this procrustean bed. The imaginary binary rule is as mindless as it is cruel.

Trump turns to the gallery to honor Payton McNabb, a former high school volleyball player who, in 2022, was injured when a transgender woman player spiked the ball into her head, causing traumatic brain injury. He also refers to a few other cases, calls them "demeaning to women," and says, "We're not going to put up with it any longer."

McNabb is one of 214,000-plus women injured playing volleyball in high school or college since 2012. Almost none of the injuries were caused by transgender athletes. McNabb is now a paid spokesperson for the Independent Women's Forum (IWF), which advocates against contraception, opposes essential healthcare for trans people, promotes outing LGBTQ+ high school students against their will, and supports lodging trans detainees in facilities of their birth gender. The IWF's former legal director now works in the White House. The issue of originally male bodies competing against women is a reasonable concern. It is also exceedingly rare. The handful of cases need to be handled with discretion, respect, and fairness. It is fundamentally irresponsible to make a political football out of a case where a volleyball player wasn't playing the game all that well.

Immediate Relief to Working Families?

> **TRUMP**: Among my very highest priorities is to rescue our economy and get dramatic and immediate relief to working families. As you know, we inherited from the last administration an economic catastrophe and an inflation nightmare.... Joe Biden especially let the price of eggs get out of control. The egg prices, out of control....

A major focus of our fight to defeat inflation is rapidly reducing the cost of energy.... That's why, on my first day in office, I declared a national energy emergency. As you've heard me say many times, we have more liquid gold under our feet than any nation on earth, and by far, and now I fully authorize the most talented team ever assembled to go and get it. It's called drill, baby, drill....

"Dramatic and immediate relief to working families"?

Maybe someday. Not yet. Probably not soon. Maybe never. Trump's first months of economic moves have produced uncertainty, a declining stock market, increased inflation, and the price of eggs keeps going up. The first quarter produced a contraction of the economy. Trump's economic analysis is simplistic, unrealistic, and rooted in fantasies designed to help his supporters, not the American people.

Trump flat-out lies when he claims that "we inherited from the last administration an economic catastrophe and an inflation nightmare...." In

January 2025, the U.S. economy was widely viewed as a model of resilience and strength, with many analysts and publications describing it as the "envy of the world" due to its strong growth and low unemployment, especially in comparison to other developed economies. Inflation was less than 3% in January, concerning but far from a "nightmare." Inflation was 2.8% for the full year ending in February.

Unmentioned, but crucial: Trump's fossil fuel policies will only speed up global warming. That is a real national emergency. Trump does nothing but make it worse. For everyone. Under Trump, political dogma determines what's considered reality. In its 2025 Annual Threat Assessment, the U.S. intelligence community did not include climate change as a national security threat, marking the first time in over a decade that it has been excluded from the list.

Trump also left unmentioned: what tariffs will do to inflation and what impact they will have on working families.

The Department of Government Efficiency

> **TRUMP**: To further combat inflation, we will not only be reducing the cost of energy but will be ending the flagrant waste of taxpayer dollars. And to that end, I have created the brand-new Department of Government Efficiency. DOGE. Perhaps you've heard of it. Perhaps. Which is headed by Elon Musk, who is in the gallery tonight.
>
> Thank you, Elon. He's working very hard. He didn't need this. He didn't need this. Thank you very much, we appreciate it. Everybody here, even this side, appreciates it, I believe. They just don't want to admit that. Just listen to some of the appalling waste we have already identified....

Trump's claim that he created a "brand-new" government department is misleading. DOGE is not a legitimate government department created by Congress, as mandated by the Constitution. Sidestepping the Constitution by executive order on January 20, 2025, Trump re-named the existing United States Digital Service (USDS) as the United States DOGE Service, with the same acronym, USDS, and established it in the Executive Office of the President. The executive order established DOGE teams throughout the government:

- "In consultation with USDS, each Agency Head shall establish within their respective Agencies a DOGE Team of at least four employees, which may include Special Government Employees, hired or assigned within thirty days of the date of this Order."
- "Each DOGE Team will typically include one DOGE Team Lead, one engineer, one human resources specialist, and one attorney."
- "[The DOGE] Administrator shall work with Agency Heads to promote inter-operability between agency networks and systems, ensure data integrity, and facilitate responsible data collection and synchronization."
- "Agency Heads shall take all necessary steps…to ensure USDS has full and prompt access to all unclassified agency records, software systems, and IT systems. USDS shall adhere to rigorous data protection standards."

The executive order says the purpose of DOGE is "to implement the President's DOGE Agenda, by modernizing Federal technology and software to maximize governmental efficiency and productivity."

What this looks like is a digital coup d'etat, designed to put the entire government, even agencies created to be independent, under the control of the Executive Office of the President. Trump has promoted DOGE as a vehicle to reduce "waste, fraud, and abuse," but that is unmentioned in the executive order.

In the early weeks of the presidency, DOGE employees swarmed through the Treasury, the Internal Revenue Service, the Veterans Administration, and other agencies, accessing the personal data on millions of Americans. They offered no explanation. Instead, they distracted attention from their main activity by firing thousands of government employees, randomly, without any stated analysis or justification. Many had to be hired back when it turned out they were too valuable to let go.

Elon Musk was generally understood to be running DOGE, as the president said here. But in court, government lawyers have told judges they don't know who is running DOGE. In effect, Trump outsourced significant government authority, with no accountability to anyone but the president.

Appalling Waste We Have Identified?

> **TRUMP**: They just don't want to admit that. Just listen to some
> of the appalling waste we have already identified.
> [To support this claim, Trump went through 19 items with val-
> ues ranging from $22 billion to $250,000. Eleven of the items
> were for foreign countries.]
> **TRUMP**: $22 billion from H.H.S. to provide free housing and
> cars for illegal aliens.

This is a lie.

The money went to legal aliens, mostly through non-profit organizations. During fiscal years 2020-2024, five years during both the Trump and Biden administrations, the Department of Health and Human Services spent approximately $22.6 billion under the Office of Refugee Resettlement (ORR). These funds were allocated to various programs supporting migrants, including cash assistance for purchasing vehicles and homes, as well as initiatives to establish credit for startup businesses. These grants were primarily provided to nonprofit organizations supporting refugees and migrants with legal status, including asylees and victims of human trafficking. The assistance provided aimed to support integration efforts, including financial literacy training and matching funds for savings towards significant purchases or education.

Trump falsely characterizes the expenditures. There is no showing of waste, fraud, or abuse. There are no savings. The money has already been spent.

> **TRUMP**: $45 million for diversity, equity, and inclusion schol-
> arships in Burma.

Trump exaggerates here. There is some saving, but not $45 million.

In August 2023, the U.S. government initiated the Diversity and Inclusion Scholarship Program (DISP), allocating $45 million over five years to support Burmese students from marginalized communities. Its primary goal was to offer educational opportunities to Burmese students affected by the ongoing conflict and political instability in Myanmar (Burma). The cancellation has raised concerns about the U.S. commitment to supporting young leaders striving for positive change in Myanmar. The program aimed to provide tuition, room, and board for up to 1,000 students pursuing degrees at universities in Thailand, Cambodia, the Philippines, Indonesia, and online courses from the University of Arizona.

In late January 2025, DOGE abruptly cancelled the program, calling it wasteful. That left many students, including those already enrolled, uncertain about their future. The Trump administration has offered no rationale for abandoning a generation of students in a country in turmoil.

TRUMP: $40 million to improve the social and economic inclusion of sedentary migrants. Nobody knows what that is.

"Nobody knows what that is," Trump says, revealing his lack of attention to detail.

Turns out that this funding refers to a program in Colombia aimed at supporting Venezuelan refugees and host communities. The initiative focuses on promoting social and economic integration by supporting local businesses and creating job opportunities, thereby deterring migration to the U.S.

The claimed $40 million savings is undocumented. The U.S. has been funding this initiative since 2018. The resulting increased cost of deportations would more than offset any savings.

TRUMP: $8 million to promote LGBTQ+ in the African nation of Lesotho, which nobody has ever heard of.

Flaunting his ignorance, Trump also appears to be wrong on the facts.

In Lesotho, People's Matrix spokesperson Tampose Mothopeng alleged that Trump's claim was baseless. He told AFP: "We are literally not receiving grants from the U.S."

Lesotho's Foreign Affairs Minister Lejone Mpotjoane also weighed in on the president's comments, saying it was "shocking" to hear the president "refer to another sovereign state in that manner."

Lesotho is a small, poor, rural, landlocked country in central Africa. In 2024, Lesotho exported $240 million in goods to the U.S. (primarily denim for jeans, with some 75% of its output going to the U.S.). Lesotho imports less than $3 million in goods from the U.S., creating a trade "imbalance" that Trump used to justify placing a 50% tariff on the country, among the highest "reciprocal" tariff rates Trump imposed on anyone (especially compared to the zero rate imposed on Russia, Belarus, North Korea, and Cuba).

No credit for any savings here.

> **TRUMP**: $60 million for Indigenous peoples and Afro-Caribbean empowerment in Central America – $60 million.

Trump claims savings for a program that has been spending for years.

Since 2011, USAID and ACDI/VOCA have been working with and for Colombia's ethnic communities to guarantee their recognition, inclusion, and empowerment. The most recent manifestation of this commitment began on December 1, 2021, with the launch of a five-year, $60 million initiative called the Indigenous Peoples and Afro-Colombian Empowerment Activity (IPACE). IPACE partners directly with ethnic-led national and local organizations to strengthen their existing initiatives and elevate their priorities on the national agenda to close gaps in racial disparity and promote ethnic pride, resulting in a more inclusive Colombia.

Cutting a $60 million program that began in 2021 doesn't save much, nowhere close to $60 million.

> **TRUMP**: $8 million for making mice transgender – this is real.

Actually, it's not real. Trump falsely characterizes the science.

While the $8 million in NIH grants is allocated for studies involving hormone therapies in mice, these studies are part of broader biomedical research efforts to understand the effects of such treatments on health outcomes. The depiction of these studies as attempts to "make mice transgender" is an oversimplification and misrepresentation of their scientific intent.

Saving $8 million, maybe, but at the cost of basic research to support human health.

> **TRUMP**: $32 million for a left-wing propaganda operation in Moldova.

Trump again claims savings for a program that has already spent at least some of its allocation. In Moldova, there is a political uproar over how the money was spent.

Regarding the $32 million allocated for Moldova, this funding was intended for initiatives supporting media as a component of democracy, inclusion, and accountability, as well as promoting the sustainability of media institutions. However, in February 2025, the U.S. Department of Government Efficiency (DOGE), led by Elon Musk, announced the cancellation of this funding, describing it as a "left-wing propaganda operation."

Again, there is no evidence to support the smear.

TRUMP: $10 million for male circumcision in Mozambique.

Trump is claiming savings for cancelling a program that directly reduces HIV/AIDS.

Since 2007, the U.S. President's Emergency Plan for AIDS Relief (PEPFAR) has facilitated over 32.5 million voluntary medical male circumcisions across various countries, including Mozambique. In Mozambique, the program has led to a significant increase in circumcision rates, with over 2.5 million procedures performed between 2010 and 2023.

The funding cut by Trump directly supports Mozambique's Voluntary Medical Male Circumcision (VMMC) program, a key component of HIV prevention efforts. Studies have shown that male circumcision can reduce the risk of HIV acquisition by approximately 60%.

Trump has called this program a "scam," even though its success has been demonstrated for decades. The real scam is calling it a waste to prevent the spread of HIV/AIDS.

TRUMP: $20 million for the Arab Sesame Street in the Middle East. It's a program. $20 million for a program.

Trump is wrong. Or lying.

The program, a collaboration between Sesame Workshop and the International Rescue Committee, received a $100 million grant from the MacArthur Foundation in 2017. In 2021, USAID contributed an additional $20 million over six years to support "Ahlan Simsim Iraq," targeting children affected by conflict and violence.

Trump's claim appears to conflate a kids' TV show featuring Sesame Street characters and broadcast in Arabic across numerous countries, including Iraq, with a USAID-funded educational project called Ahlan Simsim Iraq. An archived page from the USAID website shows the agency provided funding for Ahlan Simsim Iraq in 2021. The name "Ahlan Simsim" applies to both the TV show and an early childhood development program targeting families in conflict zones. The USAID funding was for the period 2021-2027.

There is disagreement as to how much of the funding has already been spent, but the "savings" are less than $20 million. There is no Trump administration analysis of why this project should be considered "waste."

> **TRUMP**: $1.9 billion to recently created decarbonization of homes committee, headed up – and we know she's involved – just at the last moment, the money was passed over by a woman named Stacey Abrams. Have you ever heard of her?

Trump is wrong and lying again.

The original grant was awarded in April 2024 for $2 billion. It was awarded to Power Forward Communities, a coalition of clean energy groups, by the Environmental Protection Agency (EPA). There is no analysis of how much of the original grant remains, if any.

Trump's reference to Stacey Abrams is a pure political smear. She did not "head up" Power Forward Communities. She did not receive any of the grant funds. During 2023-2024, Abrams was senior counsel for Rewiring America, one of five members of the coalition that forms Power Forward Communities. The coalition's CEO confirmed that Abrams was neither paid by the group nor directly involved in its operations.

Again, Trump lied, failed to offer any coherent analysis, and threw in a political smear for good measure.

> **TRUMP**: A $3.5 million consulting contract for lavish fish monitoring.

Trump appears to have misspoken when he said "lavish."

The DOGE website lists a contract for "larval fish monitoring," which can help assess ecosystem health and water quality. The contract was between the Department of the Interior's Bureau of Reclamation and a research company called ASIR LLC.

The monitoring focuses on larval stages of fish, which are crucial for understanding fish populations and aquatic ecosystems. This type of research is essential for informed resource management and environmental conservation efforts.

According to usaspending.gov, ASIR LLC's award from the Department of the Interior is potentially worth $6.6 million, of which $1.2 million was awarded in 2023 and 2024.

TRUMP: $1.5 million for voter confidence in Liberia.

Trump called this program "waste" and elsewhere commented sarcastically, "We want to give them confidence in Liberia?" The view from Liberia's capital, Monrovia:

> President Donald Trump's decision to suspend U.S. foreign assistance is causing concern in Liberia, where vital health, education, and community development programs depend on American funding. The move, part of Trump's broader criticism of U.S. spending on international aid, threatens to disrupt essential services and roll back progress in public health and social stability.

The Liberia Domestic Election Observation activity program was created to enhance voter confidence in the electoral processes and results, to the extent warranted, and to mitigate electoral violence and tension, through evidence-based, responsive election observation and reporting to the public. Supported by USAID, the program started in February 2023 and was scheduled to end in August 2025, saving only a fraction of $1.5 million.

The initiative was designed to promote transparency and public trust in elections as Liberia continues to strengthen its democratic institutions. Clearly a sign of waste in the MAGA world.

TRUMP: $14 million for social cohesion in Mali.

Trump is claiming savings for a contract that started in 2023 and was intended to run into 2028. There is no analysis.

The USAID Community Stabilization Activity in Mali awarded a five-year contract for $14.3 million to Chemonics International, designed to reduce conflict in the country using peacebuilding tools like mediation alongside cash transfers. The USAID Salam (translation: USAID Peace) peacebuilding activity will reduce the frequency and severity of dispute escalations in the villages of Ségou and Mopti to prevent broader-reaching or more violent conflicts. Another example of waste in the MAGA world.

TRUMP: $59 million for illegal alien hotel rooms in New York City. He's a real estate developer. He's done very well.

Trump is mostly wrong on this. Or lying.

There was no $59 million paid for hotel rooms. Payments went to New York City for approved expenses for migrants from the Department of Homeland Security's (DHS) Shelter and Services Program. The money was provided to house individuals who FEMA had decided could be in the country legally.

More than 200,000 migrants have arrived in New York since the spring of 2022. The federal payments are reimbursements for 2023 and 2024. They were deposited in city bank accounts.

In February 2025, New York City officials said the city had received two payments from the federal government as reimbursement for expenses the city incurred while providing services to migrants who arrived in New York, including $19 million for hotel expenses. But Elon Musk claimed, without evidence, that $59 million "is meant for American disaster relief and instead is being spent on high-end hotels for illegals!" This is a lie.

The White House has not provided any evidence that the funds were originally "meant for American disaster relief," as Musk said. The White House press office did not respond to an inquiry about this. A DHS spokesperson said that DHS has "clawed back the full payment" from the city and fired four FEMA employees responsible for making the payments.

In a statement on February 12, New York City Comptroller Brad Lander called the revocation of over $80 million in congressionally appropriated funds illegal and advised Eric Adams, the city's mayor, to pursue legal action.

"This is money that the federal government previously disbursed for shelter and services and is now missing," he said. "This highway robbery of our funds directly out of our bank account is a betrayal of everyone who calls New York City home."

The day after Trump's bicameral speech, federal Judge Jennifer H. Rearden in Manhattan ruled that the Federal Emergency Management Agency doesn't need to immediately return more than $80 million that it took away from New York City last month in a dispute over funding for sheltering migrants. In declining to issue a temporary restraining order, the judge said the city had failed to prove it would suffer irreparable harm. FEMA clawed back grant funding intended to reimburse the city for hotels it had leased as shelters for migrants, claiming that a violent gang had taken over a city shelter. FEMA approved and awarded the funds during the final months of President Joe Biden's administration but didn't disburse them until after Trump took office. The city argued in court that "these are extraordinary circumstances... that it was unconstitutional that the money was taken back when Congress had appropriated it."

In April, FEMA demanded the city return another $106 million.

The litigation continues.

Any savings here are New York City's loss.

> **TRUMP**: $250,000 to increase vegan local climate action innovation in Zambia.

Trump mocked this tiny effort to address global warming.

The 2024 USAID project supported climate-smart innovations. The program focuses on promoting plant-based diets, supporting such sustainable agriculture practices as agroforestry and permaculture, educating communities on the environmental impacts of animal agriculture, and advocating for policies that incentivize plant-based food production. It also promoted transitioning from intensive livestock farming to more sustainable practices like pasture-based grazing.

Clearly, to MAGA, this is waste, because climate change is a hoax.

> **TRUMP**: $42 million for social and behavioral change in Uganda.

Trump claims it's all savings, even though the allocation is two years old.

USAID allocated $42 million for Uganda in 2023 to support the country's development in sectors such as health, education, and economic growth. This funding was part of the broader U.S. government efforts to support Uganda's development priorities, including addressing such public health challenges as HIV/AIDS, improving food security, and fostering economic opportunities.

This funding was designed to encourage more women to get prenatal checks, more parents to feed their kids varied diets and have them sleep under bed nets, more high-risk people to get HIV testing, and a range of other socially beneficial behaviors.

Trump is not into "socially beneficial behaviors."

TRUMP: $14 million for improving public procurement in
Serbia.

Trump claims full savings for this five-year-old grant that was allocated
under his first presidency. No apparent savings.

In 2020, the U.S. government, through USAID, allocated $14 million to
improve public procurement in Serbia. This funding was aimed at strengthening the country's procurement systems, making them more transparent,
efficient, and accountable. This initiative was part of broader U.S. support
for democratic governance and anti-corruption efforts in Serbia, aligning
with U.S. priorities to promote good governance and the rule of law in the
Balkans.

TRUMP: $47 million for improving learning outcomes in Asia.
Asia is doing very well with learning. You know what we're doing – could use it ourselves.

Ignore the snide remark. Trump has no intention of spending money on
American education. He wants to eliminate the Department of Education.
And he wants to reduce American history to rote repetition of self-approving
lies.

Trump again claims full savings for a five-year-old grant from his previous administration. No apparent saving.

In 2020, during Donald Trump's first term, the U.S. government allocated $47 million to improve learning outcomes in Asia. This funding
was primarily aimed at enhancing education systems, improving access to
quality education, and addressing the disparities in learning outcomes across
countries in the region.

TRUMP: And $101 million for D.E.I. contracts at the
Department of Education – the most ever paid, nothing even
like it.

Trump offers this without analysis. On February 10, DOGE announced
that the Education Department cancelled 29 DEI training grants worth a
total of $101 million. This was part of an announcement the same day that
the Education Department was cancelling a total of 89 grants worth $881
million. DOGE rejected the value of a grant to train teachers to "help students understand/interrogate the complex histories involved in oppression,

and help students recognize areas of privilege and power on an individual and collective basis."

Anything that creates an informed, thoughtful populace is anathema to Trump. Trump has offered these 19 examples (11 of them foreign aid) of "appalling waste." None of them is appalling. None of them is indisputably wasteful. They are not fraud. They are not abuse. They are just things that Trump doesn't like.

Then he doubled down on his lies.

All of These 'Scams' Exposed?

> **TRUMP**: Under the Trump administration, all of these scams – and there are far worse – but I didn't think it was appropriate to talk about them. They're so bad. Many more have been found out and exposed, and swiftly terminated by a group of very intelligent, mostly young people headed up by Elon, and we appreciate it. We found hundreds of billions of dollars of fraud....

Saying "all of these scams" is a lie. Not one of his examples is a scam. No one has been charged with anything illegal. Trump has not alleged anything smacking of a scam.

Saying "and there are far worse" is not credible, unless you believe he's holding back anything that would support his argument.

DOGE agents have not found "hundreds of billions of dollars of fraud." Not even close. Everything Trump mentioned above was, by his own reckoning, "waste." Trump has offered no evidence of fraud. Or any abuse.

In mid-February, DOGE posted its first claim of finding over $100 billion in "waste, fraud, and abuse." This was supported by little evidence, much of it unreliable. DOGE claimed an $8 billion savings for cancelling a contract worth only $8 million. Other claims of savings were for contracts that had already been paid. DOGE started retracting some of its claims.

DOGE has offered zero evidence of finding any fraud or abuse. Every cancellation so far has been political and based on new administration priorities that subjectively characterize previous priorities as "waste."

Is there fraud and waste in the federal government's $6.8 trillion annual budget in 2024? Yes, according to the Governmental Accounting Office

(GAO), an independent, non-partisan agency that works for Congress and was established in 1921. GAO describes its mission as follows: "GAO examines how taxpayer dollars are spent and provides Congress and federal agencies with objective, non-partisan, fact-based information to help the government save money and work more efficiently."

That sounds like DOGE. The big difference is that DOGE is madly political. That's its only reason for existing.

In November 2024, the GAO released its fiscal year 2024 Performance and Accountability Report: "This past FY, our work yielded $67.5 billion in financial benefits for Congress and the American people – a return of approximately $76 for each dollar invested in GAO. We also identified 1,232 other benefits that cannot be measured in dollars but led to program and operational improvements across the government. These benefits included public safety, national security, and vulnerable populations such as children, veterans, and those with disabilities."

The GAO estimates the government lost in the range of $233-521 billion during the five-year period 2018-2022, primarily from unemployment and healthcare over-payments. That's an average of $46.6-$104.2 billion per year during three years under Trump and two under Biden.

> **TRUMP**: The Government Accountability Office, the federal government office, has estimated annual fraud of over $500 billion in our nation. And we are working very hard to stop it. We're going to.

Trump flat-out lies about the GAO, inflating the estimate by 1,000%, and falsely attributing it to fraud, which the GAO was very careful not to do. By lying, Trump creates an image of lost billions that is imaginary. When the real numbers appear, and they are much lower, he can claim success without having done anything.

Trump then offers massive lies about Social Security.

Fraud in Social Security? Really?

> **TRUMP**: We're also identifying shocking levels of incompetence and probable fraud in the Social Security program for our seniors, and that our seniors and people that we love rely on.

Believe it or not, government databases list 4.7 million Social Security members from people aged 100 to 109 years old. It lists 3.6 million people from ages 110 to 119. I don't know any of them. I know some people who are rather elderly but not quite that elderly. 3.47 million people from ages 120 to 129. 3.9 million people from ages 130 to 139. 3.5 million people from ages 140 to 149. And money is being paid to many of them, and we are searching right now....

But a lot of money is paid out to people, because it just keeps getting paid and paid, and nobody does – and it really hurts Social Security, it hurts our country. One-point-three million people from ages 150 to 159, and over 130,000 people, according to the Social Security databases, are age over 160 years old.... But we're going to find out where that money is going, and it's not going to be pretty. By slashing all of the fraud, waste and theft we can find, we will defeat inflation, bring down mortgage rates, lower car payments and grocery prices, protect our seniors, and put more money in the pockets of American families....

No, it's not going to be pretty.

Trump paints a truly ugly picture – and a totally dishonest one – of a Social Security system paying out billions of dollars to people who are as old as 160. He said that. And it's not true. Almost none of the centenarians he pretends to believe in are getting any payments. Almost everyone who gets payments is alive and has earned what they get. As a policy, Social Security doesn't pay anyone older than 115. That's the absolute cutoff. And they check on those to be sure they're alive.

Trump begins his riff by crying wolf about the condition of Social Security, speaking as if he cares about the program. His actions make it clear that he has targeted Social Security's annual budget of $1.6 trillion. He wants to use that money to pay for billions of dollars in tax reductions for himself and other billionaires. This money does not belong to the government. This money belongs to the people who paid it into Social Security. Trump doesn't care who it belongs to; he just wants it.

Trump then lies – repeatedly – about impossibly old people supposedly getting payments. None of his assertions is true. It's lie after lie after lie. Elon Musk has repeated the same lies on behalf of DOGE. All with the intended effect of undermining people's faith in the Social Security System. That's his political goal: to inflict real harm on some 70 million Americans who receive Social Security benefits, benefits that allow many of them to live above the poverty line. Trump doesn't care.

The reality is that improper payments by Social Security are a very small part of the total, less than 1%. The Social Security inspector general filed a report in 2024 stating that, during the eight-year period, 2015-2022, Social Security paid out $8.6 trillion in benefits. This amount included improper payments of $71.8 billion (less than 1% of the total). Most of the overpayments went to living people.

On January 25, Trump illegally fired the inspector general of Social Security. At the same time, he illegally fired 16 other inspectors general. The law requires the president to inform Congress before firing any inspector general. Trump gave no notice. The Republican controlled Congress expressed no concern for the law or the firings. The New York City Bar Association challenged the firings as illegal.

In a lawsuit filed in February by eight of the inspectors general, U.S. District Judge Ana Reyes observed: "I don't think anyone can contest that the removal of these people – the way that they were fired – was a violation of the law." But on March 27, she declined to issue any injunction or to order that the inspectors general be reinstated.

The office of inspector general is an independent position, appointed by the president and confirmed by the Senate. The office is designed to conduct audits and investigations into allegations of waste, fraud, and abuse in its agency. So why fire them? They're independent. Now, Trump can replace them with political appointees who will follow his political agenda, attack his enemies, and continue to hollow out the government.

Social Security has almost 60,000 employees. In mid-March, DOGE ordered 7,000 of them to be fired. Elon Musk told Fox News that Social Security is "the big one to eliminate." He called it a "Ponzi scheme" – a lie. He said he expects to cut $700 billion from Social Security to pay for the multitrillion-dollar tax cut for billionaires.

Vermont Senator Bernie Sanders vehemently objected to Musk's plans, calling them "beyond unacceptable." On CNN, Sanders said:

> [H]e has called Social Security a Ponzi scheme. They have already laid off 2,500 employees of the Social Security Administration.... I think this is a prelude not only to cutting benefits, but to privatizing Social Security itself.... Why do you lie so much about Social Security? Why do you make it look like it's a broken, dysfunctional system? The reason is to get people to lose faith in the system, and then you can give it over to Wall Street.

Balance the Budget With Gold Cards?

TRUMP: And in the near future, I want to do what has not been done in 24 years: balance the federal budget. We are going to balance it. With that goal in mind, we have developed in great detail what we are calling the gold card, which goes on sale very, very soon. For $5 million, we will allow the most successful job-creating people from all over the world to buy a path to U.S. citizenship.

It's like the green card but better and more sophisticated. And these people will have to pay tax in our country. They won't have to pay tax from where they came. The money that they've made, you wouldn't want to do that. But they have to pay tax, create jobs. They'll also be taking people out of colleges and paying for them so that we can keep them in our country instead of having them be – being forced out. Number one at the top school, as an example, being forced out and not being allowed to stay and create tremendous numbers of jobs and great success for a company out there.

So, while we take out the criminals, killers, traffickers and child predators who were allowed to enter our country under the open-border policy of these people, the Democrats, the Biden administration – the open border, insane policies that you have allowed to destroy our country – we will now bring in brilliant, hard-working, job-creating people. They're going to pay a lot of money, and we're going to reduce our debt with that money.

Trump promises to "balance the federal budget." Why was there no laughter from the audience of Senators and Congresspeople?

They know that the last balanced budgets were 1998-2001. That was under the Clinton administration. Never since then. Not under eight years of the Bush administration, or eight years under Obama, or four years under Trump, or four years under Biden. Not even close. The budget deficits may vary, but they don't go away under either party. And they drive the national debt to ever new heights, currently more than $36 trillion. That's equivalent to more than $106,000 for every person in America, including infants.

In 1980, the national debt was about $914 million. It's multiplied by 36 times in the past 40 years. That pattern began in the Reagan years, when the national debt more than doubled to $2.6 trillion.

On February 25, 2025, Trump announced:

We're going to be selling a Gold Card…. You have a green card. This is a Gold Card. We're going to be putting a price on that card of about $5 million, and that's going to give you green card privileges, plus it's going to be a route to citizenship. And wealthy people will be coming into our country by buying this card.

Asked about Russian oligarchs, Trump responded: "Yeah, possibly. I know some Russian oligarchs that are very nice people."

The Cato Institute, which supports the idea of a Gold Card, has expressed its doubts about the specifics of Trump's proposal. In a commentary published on the Cato Institute website, David J. Bier writes that "President Donald Trump's attempts to establish his own Gold Card program are likely to prove fruitless…."

As Bier notes, selling green cards is good in theory, but Trump's specific proposal has some problems:

President Trump cannot lawfully eliminate Congress's EB-5 investor program. He cannot lawfully sell green cards in excess of Congress's caps. People will be paying for something Trump cannot provide. Even if he could, his proposal will not sell 1 million green cards or generate $5 trillion in revenue.

On March 26, Forbes reported that U.S. Commerce Secretary Howard Lutnick announced the sale of 1,000 Gold Cards, raising $5 billion in a single day. This is unconfirmed. The Gold Card would effectively replace the EB-5 immigrant investor visa program passed by Congress. EB-5s were created in 1990 as a method for immigrants to obtain green cards if they invested $800,000 to $1 million in a company that employs at least 10 people. In 2024, more than 12,000 EB-5 visas were issued.

The U.S. national debt currently exceeds $36.22 trillion, a figure that increases an average of $4.87 billion per day, or $202.94 million per hour. Lutnick estimates that 37 million people worldwide can afford to buy the Gold Card. If 200,000 Gold Cards are sold at $5 million each, the resulting $1 trillion could make a small dent in the national debt. Scaling the program to 10 million cards would generate $50 trillion. Theoretically, that would erase the national debt and free up resources for infrastructure, education, healthcare, and other critical investments. Or just eliminating taxes on billionaires.

On April 3, 2025, Trump revealed the first physical Gold Card, now called the Trump Card, with his face on it. As of then, there had been no other announcements of further sales. Still, selling a thousand cards would offset a day's increase in the national debt. Tomorrow's another day.

On July 7, the Washington Post reported that the "gold card" visa might never happen.

Imaginary Mandate, Imaginary Unelected Bureaucrats

TRUMP: Americans have given us a mandate for bold and profound change. For nearly 100 years, the federal bureaucracy has grown until it has crushed our freedoms, ballooned our deficits, and held back America's potential in every possible way. The nation founded by pioneers and risk-takers now drowns under millions and millions of pages of regulations and debt: Approvals that should take 10 days to get instead take 10 years, 15 years, and even 20 years before you [get] rejected.

Meanwhile, we have hundreds of thousands of federal workers who have not been showing up to work. My administration will reclaim power from this unaccountable bureaucracy, and we will restore true democracy to America again.

And any federal bureaucrat who resists this change will be removed from office immediately. Because we are draining the swamp. It's very simple. And the days of rule by unelected bureaucrats are over.

Trump lies again about having a mandate. No matter what he says, he failed to get a majority of the vote. He has no clear mandate for anything.

He lies about "unelected bureaucrats." He's just making it up about federal workers not showing up for work. He offers no evidence. Reliable statistics are hard to get. The federal government has about 3 million employees, 600,000 of whom are in the Postal Service (theoretically an independent agency). The rest are employed in 15 cabinet departments and more than 2,000 agencies.

According to CNN:

> Nearly half of the more than 2.3 million civilian federal workers were eligible for telework, and 10% were in remote positions with no expectation of in-person work, according to a 2024 Office of Management and Budget report. Many workers stopped working full time in their offices during the COVID-19 pandemic, but others had long-held arrangements for working from home." Some workers returned to work only to find that they had no office. More than 80% of federal employees work outside the DC area.

"Return to In-Person Work," Trump's January 20 executive order, reads in its entirety:

> Heads of all departments and agencies in the executive branch of Government shall, as soon as practicable, take all necessary steps to terminate remote work arrangements and require employees to return to work in person at their respective duty stations on a full-time basis, provided that the department and agency heads shall make exemptions they deem necessary. This memorandum shall be implemented consistent with applicable

law.

This order is made with no rationale. It's counter to government efficiency, which is acknowledged by allowing "exemptions they deem necessary." The order creates waste. It is an effort to fix a problem that hasn't been shown to exist in reality.

When Trump claims that "the days of rule by unelected bureaucrats are over," he is again claiming to fix a problem that doesn't exist. This trope of "unelected bureaucrats" is another old and false rightwing myth about public servants. Their work is supervised by cabinet officers and dictated by the laws Congress passes. The ruling bureaucrat is a figment of a fevered mind that just doesn't like the rules Congress has enacted into law.

Oh, wait. Trump didn't end the rule of unelected bureaucrats. He made it come true. And it's not legal. Elon Musk was an unelected bureaucrat, appointed by Trump, with no vetting by Congress. With no apparent supervision, Musk was taking a chainsaw to government agencies and workers. Musk was an agent of chaos, unelected and unsupervised. His work was significantly self-serving, as he weakened or eliminated agencies that were legally supposed to be overseeing his private businesses.

Fourteen States' Lawsuit Says DOGE Is Illegal

On February 13, 2025, 14 states filed suit in federal court – Case No. 1:25 cv 00429 (TSC), U.S. Dist. Ct. (D.D.C. 2025) – with the Nevada attorney general arguing that:

> President Trump has violated the Appointments Clause of the United States Constitution by creating a new federal Department without Congressional approval and by granting Musk sweeping powers over the entire federal government without seeking the advice and consent of the Senate.

On February 21, a federal judge issued a preliminary injunction blocking DOGE's access to U.S. Treasury Department systems. DOGE first achieved access to Treasury Department systems in late January. It is not clear what DOGE accomplished with that access or what data was compromised.

DOGE has access to sensitive personal data across the whole government. No one knows how much has been downloaded into private hands.

None of that information is retrievable. The looting continues as fast as systems allow. Massive amounts of government data in private hands create immeasurable vulnerabilities. This makes the future inherently more insecure.

Litigation continues in several lawsuits. The rule of unelected bureaucrats is nowhere near over. It's just beginning. It's the start of a new Golden Age.

On July 8, the Supreme Court issued an unsigned order lifting a lower court injunction and freeing the administration to cut thousands of federal employees. The court based its ruling on its conclusion that Trump's executive order and memorandum are likely legal. As for the underlying substantive issues, the Court wrote with what has become chronic cowardice and evasion: "We express no view on the legality of any agency [reduction-in-force] and reorganization plan produced or approved pursuant to the executive order and memorandum…. Those plans are not before this court."

Tax Cuts for Everybody – Maybe

> **TRUMP**: And the next phase of our plan to deliver the greatest economy in history is for this Congress to pass tax cuts for everybody. They're in there. They're waiting for you to vote…. It's a very, very big part of our plan. We had tremendous success in our first term, with a very big part of our plan, we're seeking permanent income tax cuts all across the board. And to get urgently needed relief to Americans hit especially hard by inflation, I'm calling for no tax on tips, no tax on overtime, and no tax on Social Security benefits for our great seniors.

This is fundamentally dishonest.

There may well be something minimal that passes as "tax cuts for everybody," everybody including 99% of Americans. But the overwhelming benefit of Trump's tax cuts goes to the top 1%, people who earn more than $788,000 annually.

Trump's 2017 tax cuts in his first term mostly benefited the same rich people and corporations. The 2017 tax cuts to the wealthiest 1% were worth 50 times more than tax cuts to middle-income families. The tax cuts currently proposed provide the same benefits for the rich and little for anyone else. It's MAGA world, even though most MAGA cultists can't see it. They see a new Golden Age.

Trump's 2017 tax cuts added $1.9 trillion to the national debt. As enacted, those tax cuts would expire in 2025. They have failed to produce the job growth or economic expansion that Trump promised. "Cutting taxes creates jobs" is a very old Reagan-era Republican lie. Tax cuts have further bloated the national debt, as predicted before Republicans passed them.

Trump's 2025 tax cuts (an extension of the 2017 tax cuts) would add $4.6 trillion to the national debt over 10 years, according to the nonpartisan Congressional Budget Office. There is almost no likelihood that they would produce any more stimulus than the earlier cuts. But the rich, who pay disproportionately small taxes, would pay still less.

Senator Ron Wyden (D-OR) warns: "The Republican tax plan is to double down on Trump's handouts to corporations and the wealthy, run the deficit into the stratosphere, and make it impossible to save Medicare and Social Security or help families with the cost of living in America."

Trump's promise to lift the "tax" on Social Security is a conman's joke: there is no tax on Social Security unless the recipient has a job earning $25,000 a year or more.

Here Are Some Crumbs for Which You Should Be Grateful

TRUMP: And I also want to make interest payments on car loans tax deductible – but only if the car is made in America. And by the way, we are going to have growth in the auto industry like nobody has ever seen. Plants are opening up all over the place. Deals are being made – never seen. That's a combination of the election win and tariffs. It's a beautiful word, isn't it?

That, along with our other policies, will allow our auto industry to absolutely boom. It's going to boom. Spoke to the majors today, all three, the top people, and they're so excited. In fact, already numerous car companies have announced that they will be building massive automobile plants in America, with Honda just announcing a new plant in Indiana, one of the largest anywhere in the world. And this has taken place since our great victory on November 5, a date which will hopefully go down as one of the most important in the history of our country.

In addition, as part of our tax cuts, we want to cut taxes on domestic production and all manufacturing. And just as we did before, we will provide 100% expensing. It will be retroactive to January 20, 2025. And it was one of the main reasons why our tax cuts were so successful in our first term, giving us the most successful economy in the history of our country. First term, we had a great first term.

Cheerleading for the auto industry hasn't taken long to come apart as Trump imposed tariffs, removed tariffs, imposed tariffs, whatever. Who knows where the industry is going, with Trump removing incentives for electric vehicles? Yes, he made an exception of sorts for Elon Musk's Tesla, by performing an infomercial at the White House and promising to buy one. But public resentment over Musk mucking up the government has helped Tesla stock lose half its value. Even Tesla executives are selling, and protests (some violent) at Tesla dealers are nationwide.

Trump's policy is driving us away from "growth in the auto industry like nobody has even seen."

As for "the most successful economy in the history of our country," this is a lie. It was not. It was not even close. Annual GDP (Gross Domestic Product) growth under Trump's first term was not markedly higher than it was under President Obama. Job growth was about a million jobs fewer. With almost full employment at the end of the Obama administration, unemployment reached historic lows. Under Trump, the number of Americans without health insurance increased to 4.6 million (16%). Trump increased federal spending and cut taxes. This contributed to a 33% increase in the national debt under Trump, more than most previous administrations. Trump's tariffs produced only mixed results.

The longest economic expansion in American history (10.7 years) started in June 2009. It ended in February 2020 with the arrival of the COVID-19 pandemic. Trump's response to the pandemic was slow and inept. As a result, there were unnecessary deaths from COVID-19, variously estimated from 232,000 to more than 500,000. By April 2020, unemployment was at a 90-year high, at Great Depression levels. Trump was the only modern president to leave office with a smaller workforce (by 3 million jobs) than when he entered office. Throughout his presidency, Trump mischaracterized the economy as the best in American history.

During Trump's 2025 first quarter, the U.S. economy contracted.

On April 2, Reciprocal Tariffs Kick In

TRUMP: If you don't make your product in America, however, under the Trump administration, you will pay a tariff and, in some cases, a rather large one. Other countries have used tariffs against us for decades, and now it's our turn to start using them against those other countries. On average, the European Union, China, Brazil, India, Mexico, and Canada – have you heard of them? And countless other nations charge us tremendously higher tariffs than we charge them....

This system is not fair to the United States and never was, and so on April 2 – I wanted to make it April 1, but I didn't want to be accused of April Fools' Day – it's not – it's just one day which costs us a lot of money. But we are going to do it in April. I'm a very superstitious person. April 2, reciprocal tariffs kick in, and whatever they tariff us, other countries, we will tariff them. That's reciprocal, back and forth.

Whatever they tax us, we will tax them. If they do non-monetary tariffs to keep us out of their market, then we will do nonmonetary barriers to keep them out of our market. There's a lot of that too. They don't even allow us in their market. We will take in trillions and trillions of dollars and create jobs like we have never seen before. I did it with China, and I did it with others, and the Biden administration couldn't do anything about it because it was so much money, they couldn't do anything about it. We've been ripped off for decades by nearly every country on earth, and we will not let that happen any longer.

Trump's imposition of tariffs and threats of tariffs was just beginning to play out as he gave this speech. America is hurting its traditional friends, Europe, Mexico, and Canada. Tariffs have come and gone on Canada at a dizzying pace. Trump threatened European winemakers with a 200% tariff. The tariff war is underway, and retaliations are increasing instability. Uncertainty is becoming globalized.

Nobel Prize-winning economist Paul Krugman wrote in January:

> Economists would, if he asked, tell him that high tariffs on neighboring nations closely integrated with the United States will do major damage; businesspeople would say the same thing. But if Trump wants your opinion, he'll tell you what he wants it to be.

Another Nobel Prize-winning economist, Joseph Stiglitz, former chairman of President Clinton's Council of Economic Advisors, told the Century Foundation in January:

> Virtually all economists think that the impact of the tariffs will be very bad for America and for the world.... They will almost surely be inflationary.... It's inconceivable that other countries won't retaliate. Even if some of the governments might not want to retaliate, their citizens will demand that you can't allow yourself to be beaten up. When you make like a gorilla thumping on his chest, are countries just going to say, 'Are we chopped liver?' Their politics will demand that they do something.

On April 2, Trump unveiled his tariff program, creating much confusion, consternation, and shock around the globe. The tariffs on many countries were higher than anyone expected. The formula used to set tariffs was unorthodox. None of it made much immediate sense to a lot of people. Why were there no tariffs on Russia, Belarus, or North Korea? Why are the Heard and McDonald Islands, located 2,400 miles southwest of Australia, hit with a 10% tariff when no one lives there but seals and penguins?

'Let Donald Trump Run the Global Economy'

Commerce Secretary Howard Lutnick had a different take on CNN on April 3, 2025: "Let Donald Trump run the global economy. He knows what he's doing. He's been talking about it for 35 years. You got to trust Donald

Trump in the White House."

During those 35 years, Trump's businesses filed for bankruptcy six times.

On April 9, after a week of commercial chaos and falling markets, Trump pulled back somewhat on his tariff regime, decreeing a 90-day pause on most tariffs. He left in place across the board 10% tariffs on most countries and 145% on China. This didn't solve the problem, but it changed its shape for the moment.

For the next month, there were warnings of trouble ahead: higher costs for Americans, reduced imports, supply chain disruptions, and further economic contraction. The Trump administration made minor adjustments at the fringes but made no fundamental changes. Trump and his officials assured us that the American people understand shared sacrifice. Trump expressed that by citing the "two-doll Christmas," – saying an American girl could make do with 2 dolls instead of 30. The state of Trump's tariff policy remained uncertain, unsettled, and volatile into mid-summer.

Fentanyl – Nobody's Seen Anything Like It

> **TRUMP**: Much has been said over the last three months about Mexico and Canada. But we have very large deficits with both of them. But even more importantly, they have allowed fentanyl to come into our country at levels never seen before, killing hundreds of thousands of our citizens and many very young, beautiful people, destroying families. Nobody's ever seen anything like it. They are, in effect, receiving subsidies of hundreds of billions of dollars. We pay subsidies to Canada and to Mexico of hundreds of billions of dollars. And the United States will not be doing that any longer. We are not going to do it any longer.

Trump's big lie here is about fentanyl, a potent synthetic opioid drug approved by the Food and Drug Administration (FDA) for use as an analgesic (pain relief) and an anesthetic. It was first synthesized in 1959 by a Belgian chemist. Fentanyl is approximately 100 times more potent than morphine and 50 times more potent than heroin as an analgesic. As a street drug, it has many names such as Apache, China Town, Great Bear, King Ivory, and Poison. It is snorted/sniffed, smoked, taken orally by capsule or tablet, spiked onto blotter paper, patches, and sold alone or in combination with heroin and other substances. It has been identified in fake pills, mimicking pharmaceutical drugs such as oxycodone. Similar to other opioid analgesics, fentanyl produces effects such as relaxation, euphoria, pain relief, sedation, confusion, drowsiness, dizziness, nausea and vomiting, urinary retention, pupillary constriction, and respiratory depression. An overdose can kill you. Keep your Narcan handy.

According to the Drug Enforcement Administration (DEA), "Illicit fentanyl, primarily manufactured in foreign clandestine labs and smuggled into the United States through Mexico, is being distributed across the country and sold on the illegal drug market." Most fentanyl labs are thought to be in Mexico or China, and at least eight U.S. states, listed by the DEA: California, Arizona, Florida, Ohio, Indiana, Kentucky, Michigan, Missouri, and North Carolina.

According to the DEA, "The Sinaloa Cartel and Jalisco Cartel in Mexico, using chemicals largely sourced from China, are primarily responsible for the vast majority of the fentanyl that is being trafficked in communities across the United States."

The Centers for Disease Control (CDC), recently downsized by the Trump Administration, estimates that over 110,000 people in the U.S. died from drug overdoses in 2022, and almost 70% of these deaths were caused by fentanyl and other synthetic opioids. National Public Radio (NPR) reports that during the past four years, illicit fentanyl has been found as a factor in more than 70,000 deaths annually. According to the Council on Foreign Relations, "The opioid crisis has been ravaging the United States for the past several years, although fatalities sharply declined in 2024. At the crisis's peak in 2022 and 2023, drug overdoses caused more than 110,000 fatalities per year, most of them driven by fentanyl." No one has a good handle on the precise statistics for fentanyl alone.

The current opioid crisis began about 30 years ago when the FDA approved Purdue Pharma's blockbuster painkiller OxyContin. Spurred in part by Purdue Pharma's false claim that the addiction risk of OxyContin was low, the U.S. healthcare system significantly increased the prescribing of opioid painkillers. Years of Purdue Pharma's promotion of OxyContin eventually led to lawsuits against the company and the Sackler family that owned it. In January 2025, Purdue Pharma and the Sackler family settled the lawsuits for $7.4 billion, as partial compensation to thousands of victims of the opioid crisis. The final settlement is still pending.

So, where is Trump lying? Accusing Mexico and Canada of "allowing" fentanyl to come into the U.S. is as much of a lie as saying the U.S. "allows" it. The main supplier of fentanyl ingredients appears to be China. Both China and Mexico have increased efforts to stop it. Almost no fentanyl comes into the U.S. from Canada, which has also promised to work harder. There is no evidence that fentanyl is coming in "at levels never seen before."

Trump says, "Nobody's ever seen anything like it." Well, he has. The opioid crisis was raging during his first presidency before peaking two years later.

In 2018, the Trump White House issued a statement saying, in part:

Since President Donald J. Trump issued a nationwide call to action, the results offer hope that America can solve the worst drug crisis in U.S. history. When President Trump took office, the opioid crisis was devastating communities across America. Nearly 64,000 Americans died from a drug overdose in 2016 alone. Opioid overdoses accounted for more than 42,000 of these deaths, more than any previous year on record. In October 2017, President Trump declared the opioid crisis a public health emergency. Ever since, the Trump Administration applied an all-of-Government approach to the epidemic, taking an extraordinary range of actions that reflect the President's commitment to stopping the crisis in its tracks.

As Trump might say: how'd that work out? The crisis got worse. For another five years.

On April 2, 2025, Trump posted on Truth Social calling on Republicans to "fight the Democrats wild and flagrant push to not penalize Canada for the sale, into our Country, of large amounts of Fentanyl, by Tariffing [sic] the value of this horrible and deadly drug in order to make it more costly to distribute and buy.... Why are they allowing Fentanyl to pour into our Country unchecked, and without penalty?"

This is a nest of lies. It is dishonest and divorced from reality. Almost no fentanyl (a suitcase full in a year) enters the U.S. through Canada. Canada does its share of enforcement. And the last time drug traffickers were impacted by tariffs was... never. To claim that tariffs can make any difference to drug trafficking is delusional.

On April 29, Attorney General Pam Bondi claimed on X: "In President Trump's first 100 days, we've seized over 22 million fentanyl laced pills, saving over 119 million lives." This was widely dismissed as an exaggeration by knowledgeable drug officials such as DEA veteran Jim Crotty: "We know that as of the last 12 months, there have been something like 80,000 overdose deaths. That number, while unacceptably high, is nowhere near 119 million. So, it's hard to square the math on that."

On April 30, as cabinet members competed to praise Trump, Bondi claimed: "Since you have been in office, President Trump, your DOJ agencies have seized more than 22 million fentanyl pills, 3,400 kilos of fentanyl, since your last 100 days, which saved – are you ready for this, media? – 258 million lives,...because of you. What you've done."

Saving 258 million lives in a nation of 340 million is no mean trick. It's pure demagoguery.

On May 6, a Department of Justice (DOJ) press release announced "the single largest seizure of fentanyl pills in DEA history" in Albuquerque, NM – "2.7 million fentanyl pills in New Mexico's largest city.... this single seizure of 2.7 million fentanyl pills equates to nearly 1.5 million potentially deadly doses of fentanyl taken out of circulation. In total, DEA seized more than 3 million fentanyl pills and 11.5 kilograms of fentanyl powder." The press release also announced seizures in Salem, OR; Layton, UT; Phoenix, AZ; and Las Vegas, NV.

In February, Bondi quietly set about defending Americans in a very different way, by reducing efforts to check foreign interference.

As NBC News reported: "In a little-noticed directive on her first day in office, Attorney General Pam Bondi ordered a halt to a years-old federal law enforcement effort to combat secret influence campaigns by China, Russia, and other adversaries that try to curry favor and sow chaos in American politics."

Buried on the fourth page of one of 14 policy memos Bondi issued on February 5, the order disbands the FBI's Foreign Influence Task Force and pares back enforcement of the Foreign Agents Registration Act, despite years of warnings by U.S. intelligence agencies that foreign malign influence operations involving disinformation were a growing and dangerous threat.

"To free resources to address more pressing priorities, and end risks of further weaponization and abuses of prosecutorial discretion, the Foreign Influence Task Force shall be disbanded," the order states.

It also states that criminal charges for violating the Foreign Agents Registration Act, which requires people to register when lobbying on behalf of a foreign nation, "shall be limited to instances of alleged conduct similar to more traditional espionage by foreign government actors." The order adds that DOJ prosecutors instead "shall focus on civil enforcement, regulatory initiatives, and public guidance."

A separate Bondi directive also disbanded efforts to seize the assets of Russian oligarchs, including Task Force Klepto Capture and the Kleptocracy Asset Recovery Initiative.

The order said the personnel working on those projects will be reassigned to target drug cartels and transnational criminal organizations.

That's kind of a nifty summary of Trump administration priorities. Go after drug dealers; everyone hates drug dealers. That's popular and politically low risk.

As for foreign actors intervening in the basic function of the United States as a free democracy, not so much. That's low priority. After all, aren't these the people who helped put us in power?

Is the CHIPS Act a Horrible Thing?

TRUMP: ... just yesterday, Taiwan Semiconductor, the biggest in the world, most powerful in the world, has a tremendous amount, 97% of the market, announced a $165 billion investment to build the most powerful chips on earth, right here in the U.S.A.

And we are not giving them any money. Your CHIPS Act is a horrible, horrible thing. We give hundreds of billions of dollars, and it doesn't mean a thing. They take our money, and they don't spend it. All that meant to them – we giving them no money – all that was important to them was that they didn't want to pay the tariffs, so they came and are building, and many other companies are coming.

We don't have to give them money; we just want to protect our businesses and our people, and they will come because they won't have to pay tariffs if they build in America. That feels like it's amazing. You should get rid of the CHIP Act, and whatever's left over, Mr. Speaker, you should use it to reduce debt. Or any other reason you want to.

Trump doesn't seem to understand the CHIPS Act of 2022. According to Wikipedia:

The CHIPS and Science Act is a U.S. federal statute enacted by the 117th United States Congress and signed into law by President Joe Biden on August 9, 2022. The act authorizes roughly $280 billion in new funding to boost domestic research and manufacturing of semiconductors in the United States, for which it appropriates $52.7 billion. The act includes $39 billion in subsidies for chip manufacturing on U.S. soil, along with 25% investment tax credits for costs of manufacturing equipment, and $13 billion for semiconductor research and workforce training, with the dual aim of strengthening American supply chain resilience and countering China. It also invests $174 billion in the overall ecosystem of public sector research in science and technology, advancing human spaceflight, quantum computing, materials science, biotechnology, experimental physics, research security, social and ethical considerations, workforce development, and diversity, equity, and inclusion efforts at NASA, NSF, DOE, EDA, and NIST....

By March 2024, analysts estimated that the act incentivized between 25 and 50 separate potential projects, with total projected investments of $160–$200 billion and 25,000–45,000 new jobs. However, these projects are faced with delays in receiving grants due to bureaucratic hurdles and shortages of skilled workers, both during the construction phase and upon completion in the operational/manufacturing stage, where 40% of the permanent new workers will need two-year technician degrees and 60% will need four-year engineering degrees or higher. In addition, Congress had routinely made several funding deals that underfunded key basic research provisions of the Act by tens of billions of dollars.

So why does Trump speak so harshly and inaccurately about the CHIPS Act? Because Biden passed it? Because it doesn't discriminate against women, ethnic minorities, disabled people, or others covered by DEI?

Or maybe it had something to do with the Taiwan Semiconductor investment he touted just moments earlier. That investment was made under the auspices of the CHIPS Act.

'I Love the Farmer'

TRUMP: Our new trade policy will also be great for the American farmer – I love the farmer – who will now be selling into our home market, the U.S.A., because nobody is going to be able to compete with you. Because those goods that come in from other countries and companies are really, really in a bad position in so many different ways.

They are uninspected, they may be very dirty and disgusting when they come in, and they pour in and they hurt our American farmers. The tariffs will go on agricultural product coming into America and our farmers starting on April 2, may be a little bit of an adjustment period. We had that before when I made the deal with China. $50 billion of purchases, and I said, just bear with me, and they did. They did. Probably have to bear with me again. And this will be even better. That was great. The problem with it was that Biden didn't enforce it. He didn't enforce it.

$50 billion of purchases, and we were doing great, but Biden did not enforce it, and it hurt our farmers. But our farmers are going to have a field day right now. So, to our farmers, have a lot of fun. I love you too. I love you too....

If Trump says he loves you, you've been warned.

Farmers took an early hit when Trump disabled USAID programs to feed hungry people around the world. He cut $2 billion earmarked to buy commodities from American farmers for the Food for Peace program. Established in 1954, the program helps ensure that U.S. farmers have a market for their products and that food aid is sourced domestically.

This money had already been committed. U.S. District Judge Amir Ali ordered the government to promptly release funding to contractors and recipients. The administration appealed. On March 5, the Supreme Court (5-4) upheld the lower court order that the money be paid. But the court left it to Judge Ali to sort out the details. The case remained unresolved months later.

Destroying USAID Kills People – And It's Illegal

As of April 2, 2025, the government had not complied. CNN reported that:

[S]cores of organizations grappling with canceled USAID contracts and little to no payment from the agency.... USAID said in a letter sent to Congress last week that it issued more than $250 million in payments between March 10 and March 21 [leaving almost 90% of the allocated money unpaid]. However, sources who spoke to CNN said payments to aid groups have trickled in – if they have arrived at all. Several humanitarian officials told CNN they are still owed money for work they had completed.... Because of slow payment or funding cuts, many humanitarian organizations have had to furlough or lay off staff. Nearly 19,000 American jobs have been lost, and more than 166,000 global jobs have been lost, according to USAID Stop Work.... With the suspension of assistance and stop-work orders put in place in late January, efforts to combat infectious diseases like tuberculosis and to treat people, including children, with HIV/AIDS have been stymied. Local employees who worked with nonprofit organizations abroad may now be at risk in countries where affiliation with the U.S. makes them a target.

On March 18, U.S. District Judge Theodore Chuang in Maryland ruled that the dismantling of the USAID by billionaire Elon Musk's DOGE likely violated the Constitution. The judge indefinitely blocked DOGE from making further cuts to the agency. The order required the Trump administration to restore email and computer access to all employees of USAID, including those put on administrative leave, though it stopped short of reversing firings or fully resurrecting the agency. Judge Chuang rejected the Trump administration's position that Musk is merely President Donald Trump's adviser. Musk's public statements and social media posts demonstrate that he has "firm control over DOGE," the judge found, pointing to an online post where Musk said he had "fed USAID into the wood chipper."

On March 28, a federal appeals court lifted Judge Chuang's injunction. The administration, with Musk's and DOGE's support, went on to order all but a fraction of the agency's staffers off the job through forced leaves and firings, and terminated what the State Department said was at least 83% of USAID's program contracts. The judge said it's likely that USAID is no longer capable of performing some of its statutorily required functions: "Taken together, these facts support the conclusion that USAID has been effectively eliminated."

Unconstitutional, brutal, but effective, the destruction of USAID was accomplished quickly, before any court could act beyond preserving some of the pieces.

This is a stark example of Trump's policy of cruel and inhumane treatment of vulnerable populations. The administration makes no effort to explain or defend its policy, it slow-walks humane programs to death, and pretends its victims are just more waste, fraud, or abuse.

Worse, the administration's actions are clearly in violation of court orders, including the Supreme Court. And the Constitution. Without consequence.

American farmers are just collateral damage in an ideological war on government functions. Trump says, "I love the farmer." That's a warning sign.

Trump's first-term tariffs hurt farmers, costing them more than $2.7

billion, according to the Department of Agriculture (USDA). Farmers still have not recovered their previous market share of selling soybeans to China. The chaos of Trump's current tariff policy is creating uncertainty now, with the likelihood of financial pain in the future. Farmers are going to suffer more.

Trump's squeamishness over germs and dirt manifests itself in his fear that imported foods "may be very dirty and disgusting." He offers no evidence of this. He says they are "uninspected," which is a lie. The cleanliness and safety of imported food are overseen by agencies like the FDA and USDA, with programs like the FSVP (Foreign Suppliers Verification Program) ensuring foreign suppliers meet U.S. standards and that imported food is safe, sanitary, and properly labeled. Trump and DOGE have been undermining those agencies.

The USDA usually helps farmers with billions of dollars in grants. Many were frozen by the Trump administration in January. One analysis, by former USDA employees, says the agency currently owes nearly $2 billion in promised grants and unpaid funds for conservation and energy efficiency programs to more than 22,000 farmers. Another, by an agricultural economist at the University of Illinois Urbana-Champaign, finds that farmers stand to lose $12.5 billion from the agency's most popular and widely used programs.

The Trump administration now considers some traditional farming practices, which include limiting tillage, planting soil-enriching cover crops, or installing water chutes to control erosion, to be "far-left climate" activities, justifying the funding freeze. USDA has removed climate information from its website.

As for Trump's deal with China. He lied. President Biden maintained Trump's tariffs on China.

Securing America's Borders

> **TRUMP**: And I have also imposed a 25% tariff on foreign aluminum, copper, lumber, and steel because if we don't have, as an example, steel, and lots of other things, we don't have a military, and frankly, we won't have – we just won't have a

country very long….

Trump then introduced a steelworker in the gallery, lied about the state of the economy under Biden, complimented the first lady for her work in foster care, and introduced two women who benefited from that work. He went on to praise the Take It Down Act, passed by the Senate in December 2024, to deal with online harassment. It awaits House action.

TRUMP: But if we truly care about protecting Americans' children, no step is more crucial than securing America's borders. Over the past four years, 21 million people poured into the United States – many of them were murderers, human traffickers, gang members, and other criminals from the streets of dangerous cities all throughout the world. Because of Joe Biden's insane and very dangerous open border policies, they are now strongly embedded in our country. But we are getting them out and getting them out fast.

One reason immigration has been such a fraught subject for decades is that people like Donald Trump shamelessly demagogue it. Trump's claim of 21 million immigrants over four years is a lie. It is false by more than 10 million. There is no credible basis for claiming they were all "murderers, human traffickers, gang members, and other criminals." The only credible basis for such false claims is to scare people. That's unprincipled. In reality, immigration has been dropping since March 2024, under Biden.

Yes, immigration is a real problem. There are an estimated 11 million or so undocumented immigrants in the country. Most of them cause no trouble and pay their own way. But they are outside the system. Congress has been struggling to find answers for decades.

The realities of immigration to the U.S. include the following corrections to popular myths compiled by the Cato Institute:
- Immigrants don't take American jobs, lower wages, or push the poor out of the labor market.
- It's very difficult to immigrate legally to the United States. Immigration law is second only to the income tax code in legal complexity.
- Immigrants use significantly less welfare than native-born Americans. Immigrants in the United States have about a net-zero effect on

government budgets – they pay about as much in taxes as they consume in benefits.

■ Immigrants to the United States – including Mexicans – are assimilating as well as or better than immigrant groups from Europe over a hundred years ago.

■ Immigrants, including illegal immigrants, are less likely to be incarcerated in prisons, convicted of crimes, or arrested than native-born Americans.

■ The annual chance of being murdered in a terrorist attack committed by a foreign-born person on U.S. soil from 1975 through the end of 2017 was about 1 in 3.8 million per year.

■ America's current immigration laws violate every principal component of the Rule of Law. Enforcing laws that are inherently capricious and that are contrary to our traditions is inconsistent with a stable Rule of Law.

■ Different immigration policies do not reduce the U.S. government's ability to defend American sovereignty.

■ There is no evidence that immigrants weaken or undermine American economic, political, or cultural institutions.

Realities don't matter to Trump. In mid-March, the Trump Administration escalated its unlawful attacks on immigrants.

U.S. Police State Sends Mahmoud Khalil to Jena Gulag

On March 8, ICE (Immigration and Customs Enforcement) agents arrested Columbia University graduate student Mahmoud Khalil. It was pure police state activity. They had no warrant. They showed no identification. They didn't know he had a green card. He was not accused of any crime. He was afforded no due process of law, his constitutional right. Plain clothes officers swept him up and sent him from New York to New Jersey to a gulag in Jena, Louisiana. After months of litigation, Khalil was released on June 20 and returned to New York.

Khalil's arrest was soon followed by more police state terror, the snatch and grab deportations of hundreds of Venezuelans with no due process, no convictions, no warrants. The U.S. sent them to a foreign concentration camp in El Salvador. ICE acted in direct defiance of a federal court order by Judge James E. Boasberg, the chief judge of the Federal District Court in Washington.

We have no idea who those Venezuelans are; they were deported without any due process of law. No one even proved that they were illegal. The administration insists they are violent criminals and that anyone trying to protect the rule of law is somehow siding with rapists and murderers. This is a lie. Attorney General Pam Bondi issued a statement preposterously claiming that the judge insisting on the rule of law was supporting "terrorists over the safety of Americans." That is unsupported by any evidence.

In response to Judge Boasberg's order, Trump posted with manic dishonesty:

> This Radical Left Lunatic of a Judge, a troublemaker and agitator who was sadly appointed by Barack Hussein Obama, was not elected President - He didn't WIN the popular VOTE (by a lot!), he didn't WIN ALL SEVEN SWING STATES, he didn't WIN 2,750 to 525 [sic] Counties, HE DIDN'T WIN ANYTHING! I WON FOR MANY REASONS, IN AN OVERWHELMING MANDATE, BUT FIGHTING ILLEGAL IMMIGRATION MAY HAVE BEEN THE NUMBER ONE REASON FOR THIS HISTORIC VICTORY. I'm just doing what the VOTERS wanted me to do. This judge, like many of the Crooked Judges I am forced to appear before, should be IMPEACHED!!! WE DON'T WANT VICIOUS, VIOLENT, AND DEMENTED CRIMINALS, MANY OF THEM DERANGED MURDERERS, IN OUR COUNTRY. MAKE AMERICA GREAT AGAIN!!!

On March 18, Robert Reich reported:

> Federal courts are now hearing more than 100 lawsuits challenging Trump's and Musk's initiatives. Since the end of January, Musk has blasted judges in more than 30 posts on his social media site X, calling them "corrupt," "radical," "evil" and deriding the "TYRANNY of the JUDICIARY" after judges blocked parts of the federal downsizing he has led. As a result, there has been a rise in violent threats against judges across the United

States. Judges are expressing mounting alarm over their physical safety. Several judges describe phone calls promising personal harm to them and their families.... How will this end? Will they stop when a federal judge is murdered?

A police state is not concerned with murdered judges. How is that a bad thing for them?

Let's Trot Out Some Victims to Tug Heart Strings

TRUMP: What a job they've all done – everybody, Border Patrol, ICE, law enforcement in general is incredible, we have to take care of our law enforcement. We have to....

Trump then turned to the case of Laken Riley, a 22-year-old nursing student who was murdered in February 2024 by an illegal immigrant from Venezuela, now serving a life sentence. Trump used the case to attack the Biden administration's immigration policy, as he had during his campaign. The murderer had been caught and released by ICE near the Mexican border, then caught and released by New York City authorities, then caught and released by Georgia authorities. Trump honored Laken Riley's mother and sister in the gallery.

He then honored a woman in the gallery whose 12-year-old daughter had been sexually assaulted and murdered in June 2024 by two Venezuelan illegal immigrants in their 20s, who now face the death penalty in Texas. Trump formally re-named the Anahuac National Wildlife Refuge to the Jocelyn Nungaray National Wildlife Refuge in her memory.

TRUMP: All three savages charged with Jocelyn and Laken's murderers were members of the Venezuelan prison gang, the toughest gang, they say, in the world, known as Tren de Aragua. Two weeks ago, I officially designated this gang, along with MS-13 and the bloodthirsty Mexican drug cartels, as foreign terrorist organizations. They are now officially in the same category as ISIS, and that is not good for them. Countless thousands of these terrorists were welcomed into the U.S. by the Biden administration. But now every last one will be rounded up and forcibly removed from our country, or if they are too dangerous, put in jails, standing trial in this country because we don't want them to come back ever....

Trump then honored a Border Patrol agent in the gallery for his bravery in a shootout, saving his partner's life.

TRUMP: The territory to the immediate south of our border is now dominated entirely by criminal cartels that murder, rape, torture, and exercise total control. They have total control over a whole nation, posing a grave threat to our national security. The cartels are waging war in America, and it's time for America to wage war on the cartels, which we are doing.

Five nights ago, Mexican authorities, because of our tariff policies being imposed on them, think of this, handed over to us 29 of the biggest cartel leaders in their country. That has never happened before. They want to make us happy. First time ever....

This is a lie. It was not the first time. Mexico has extradited drug cartel members to the U.S. for years, including during Trump's first term. From 2019 to 2023, Mexico extradited about 65 people to the U.S., Reuters reported.

Trump's exploitation of the victims of crimes to smear everyone else of the same ethnicity as the criminal is a familiar tactic. It seems to work. But it's dishonest. And corrupt. This is pure demagoguery.

It would be just as valid to use Trump as an example to show that all white men are tax cheats, bankrupts, draft dodgers, felons, and finger rapists.

'Bring Back Law and Order'

TRUMP: And as we reclaim our sovereignty, we must also bring back law and order to our cities and towns. In recent years, our justice system has been turned upside down by radical left lunatics. Many jurisdictions virtually ceased enforcing the law against dangerous repeat offenders while weaponizing law enforcement against political opponents, like me. My administration has acted swiftly and decisively to restore fair, equal, and impartial justice under the constitutional rule of law, starting at the FBI and the DOJ.

We are also once again giving our police officers the support, protection, and respect they so dearly deserve. They have to get it. They have such a hard, dangerous job, but we're going to make it less dangerous....

When it comes to law and order, what are we supposed to make of Trump's willingness to violate the Constitution? Or his willingness to ignore laws passed by Congress? Or his willingness to show contempt for judicial orders? What are we to make of his 34 felony convictions?

Trump demonstrated his "support, protection, and respect" for police officers by pardoning people who attacked police officers in the Capitol riot on January 6, 2021. They were violating law and order by trying to upset the 2020 election. Trump pardoned some 1,500 of his supporters who engaged in this riot, including about 600 who attacked police officers and committed other violent offenses. Those rioters caused about $3 million in damage to the Capitol. Those convicted of felonies or misdemeanors were required to pay restitution totaling almost $500,000. On April 8, 2025, in a federal court filing, Trump's Justice Department agreed that one of the pardoned rioters "is entitled to the return" of the $500 he paid in restitution. The Trump administration has displayed "support, protection, and respect" for criminals.

In his January 20, 2025, executive order, "Ending the Weaponization of the Federal Government," Trump claimed the prior administration "engaged in an unprecedented, third-world weaponization of prosecutorial power." His only specific example was the claim that "the Department of Justice (DOJ) has ruthlessly prosecuted more than 1,500 individuals associated with January 6, and simultaneously dropped nearly all cases against BLM (Black Lives Matter) rioters."

That's as clear as black and white.

Trump's claim is a longstanding right-wing trope. And it's a lie. All the cases against Trump personally were supported by substantial evidence. There's no telling how a jury might have assessed them. Trump chronically complains that law enforcement was weaponized against him. That ignores his convictions. It also ignores the strength of the cases against him that never came to trial. And it ignores the reality that no jury has ever found him "not guilty" of any accusation. The exception to that would be the "jury" of Republican Senators who acquitted him twice in impeachment trials.

In the aftermath of the protests over the George Floyd killing in 2020, the DOJ charged more than 300 people with crimes, including rioting, arson, and conspiracy. More than 120 pleaded guilty or were convicted.

Weaponization of the government is widespread under Trump. The targets include government agencies and employees, media companies, law firms, the Kennedy Center, and federal judges, among others – perhaps most of all, immigrants (real or imagined).

On March 17, the U.S. illegally deported hundreds of Venezuelans. They were deported without any due process of law. They were deported without any evidence that they had criminal records. They were deported to a maximum-security prison in El Salvador, known for its inhumane treatment of its prisoners. The U.S. subsidizes this inhumanity. The U.S. pays El Salvador $6 million a year for its gulag-for-hire.

Asked about the deportees' absence of criminal records, Acting Field Office Director for Immigration and Customs Enforcement (ICE), Robert L. Cerna, offered this wonderland rationale:

> The lack of criminal record does not indicate they pose a limited threat. In fact, based upon their association with TdA [Tren de Aragua gang], the lack of specific information about each individual actually highlights the risk they pose. It demonstrates that they are terrorists with regard to whom we lack a complete profile.

In Trump's America, evidence of your innocence is proof of your guilt.

'Making America Healthy Again'

Trump honored the widow of a New York police officer who was murdered and DJ, a 13-year-old with cancer. DJ has dreamed of becoming a police officer. Trump promised to make him an honorary Secret Service agent.

TRUMP: DJ's doctors believe his cancer likely came from a chemical he was exposed to when he was younger. Since

1975, rates of child cancer have increased by more than 40%. Reversing this trend is one of the top priorities for our new presidential commission to Make America Healthy Again, chaired by our new Secretary of Health and Human Services, Robert F. Kennedy Jr....

Our goal is to get toxins out of our environment, poisons out of our food supply, and keep our children healthy and strong. As an example, not long ago, and you can't even believe these numbers, one in 10,000 children have autism. One in 10,000. And now it's one in 36. There's something wrong. One in 36. Think of that. So, we're going to find out what it is, and there's nobody better than Bobby...

Trump Falsifies the Autism Spectrum Disorders (ASD) Statistics

The 1 in 36 autism estimate comes from the Centers for Disease Control (CDC), which Trump is dismantling. This is an increase from 1 in 150 in 2000. The CDC cautions: "It is unclear how much this is due to changes to the clinical definition of ASD (which may include more people than previous definitions) and better efforts to diagnose ASD (which would identify people with ASD who were not previously identified)."

In other words, Trump misrepresents the problem, then suggests it will be solved by someone who thinks autism is caused by vaccines. This is no longer about science. This is about inventing imaginary threats to frighten people and make them less safe. This is about discrediting science as an authority. This is about discrediting rational thought as an authority. Trump recognizes no authority but his own.

Trump engages in similar magical thinking when he sets out to "get toxins out of our environment, poisons out of our food supply" by disabling the agencies that do that job. Disabling the FDA or the EPA will not make anyone safer. Cuts at the United States Department of Agriculture (USDA) have decimated the teams that inspect plant and food imports, creating risks from invasive pests and leaving food to rot as it waits for inspection.

TRUMP: My administration is also working to protect our children from toxic ideologies in our schools. A few years ago,

January Littlejohn and her husband discovered that their daughter's school had secretly socially transitioned their 13-year-old little girl, teachers and administrators conspired to deceive January and her husband while encouraging her daughter to use a new name and pronouns. They/them pronoun actually. All without telling January, it was here tonight and is now a courageous advocate against this form of child abuse. January, thank you. Thank you very much. Thank you. Stories like this are why shortly after taking office, I signed an executive order banning public schools from indoctrinating our children with transgender ideology.

Trump lies about this case.

Having issued an executive order that there are only two sexes/genders, he's on record admitting he has no understanding of transgender issues, or how complex they can be. Biology cannot be allowed to interfere with politics.

According to The New York Times, what happened in Florida was that, in the fall of 2020, the Littlejohns' 13-year-old daughter asked her parents to use a more masculine name and to change her pronouns to they/them. The parents agreed to use a different name as a nickname, but not the pronouns. They informed the school of these views. Mrs. Littlejohn emailed her child's homeroom teacher about the child's "gender confusion," and she sought a private counsellor for her child.

The school, following protocol, proceeded to counsel the child without involving the parents. The child did not request to include her/his parents. The school relied on a 2018 guide that advised that "outing a student, especially to parents, can be very dangerous" for a student's well-being. That guide allowed for a support plan that documented, in part, whether parents were "supportive" of a student's identity or whether they were to be identified as LGBTQ+ to their parents. There was no law requiring the school to involve the parents.

In September 2020, the school worked with the child to develop a support plan. The parents were not included as the child did not request to include them. The child later shared the plan with their parents. At the end of October, Mrs. Littlejohn met with a school official, but she rejected an offer of further meetings.

Subsequently, the Littlejohns sued the School Board of Leon City, Florida, and individual members of the school staff in federal district court. On December 22, 2022, the court dismissed the case without prejudice. The Littlejohns appealed.

This reality is a far cry from Trump's completely false claim that their daughter's school had "secretly socially transitioned their 13-year-old little girl, that teachers and administrators conspired to deceive January and her husband while encouraging her daughter to use a new name and pronouns. They/them pronoun actually. All without telling January..." Trump not only lies about the case throughout, but he also omits the fact that the Littlejohns lost their lawsuit.

After Trump's March 4 speech, one of the defendants in the lawsuit, Rocky Hanna, the Leon County Schools superintendent, responded: "To blatantly lie and disparage our teachers and our public schools to simply gain notoriety or political power is reprehensible. I only hope that truth and honesty matter more to our federal courts than it does to Ms. Littlejohn, our current governor, and our current president."

On March 12, the U.S. Circuit Court of Appeals for the 11th Circuit, in a 2-1 decision, rejected the argument made by the Littlejohns on appeal. They upheld the district court's decision to dismiss the case.

'Wokeness is Trouble, Wokeness is Bad'

> **TRUMP**: I also signed an order to cut off all taxpayer funding to any institution that engages in the sexual mutilation of our youth. Now I want Congress to pass a bill permanently banning and criminalizing sex changes on children and forever ending the lie that any child is trapped in the wrong body. This is a big lie. And our message to every child in America is that you are perfect, exactly the way God made you.
>
> Because we are getting wokeness out of our schools and out of our military, and it's already out, and it's out of our society, we don't want it. Wokeness is trouble, wokeness is bad, it's gone.

It's gone. And we feel so much better for it, don't we? Don't we feel better?

... I am pleased to report that in January, the U.S. Army had its single best recruiting month in 15 years. And that all armed services are having among the best recruiting results ever in the history of our services. What a difference.

And you know it was just a few months ago where the results were exactly the opposite. We could not recruit anywhere; we couldn't recruit. Now we are having the best results – just about that we ever had. What a tremendous turnaround. It's really a beautiful thing to see. People love our country again. It is very simple. They love our country, and they love being in our military again. So, it's a great thing and thank you very much. Great job. Thank you....

Turning again to the gallery, Trump announced that Jason Hartley, a 17-year-old high school senior from Whittier, California, would be accepted into West Point.

It is a big lie to claim "that you are perfect exactly the way God made you." If that were true, no one would have gender dysphoria. Trump's assertion is also a violation of the constitutional separation of church and state. It is an attempt to impose religious dogma on both the law and reality. The assumption that people are born male or female is generally true, but it is not an absolute. The claim is ideology, not rational thought. It imposes mindless cruelty on those whose actual lives don't conform to a rigid dichotomy that tries to coerce reality into a simplicity it will never allow. The Littlejohns' daughter is living proof that the big lie, the bigotry, is more destructive than tolerance and kindness.

Trump says, "wokeness is bad." He wants it "out of our society." But what is it? Why does he want it gone? Why doesn't he explain what he thinks it means? Whatever Trump means by "wokeness," he's replacing it with prejudice. He's re-establishing traditional American bigotries against women, against ethnic minorities, against old people, against immigrants, against handicapped people, against LGBTQ+ and trans people – a new golden age of hate. Some call it the "woke right."

As for his imaginary military recruiting numbers, Army Times, a U.S.-based bi-weekly newspaper, reported on January 17, 2025:

> In fact, according to Army data, recruiting numbers have been increasing steadily over the past year, with the highest total coming in August 2024 – before the November election. Army officials closely track recruiting numbers. A significant driver of the recruiting success was the Army's decision to launch the Future Soldier Prep Course at Fort Jackson, South Carolina, in August 2022. That program gives lower-performing recruits up to 90 days of academic or fitness instruction to help them meet military standards and move on to basic training.

Translation: We have to do more to induct the under-qualified. In other words, the military has to rely on DEI and call it something else. Recruiting goals have improved in part by lowering targets and lowering standards. This is a problem that has developed over decades. The all-volunteer army is running out of volunteers who are qualified to serve.

In the February 10, 2025, issue of The New Yorker, Dexter Filkins wrote:

> Recruiters are contending with a population that's not just un-enthusiastic but incapable. According to a Pentagon study, more than three-quarters of Americans between the ages of seventeen and twenty-four are ineligible because they are overweight, unable to pass the aptitude test, afflicted by physical or mental health issues, or disqualified by such factors as a criminal record. While the political argument festers, military leaders are left to contemplate a broader problem: Can a country defend itself if not enough people are willing or able to fight?

> After a decade of downward trends in enlistment numbers, the Army hit its recruitment goal in 2024 for the first time since 2021. It's on track to meet its goal again in 2025. Pentagon officials estimate just 23% of Americans aged 17 to 24 qualify to serve, citing rising obesity rates and poor performance on aptitude tests.

A Golden Dome for a Golden Age?

TRUMP: I'm asking Congress to fund a state-of-the-art Golden Dome missile defense shield to protect our homeland – all made in the U.S.... We want to be protected, and we are going to protect our citizens like never before.

To boost our defense industrial base, we are also going to resurrect the American shipbuilding industry, including commercial shipbuilding and military shipbuilding.... We used it to make so many ships. We don't make them anymore very much, but we're going to make them very fast, very soon. It will have a huge impact.

To further enhance our national security, my administration will be reclaiming the Panama Canal.... We didn't give it to China; we gave it to Panama, and we're taking it back....
I also have a message tonight for the incredible people of Greenland. We strongly support your right to determine your own future. And if you choose, we welcome you into the United States of America. We need Greenland for national security and even international security.... And I think we're going to get it – one way or the other, we're going to get it....

In the Middle East, we're bringing back our hostages from Gaza.... And now we're going to build on that foundation to create a more peaceful and prosperous future for the entire region....

I'm also working tirelessly to end the savage conflict in Ukraine.... The United States has sent hundreds of billions of dollars to support Ukraine's defense with no security, with no anything.... Meanwhile, Europe has sadly spent more money buying Russian oil and gas than they've spent on defending Ukraine, by far....

There's Trump's foreign policy in a nutshell: build a "Golden Dome" over the entire U.S., build more warships, reclaim the Panama Canal, take over Greenland, maintain the Gaza genocide, and abandon Ukraine to Russian dismemberment.

Elsewhere, he has offered (and then denied) Elon Musk a top-secret Pentagon briefing on plans for a future war with China; hinted at military action against Mexico; pushed for Canada to become the 51st U.S. state; and signaled he's ready to abandon Europe, among other, lesser actions constituting an incoherent approach to the world. And tariffs on, tariffs off, tariffs on, tariffs off.…

On January 27, Trump issued an executive order ("The Iron Dome for America") ordering Defense Secretary Pete Hegseth to submit a plan for developing and implementing the next-generation missile defense shield by March 28 (not yet accomplished by mid-July). The estimated cost of this as yet undesigned and untested technology is half a trillion dollars, give or take a few hundred billion. That's the "Golden Dome" that remains undefined beyond the name, a reference to the "Iron Dome" that defends Israel (the size of New Jersey).

In his executive order, Trump called for a far more complex and robust system, with space-based interceptors capable of downing a target moments after it launches. With the Pentagon saying it's cutting its budget, any Golden Dome project would cost billions if not trillions of dollars, busting any budget for years if not decades. At present, there is no existing technology that could protect the entire U.S. The Pentagon has been working on a missile defense for the Island of Guam for more than 20 years, achieving its first interception test only in December 2024.

At the same time that Trump spoke of a Golden Dome, Elon Musk's work at DOGE threatened U.S. security: cuts to the top secret National Nuclear Security Administration have meant the loss of critical employees, from scientists and engineers to accountants and lawyers, at the agency that manages the nation's 3,748 nuclear bombs and warheads. The agency was already shorthanded as it worked to modernize the arsenal and was in the midst of hiring personnel to handle the additional workload.

Resurrecting the American shipbuilding industry, commercial and military, seems to be a reasonable goal. As analyst Colin Grabow wrote in September 2024 on War on the Rocks, an online platform focusing on foreign policy and national security issues:

Although numerous metrics demonstrate the maritime

industry's descent into mediocrity, few capture it more starkly than the state of commercial shipbuilding. Despite American manufacturing and technological prowess, U.S. shipyards' output in recent years has ranked just 15th in the world. So gross is the industry's lack of competitiveness – building ships for four or more times the average world price – and so paltry is the demand for its offerings that the sector's collective output amounts to just a fraction of 1% of the global total. Not only a far cry from the dominant shipbuilding triumvirate of China, Japan, and South Korea, U.S. numbers also trail the likes of much smaller players such as Finland, the Netherlands, and Norway.

Panama, Denmark, Ukraine, Allies, Who Cares?

About the Panama Canal, Trump says: "We're taking it back." Panama has made it clear that it's not giving the canal to anyone. Trump has not made it clear how he intends to overcome Panamanian sovereignty. He did make it clear that he would blame Marco Rubio "if anything goes wrong."

Greenland, with a population of roughly 56,000 people, probably has more to worry about (along with NATO member Denmark, of which Greenland is an autonomous territory). Trump's mixed message here is: "We strongly support your right to determine your own future," and "I think we're going to get it – one way or the other, we're going to get it."

When it comes to Gaza, Trump maintains U.S. support for the Israeli genocide of the Palestinian population. He has spoken carelessly of ethnic cleansing, removing all Palestinians from Gaza. He has talked about creating a "new Riviera" in Gaza.

Beyond supporting Israel no matter what it does (including occupying parts of Lebanon and Syria, and bombing them at will), Trump has not indicated any coherent policy for the Middle East. Or anywhere else, except maybe giving Russia whatever Putin wants.

Trump claims to be "bringing back our hostages from Gaza." There was one American hostage when Trump spoke. He was released on May 12. Trump fails to mention other American hostages (Americans wrongfully imprisoned) anywhere else. There is one each in Venezuela, Cuba, the United

Arab Republic, Syria, Iran, and Cambodia. There are two in Afghanistan and three in the Democratic Republic of the Congo. There are 12 American hostages in Russia.

Trump calls the war in Ukraine a "horrific and brutal conflict with no end in sight" while claiming he's trying to end it. But he blames Ukraine for starting the war when Russia invaded. He attacks Ukrainian President Zelensky in the Oval Office. And he lies about U.S. support: "The United States has sent hundreds of billions of dollars to support Ukraine's defense." The actual amount is hard to pin down. Trump claims $350 billion, but others, using different definitions, put the amount of U.S. aid at between $110 billion and $182 billion (which includes money appropriated by Congress, but not disbursed). Europe has spent roughly $140 billion.

Trump has continued to withhold aid to Ukraine, knowing that Ukraine's ability to fight back is critical to ending the war.

You Have to be Able to Play Both Sides

TRUMP: Earlier today, I received an important letter from President Zelensky of Ukraine. The letter reads: "Ukraine is ready to come to the negotiating table as soon as possible to bring lasting peace closer.... Nobody wants peace more than the Ukrainians. My team and I stand ready to work under President Trump strong leadership to get a peace that lasts. ... We do really value how much America has done to help Ukraine, maintain its sovereignty and independence.... Regarding the agreement on minerals and security, Ukraine is ready to sign it at any time."

... I appreciate that he sent this letter. I just got it a little while ago. Simultaneously, we've had serious discussions with Russia. Then I've received strong signals that they are ready for peace. Wouldn't that be beautiful? Wouldn't that be beautiful? Wouldn't that be beautiful? It's time to stop this madness. It's time to halt the killing. It's time to end the senseless war. If you want to end wars, you have to talk to both sides....

The Trump administration began by talking to only one side, Russia, the aggressor that invaded Ukraine in February 2022.

Trump officials publicly said that Ukraine should give up territory to Russia, that Ukraine should be denied NATO membership, and that Ukraine should not seek security guarantees. These are all Russian demands. Why are U.S. officials promoting a plan that is tantamount to telling Ukraine to surrender? Trump himself even said that Ukraine started the war, and he called Ukrainian President Zelensky a "dictator" while falsely claiming Zelensky's popular support in Ukraine was near rock-bottom. Some of these comments echoed Russian negotiating demands. Others just undermined Ukraine's position. All of them undercut Ukrainian leverage in any negotiations.

On February 18, a U.S. delegation met with Russians in Saudi Arabia to negotiate over Ukraine. Ukraine was not allowed to participate. This was followed by the infamous February 28 Oval Office meeting where Zelensky was ambushed by Trump, Vice-President Vance, and several members of the Trump Cabinet – all in full view of assembled reporters, some of whom joined in the attack on the Ukrainian president on live television. So much for talking with "both sides."

Trump and his cabinet members demonstrated an inability to talk to even one side. Diplomatically, the Oval Office meeting was an appalling display that created the context for Zelensky's letter that Trump read from during his speech to the joint session of Congress. Trump's bullying tactics help explain the humble, almost fawning tone of Zelensky's letter.

On March 24, The New York Times published an Associated Press story saying that:

> The United States is holding separate talks with Russia and Ukraine in Saudi Arabia to iron out details of a possible limited ceasefire in what could be a crucial step toward a full cessation of hostilities in the war.... The talks – held in Riyadh, the Saudi capital, with American representatives mediating – are expected to focus on hammering out those details [attacks on energy infrastructure and a limited ceasefire] and on safety for shipping in the Black Sea.

By June 30, there was no sign that the fighting in Ukraine was close to coming to an end.

'I Was Saved by God'

Trump honors two more people in the gallery: history teacher Marc Fogel and his mother. Fogel, in possession of 0.6 ounces of medical cannabis, had been arrested in Russia in 2012 and convicted of drug trafficking. He was sentenced to 14 years in prison. In 2022, U.S. Senators of both parties lobbied for the U.S. to assert that Fogel was wrongfully detained. The campaign to free Fogel grew and eventually included President Biden's national security advisor, Jake Sullivan, the first U.S. official to assert that Fogel was wrongfully detained. The Russians released Fogel on February 11, 2025, following negotiations with Trump administration officials. In exchange, the U.S. released Russian citizen Alexander Vinnik, a computer expert convicted of money laundering $4 billion in bitcoin.

> **TRUMP**: As fate would have it, Marc Fogel was born in a small rural town in Butler, Pennsylvania, where his mother has lived for the past 78 years. I just happened to go there last July 13 for a rally. That was not pleasant. And that is where I met his beautiful mom right before I walked onto that stage, and I told her I would not forget what she said about her son, and I never did, did I? Never forgot. Less than 10 minutes later, at that same rally, gunfire rang out and a sick and deranged assassin unloaded 8 bullets from his sniper's perch into a crowd of many thousands of people. My life was saved by a fraction of an inch....

Trump then honors others in the gallery – the family of Corey Comperatore, who "was a firefighter, a veteran, a Christian, a husband, a devoted father, and, above all, a protector." He had lost his life protecting his family. His wife and two daughters were in the gallery.

> **TRUMP**: I believe that my life was saved that day in Butler for a very good reason. I was saved by God to make America great again. I believe that. I do. Thank you. Thank you very much.

Trump claims: "I was saved by God to make America great again."

People who claim to be saved by God for a special purpose tend to be saints or madmen.

On April 10, Yale history professor Timothy Snyder offered this assessment of Trump's character:

> We all have our foibles, our whims, our vulnerabilities. But when one person has unchecked power, irrationality becomes unchecked. Donald Trump thinks that everyone is always ripping him off. If he were the president in a normal situation, this would be a minor problem. But in a situation in which he has gotten away with an attempted coup, in which the Supreme Court has told him he is immune from prosecution, in which members of his own party rarely challenge him, in which Congress no longer sees the need to pass laws, in which too much of the media normalizes him, Trump's vulnerability can bring about the destruction of the country.
>
> We have thousands of years of political theory and indeed great literature to instruct us on this point: too much power brings out the worst in people – especially among the worst of people. As the Founders understood, the purpose of the rule of law, of checks and balances, of regular elections, is to prevent precisely such a situation. Allowing our republic to be compromised has many costs, for example, to our rights and to our dignity. But it also has costs in a very basic economic sense.
>
> When you elevate the mad king, you elevate the madness.

On March 27, the Yale Daily News announced that three Yale professors were leaving Yale and the United States to take positions at the University of Toronto, in Canada. The three are Snyder, his wife, Marci Shore, also a history professor, and philosophy professor Jason Stanley. Stanley said his decision to leave was "entirely because of the political climate of the United States." He is the author of the book How Fascism Works. Shore wrote that she believes other professors will consider relocating in the face of the "American descent into fascism."

'The Golden Age of America Has Just Begun'

TRUMP: Americans have always been the people who defied all odds, transcended all dangers, made the most extraordinary sacrifices, and did whatever it took to defend our children, our country, and our freedom.... Despite the best efforts of those who would try to censor us, silence us, break us, destroy us, Americans are today a proud, free, sovereign, and independent nation that will always be free. And we will fight for it till death. We will never let anything happen to our beloved country, because we are a country of doers, dreamers, fighters, survivors. Our ancestors crossed a vast ocean, strode into an unknown wilderness, and carved their fortunes from the rock and soil of a perilous and very dangerous frontier. They chased our destiny across a boundless continent....

Now it is our time to take up the righteous cause of American liberty. And it's our turn to take America's destiny into our own hands and begin the most thrilling days in the history of our country. This will be our greatest era; with God's help over the next four years, we are going to lead this nation even higher, and we are going to forge the freest, most advanced, most dynamic, and most dominant civilization ever to exist on the face of this Earth.

We are going to create the highest quality of life, build the safest and wealthiest and healthiest and most vital communities anywhere in the world. We are going to conquer the vast frontiers of science, and we are going to lead humanity into space and plant the American flag on the planet Mars and even far beyond. And through it all, we are going to rediscover the unstoppable power of the American spirit, and we are going to renew unlimited promise of the American dream. Every single day, we will stand up, and we will fight, fight, fight for the country our citizens believe in and for the country our people deserve.

My fellow Americans, get ready for an incredible future because the Golden Age of America has only just begun. It will be like nothing that has ever been seen before. Thank you, God bless you, and God bless America.

Trump's peroration relies on traditional tropes of American exceptionalism. Pre-woke America. Defied all odds. Proud. Free. Dreamers. Righteous. The greatest nation on Earth (if you keep your mind closed). But there are other notes.

Planting "the American flag on the planet Mars" in the next four years kind of jumps out. That's impossible. The claim is probably an accident of grammar. It's also a tip of the hat to Elon Musk and his obsession with starting a new Earth civilization on Mars. Insofar as it's a serious commitment, it's a commitment to spending more money than the U.S. has, or likely will ever have, on a project that most scientists consider a fantasy.

The real warning comes at the end, when Trump promises – or warns – "get ready for an incredible future because the Golden Age of America has only just begun. It will be like nothing that has ever been seen before."

The incredible future is here already, and it is like nothing Americans have seen before.

Our new Golden Age started on day one, January 20, with an executive order illegally presuming to rewrite the Constitution's Fourteenth Amendment by fiat.

The Golden Age continues to unfold with the illegal Department of Government Efficiency invading and destroying government agencies, illegal deportations of random people without due process of law, illegal government firings without due process of law, illegal threats to universities and powerful law firms who capitulate, illegal threats to judges who issue orders that check the illegal actions of the administration, and an inchoate foreign policy that is no policy beyond offending our allies and embracing our enemies.

Atop this looming Golden Age sits President Trump, asserting that as president, he is the law, and no one has the authority to disobey him. That would include the Supreme Court, which has done so much to create this monstrous new America and, maybe – ironically – our last, best hope to survive it with something like constitutional government intact. But don't bet on it. The court has already ruled in Trump's favor in several cases.

This is no longer American exceptionalism, the hope (no matter how deluded at any given moment) to make America better. This is MAGA, the determination to manipulate nostalgia for a past that never existed to create a "Golden Age" of authoritarianism and suffering.

We can't all move to Canada. So, what can we do?

Part 3

Taking Justice to the People – Or the New Chronicle of American Justice

On March 14, 2025, Trump made a rare presidential appearance in the Great Hall of the U.S. Department of Justice (DOJ), where he spoke for about 70 minutes. He talked about his plans for the DOJ, which he claimed falsely that his predecessors had turned into a department of "injustice." An edited transcript appears below, with commentary..

Introducing the Greatest President in History

Attorney General Pam Bondi introduced the President, commenting:

> We are going to fight to keep America safe again. President Trump has prioritized tackling our nation's fentanyl crisis, and he has taken decisive action to fight it.... I see all my friends out there, my colleagues, who will work to prosecute violent criminals, get the drugs off our streets, get the gangs off our streets, and get the illegal aliens out of our country.... And thanks to Donald Trump, they will all be deported very soon. Thanks to his work, Homeland Security and I say the unsung hero, Stephen Miller.... we all work for the greatest president in the

history of our country. We are so proud to work at the directive of Donald Trump. He will never stop fighting for us, and we will never stop fighting for him and for our country. It is an honor to welcome to the Department of Justice, the 45th and the 47th president....

TRUMP: Well, thank you very much. Thank you. Thank you, Pam, very much. What a job you're doing. And it's a true honor to be with you today. This is a storied hall, if there ever was one. And based on the crowd, I think we broke the all-time record.

But as we begin a proud new chapter in the Chronicles of American Justice, this really is something we're turning the page on four long years of corruption, weaponization, and surrender to violent criminals. And we are restoring fair, equal, and impartial justice under the constitutional rule of law. And you're the people that are doing it, very, very proud of all of you. Under the Trump administration, the DOJ and the FBI will once again become the premier crime-fighting agencies on the face of the earth....

This is a lie. A big lie.

The Trump administration had already begun deporting people illegally, with no due process of law, as required by the Constitution. These were mostly people who had committed no offense or only a misdemeanor immigration offense, the equivalent of trespassing. Led by ICE agents wearing masks, offering no identification, showing no warrant, and using brute force, the Trump administration was well on its way to establishing a police state. "Homeland security" was becoming an oxymoron under the ICE-STAPO.

Trump claimed to be "restoring fair, equal, and impartial justice under the constitutional rule of law." None of that is true. The opposite is true, checked only by federal judges during the first few months.

Trump spent the next five minutes or so praising Pam Bondi, FBI Director Pash Katel, Deputy Attorney General Todd Blanch, Principal Associate Deputy Attorney Emil Bove, and several other officials in the room, all of whom were participants in the new weaponization of "justice."

TRUMP: But with you leading the way, it'll soon be the most admired and most respected of all. You're going to be more respected, and I really believe that there's also a lot of things to solve, a lot of problems to solve. But that's going to put you in the upper tier and maybe the top tier. And I believe that's going to happen. I'm so proud of the people in this room.

But first, we must be honest about the lies and abuses that have occurred within these walls. Unfortunately, in recent years, a corrupt group of hacks and radicals within the ranks of the American government obliterated the trust and goodwill built up over generations. They weaponized the vast powers of our intelligence and law enforcement agencies to try and thwart the will of the American people. You remember the 51 Intelligence agents that said as an example that Hunter Biden's laptop from hell came from Russia when they knew it came right from his bedroom.

This screed is one of Trump's chronic, dishonest assertions, offered with no evidentiary support, laced with distortions and lies.

In October 2020, 51 former U.S. intelligence officials published a letter suggesting that the story about Hunter Biden's laptop had "all the classic earmarks of a Russian information operation." The letter didn't assert the laptop was definitively Russian disinformation. It stated that the circumstances around its release resembled past Russian influence campaigns. These officials were not in government positions at the time; they were former CIA, NSA, and other intelligence agency personnel. The laptop was later authenticated by several outlets, and reporting has confirmed that significant parts of it, including many of the emails, were genuine.

Hunter Biden's Laptop? In 2025? Seriously? Yep.

Hunter Biden's laptop is an old story at best, albeit with suspicious aspects. In 2019, the water-damaged laptop was dropped off at a computer repair shop. No one came back for it for about six months. The shop owner made two copies of the hard drive. Then he contacted the FBI, which seized the laptop. The shop owner then gave a copy of the hard drive to Rudy Giuliani's lawyer. In October 2020, the laptop story broke in the media, but it did not get spectacular play because it never revealed anything like a smoking gun against anyone. Neither Rudy Giuliani nor anyone else in the Trump campaign made a laptop-based claim that could have affected the election. In 2024, in unrelated proceedings, Hunter Biden was convicted of felony firearms charges and pled guilty to tax charges.

Trump clings to the story not for its relevance, but as a wedge to claim persecution by the media, the intelligence agencies, the FBI, and who knows who else. And it's a cudgel he can use for his constant treatment of Biden as a political piñata. But no matter how often he invokes the tale, it's still not true.

> **TRUMP**: They knew that, it was a big lie, and they knew it so well. They spied on my campaign, launched one hoax and dis-information operation after another, broke the law on a colossal scale, persecuted my family, staff, and supporters. Raided my home, Mar-a-Lago, and did everything within their power to prevent me from becoming the President of the United States. With the help of radicals like Marc Elias, Mark Pomerantz. And these are people that nobody's ever seen anything like it.

Trump creates a false narrative by expanding the time frame to include years after the 2020 election. Mostly, his claims are not supported by specific evidence. And insofar as there is specific, public evidence, it all points toward his guilt in the crimes charged.

Trump Took the Documents. And He Beat the Rap.

On August 8, 2022, the FBI conducted a raid on Mar-a-Lago under a search warrant authorized by Attorney General Merrick Garland and signed by Magistrate Judge Bruce Reinhart, following a criminal referral by the National Archives and Records Administration (NARA). NARA claimed Trump was illegally withholding government documents. The FBI obtained the search warrant as part of an investigation into Trump relating to three criminal statutes:

■ Violations of the Espionage Act regarding unauthorized retention of national defense information.

- Destroying or concealing records "with the intent to impede, obstruct or influence" federal government activity.
- Illegal removal or destruction of federal government records (without respect to cause).

More than 13,000 government documents were recovered. They included nuclear-related information and FBI, CIA, and NSA information about national security interests. Of these documents, 337 were classified: 197 were handed over in January 2022, 38 were turned over under subpoena in June 2022, and 102 were seized in the August search of Mar-a-Lago. Months later, at least two more documents with classified markings were uncovered at Trump locations. Trump had no legal right to retain these documents personally.

In June 2023, Trump was indicted, arrested, booked, processed, and arraigned in the U.S. District Court of South Florida. He pleaded not guilty to all 40 charges.

In July 2024, Trump-appointed U.S. District Judge Aileen Cannon dismissed the case against Trump, ruling: "The Superseding Indictment is dismissed because Special Counsel Smith's appointment violates the Appointments Clause of the United States Constitution."

Special Counsel Jack Smith, appointed by the attorney general, contested the decision, noting that other federal courts had upheld the constitutionality of special counsels appointed by the attorney general. The special counsel appealed the ruling, then dropped it after Trump's 2024 election, before the appeal could be heard.

Trump claims they "did everything within their power to prevent me from becoming the president," but that does not hold up to close scrutiny. In reality, for whatever reason, the Biden administration slow-walked the case, taking more than a year from the FBI raid to the indictment, even though the raid produced 13,000 smoking guns. Another year of legal delays, abetted by Judge Cannon, led to the dismissal of the Florida case just four months before the election. Despite overwhelming evidence against Trump, the American justice system failed to produce a conviction, thanks greatly to Judge Cannon, who really did do "everything within her power" (in Trump's words) to shield Trump from judgment and allow him to be re-elected.

On the face of it, this situation looks like a judicial system with corrupt actors acting corruptly to enable a corrupt president to be corruptly re-elected. So maybe Trump's right: "And these are people that nobody's ever seen anything like it."

> **TRUMP:** So many others, but these are people that are bad people, really bad people. They tried to turn America into a corrupt, communist, and Third World country. But in the end, the thugs failed, and the truth won. Freedom won. Justice won. Democracy won. And above all, the American people won. There could be no more heinous betrayal of American values than to use the law to terrorize the innocent and reward the wicked.

This is an appalling inversion of the truth. Freedom, justice, democracy, and the American people – they all lost.

During Trump's first hundred days, America had become exactly that, a "heinous betrayal of American values… [using] the law to terrorize the innocent and reward the wicked."

The Cases Against Trump Were Justified, But…

Besides Trump's indictment for mishandling national security documents, he was subject to three other serious criminal charges.

On March 30, 2023, New York County District Attorney Alvin Bragg indicted Trump on 34 counts of falsifying business records. At the end of a jury trial presided over by Justice Juan Merchant of the New York Supreme Court, a jury found Trump guilty on all 34 counts on May 30, 2024. Sentencing was scheduled for September 18, then postponed till November 26, after the election. Postponed again till January 10, 2025, Trump received an unconditional discharge of his sentence.

On August 1, 2023, special prosecutor Jack Smith secured an indictment of Trump in the U.S. District Court for the District of Columbia for attempting to overturn the 2020 U.S. presidential election. Trump faced four criminal charges of conspiring to defraud the government, to disenfranchise voters, and to corruptly obstruct an official proceeding.

On July 1, 2024, in *Trump v. United States*, the Supreme Court perpetrated a constitutional travesty by sanctioning criminal behavior by a president. The court voted 6-3, with three Trump appointees in the majority, ruling that Trump had absolute immunity for acts he committed as president that were considered official acts, with presumptive immunity for other acts (but no immunity for unofficial acts, left undefined). This decision reversed the rulings of the district court and the appeals court, both of which held that presidents could be held accountable for their criminal acts.

On August 2, the case was returned to federal district court judge Tanya Chutkin to sort out. On November 24, after the election, Judge Chutkin dismissed the case without prejudice. While that means, technically, that the case might be brought again in the future, for now, Trump has escaped accountability for his actions on January 6, 2021, when his supporters sacked the Capitol. He has since pardoned some 1,500 of them, including some 600 guilty of violence and attacking police officers.

On August 14, 2023, District Attorney Fani Willis of Fulton County, Georgia, secured a 41-count grand jury indictment of Trump and accomplices for racketeering in their attempt to overturn the 2020 U.S. presidential election in Georgia. Also charged were 18 co-conspirators. Four defendants pleaded guilty to some charges and agreed to cooperate with the prosecution. The case was paused when unrelated issues were brought against the prosecutor. On December 19, 2024, the Georgia Supreme Court disqualified the prosecutor.

The Georgia Supreme Court did not dismiss the case, however. *The State of Georgia v. Donald J. Trump et al* sits in limbo while the authorities decide whether a state-level prosecutor can prosecute a sitting president. No new trial date has been set. Once again, Trump has escaped accountability for his actions on January 6, 2021, attempting to overturn the 2020 presidential election.

For Trump, this is a situation in which he claims, "Freedom won. Justice won. Democracy won."

Does it get more Orwellian than that?

> **TRUMP**: And that's what they were doing at a level that's never been seen before. And it's exactly what you saw with Joe Biden,

Merrick Garland, and their cronies to do the building of the last four years, they ripped.... What they've ripped down is incalculable, but what you're going to build up is likewise something that will be breaking all sorts of records. They set loose violent criminals while targeting patriotic parents at school board meetings. They drop charges against Antifa and Hamas supporters while labeling traditional Catholics as domestic terrorists. The Catholics, we did very well with the Catholic votes. So, I want to thank them for that. They imported, they really did record numbers.

Did All of That Really Happen That Way?

Trump continues to lie, to misrepresent reality.

Trump's claim that "They set loose violent criminals," while unsupported here, has some traction in reality. A few real criminals go a long way politically. Crime has been a highly demagogued issue since the 1960s. Even when crime rates drop, as they currently have, Republicans tend to evoke fear with claims of predators on the loose. It doesn't help that a predator is always on the loose somewhere. If our politics can ever have a rational discussion of crime and justice, we will have evolved.

What about Trump claiming that the Biden administration was "targeting patriotic parents at school board meetings"? More demagoguery, to be sure. It seems to be rooted in a 2021 memo by Attorney General Merrick Garland, addressing the rise of threats and violence against school officials. While defending the right to free speech, Garland also directed the FBI to work with local law enforcement to address violence and intimidation. Garland also referred to a letter from the National School Boards Association, suggesting that some incidents amounted to domestic terrorism (the Association's language, not Garland's). Trump and others overreacted, claiming the memo equated parental advocacy with domestic terrorism. It didn't. Trump vowed to make the ending of the virtually non-existent targeting of parents who express dissenting views at school board meetings a priority of his incoming second administration, adding, "You are not a domestic terrorist, or a terrorist."

When Trump claims, "They drop charges against Antifa," he's pretty much lying. While some cases involving alleged Antifa members have been dismissed or resulted in acquittals, these outcomes are typically due to legal reasons such as insufficient evidence, procedural errors, or the discretion of local prosecutors. Trump, as usual, offers no specific case in support of his claim. What he's really objecting to is due process of law.

Trump claims, "They drop cases against… Hamas," again with no specifics. This appears to be a flat lie. The Biden administration spent billions of dollars supporting the Israeli genocide in Gaza, in its attempt to destroy Hamas. The Trump administration continues this policy with billions of dollars of support for Israel in its genocide in Gaza. Historically, genocide in Gaza is a bipartisan priority. The genocide in Gaza is also a war crime and a crime against humanity.

Trump blames the Biden administration for "labeling traditional Catholics as domestic terrorists." He offers no evidence. This, too, appears to be a flat lie. Biden is Catholic. In 2021, the Biden Justice Department denounced anti-Catholic violence and vandalism.

When it comes to "domestic terrorists," Trump pardoned some 1,500 of them, the ones who attacked the U.S. Capitol on January 6, 2021.

> **TRUMP:** I would say, what's with the Catholics? They're really after the Catholics. So, I don't know, [inaudible 00:15:26] a lot of people, maybe they didn't even know why. They imported illegal alien murderers, drug dealers, and child predators from all over the world to come into our country while putting elderly Christians and pro-life activists on trial for singing hymns and for saying prayers. They went to jail for that.

No matter how often Trump claims "they imported illegal alien murderers, drug dealers, and child predators from all over the world," it's never going to be more than a dishonest distortion of reality. Especially "from all over the world" – seriously? But he gets away with it because there's too little pushback in the media or elsewhere. Too often, his lies go unchallenged. But as the grotesque ICE raids continue, deporting nursing mothers, legal gardeners, children with cancer, the American people are beginning to realize how disgustingly they are being lied to every day.

As for "putting elderly Christians and pro-life activists on trial for singing hymns and for saying prayers," this is false. It's another deliberate lie.
Some pro-life activists have been prosecuted for illegally blocking access to
abortion clinics, but not for singing hymns or praying. Trump cites no cases.

Lauren Handy was arrested on March 25, 2022, for an October
2020 blockade. She is a full-time activist with Survivors of the Abortion
Holocaust. She defines herself as an "anarcho-mutualist" and opposes both
abortion and the death penalty. Her message as a counsellor is LGBT+ inclusive. Handy says that when she is arrested, the charges are often dropped
or sentences are suspended. She purposely does not earn wages, so her wages
cannot be garnished in a lawsuit. On May 14, 2024, Handy was sentenced
to 57 months in prison and three years of supervised release for violating
the Freedom of Access to Clinic Entrances Act. This stemmed from her
participation in the October 2020 action when she and others went into an
abortion clinic and used their bodies, chains, ropes, and furniture to block
the clinic's doors. One of the pregnant women blocked from the clinic was
carrying a fetus that had no chance of survival; the woman collapsed in pain
outside the clinic. On January 23, 2025, Trump pardoned Lauren Handy
and nine co-defendants.

> **TRUMP**: Our predecessors turned this Department of Justice
> into the Department of Injustice. But I stand before you today
> to declare that those days are over, and they are never going to
> come back. They're never coming back. So now, as the chief
> law enforcement officer in our country, I will insist upon and
> demand full and complete accountability for the wrongs and
> abuses that have occurred. The American people have given us
> a mandate, a mandate like few people thought possible. We won
> every single swing state. We won the popular vote by millions
> and millions of people. We won districts, 2,750. Think of that,
> 2,750 districts compared to 505. So, we want it at levels that
> have... I don't believe ever seen before. That's the one where
> you see the map of the United States and it's all red, red for
> Republican, not for Communist. Red for Republican. They
> would like it to turn red for communists, but it didn't work out

that way. The American people have given us a mandate and really just a far-reaching investigation is what they are demanding into the corruption of our system.

The Imaginary 'Mandate' Still Doesn't Exist

Trump's ritual fabrication of a mandate will never be true, no matter how he manipulates the details of the vote. The reality is that he lost more than half the vote. He won 49.8% of the popular vote, with just over 77 million votes. The actual winner was NOBODY, who got 89 million non-votes from 89 million non-voters. There is no rational basis, in an election this close, for anyone claiming a mandate for anything.

As he approached the end of his first hundred days in office, Trump's approval rating was 40%, down from 47% on January 20. His disapproval rating was 48% then and had risen to 59% in less than two months, according to The Hill. As for Democrats, their approval rating is only 38%, compared to 43% for Republicans. People are not happy with their "leadership." No one knows where acceptable leadership might come from.

To Trump, leadership is turning the government into an instrument for carrying out his personal vendettas.

TRUMP: And that's exactly, I'm sure what Pam [Bondi] and Kash [Patel] and everyone else mentioned here and not mentioned is going to be doing. We will expel the rogue actors and corrupt forces from our government. We will expose, very much expose, their egregious crimes and severe misconduct, of which was levels – you've never seen anything like it. It's going to be legendary. And it's going to also be legendary for the people that are able to seek it out and bring justice. We will restore the scales of justice in America, and we will ensure that such abuses never happen again in our country.

This looks and sounds for all the world like projection. Trump invents an imaginary weaponization of government under Biden to mask his own weaponization of government.

Trump initiated a constitutional crisis on day one. He issued an executive order, asserting the right to revise the Constitution on his own authority, eliminating birthright citizenship from the Fourteenth Amendment. This was immediately challenged in court and blocked by several federal courts. After hearing the case on May 15, the Supreme Court issued a 6-3 decision on June 27. They did not decide the fundamental question of birthright citizenship, leaving that to some future case. Here, in *Trump v. CASA*, the court restricted the use of national injunctions by federal district courts. The decision is cowardly, avoiding the fundamental issue. And it is dishonest, allowing the suspension of birthright citizenship to continue, regardless of the reality that it's unconstitutional.

How Many Illegalities Can Our Judicial System Handle?

During his first hundred days, Trump flooded the zone with patently illegal actions, including hundreds of executive orders that led to hundreds of lawsuits, most of which led to temporary restraining orders and further litigation that is still playing out. The lower courts have been a bulwark of constitutional democracy, but the Supreme Court has been unreliable.

On July 10, New Hampshire Federal District Judge Joseph Laplante ruled in a case brought by the American Civil Liberties Union that the lawsuit qualified as a class action. This created a nationwide injunction against Trump's revision of the Fourteenth Amendment and preserved birthright citizenship for the time being.

The organization Just Security has a section on its website (justsecurity.org) called "Litigation Tracker: Just Security's Coverage of the Trump Administration's Executive Orders." As of mid-July, this site was tracking 330 separate cases (appeals included in the same case), including 7 that had been closed.

The Litigation Tracker treats as one case all the lawsuits involving the removal of F-1 foreign student visa registration. According to Politico, there were "more than 100 lawsuits and 50 restraining orders from dozens of federal judges" before the government reversed its decision and restored the F-1 registrations on or about April. 25, 2025.

As Trump says, "You've never seen anything like it."

> **TRUMP**: And that's why on day one, I signed an executive
> order banning all government censorship and directing the

removal of every bureaucrat who conspired to attack free speech and many other things and values in America. My administration stripped the security clearances of the disgraced intelligence agents who lied about Hunter Biden's laptop from hell. We revoked the clearances of deranged Jack Smith, Alvin Bragg, Letitia James, and the crooked law firms that aided their partisan persecutions, and I went through it. These are state and city courts, and the corruption is unbelievable. We also terminated the clearances of the Biden crime family and Joe Biden, himself, he didn't deserve it. In fact, he was essentially found guilty, but they said he was incompetent and therefore let's not find him guilty, I guess. Nobody knows what that ruling was, but I didn't want any part of it. I think I would've rather been found guilty than what they found with him. They said he didn't know what the hell he was doing and therefore, he's let him go.

Yes, Trump did a number of these things, some of which are in litigation, and all of which are forms of revenge against his political enemies, for no useful purpose. Retribution is alive and well and unfinished in the Trump administration.

But one of Trump's claims is hilarious, in a very dark way. He claims credit for "an executive order banning all government censorship." Then his administration banned the use of hundreds of words and phrases in documents, websites, or other government communications.

Things You Can't Say, Like 'Women'

Regardless of the subject, government officials are banned from using these words in official communication: accessible, activists, advocate, antiracist, assigned at birth, barrier, bias, Black, clean energy, climate crisis, climate science, community equity, cultural heritage, disabilities, discrimination, diversity, equal opportunity, equity, expression, female, gender, Gulf of Mexico, hate speech, health equity, historically, identity, immigrants, inclusion, indigenous community, inequitable, LGBTQ+, marginalize, mental health, minority, multicultural, Native American, nonbinary, oppression, polarization, political, pollution, pregnant person, prejudice, privilege, pronoun, prostitute, race, segregation, sex, social justice, status, stereotype, systemic, trans, trauma, tribal, underprivileged, underserved, victim, and women.

This is only a partial list. The list is from The New York Times. Other lists are at barnraisingmedia.com, newrepublic.com, and pen.org, which calls the Trump administration effort a "chilling act of censorship."

You've never seen anything like it, right?

> **TRUMP**: I said, "You know, I'd rather be convicted, Pam." I think that that was not... I said, "Please convict me. Don't say that." I pardoned hundreds of political prisoners who had been grossly mistreated. We removed the senior FBI officials who misdirected resources to send SWAT teams after grandmothers and J6 hostages, and it was a great honor for me to fire, I will tell you this, a great honor to fire James Comey, a great, great honor. That was nothing. There was no better day. A lot of people said, "Oh, that's too bad you did that." And they said, "That's going to be..." And you know what? A year later, they said, "That actually saved the administration because the level of corrupt things that we learned after that turned out to be that they were doing, in fact, really bad things. He was a terrible person, did terrible things and persecuted people and all in the guise of being an angel, but he wasn't an angel."

Trump "pardoned hundreds of political prisoners" is a lie. The rioters at the Capitol were not political prisoners. They were duly convicted criminals.

On January 6, 2021, the U.S. Capitol was full of Senators and House members who ran for their lives when Trump supporters broke in, vandalized the place, and attacked anyone in their way, especially Capitol police. The event resulted in 10 deaths – 5 rioters and 5 police officers.

The "political prisoners" Trump pretends to see are the convicted rioters who overran the U.S. Capitol on January 6, trying to overturn the 2020 election. They were MAGA Trump supporters. Trump called them "patriots."

On January 20, 2025, he issued an executive order titled "Granting Pardons and Commutation of Sentences for Certain Offenses Relating to the Events at or Near the United States Capitol on January 6, 2021," claiming that "This proclamation ends a grave national injustice that has been perpetrated upon the American people over the last four years and begins a process of national reconciliation."

These were not political prisoners by any rational standard. They were rioters who besieged the Capitol. Some 600 of them committed violent acts, including attacking and injuring police officers. There is no evidence that any of these people was "grossly mistreated." They were all afforded due process of law. Some who were accused were acquitted.

Trump's claim that the FBI sent "SWAT teams after grandmothers" is a lie.

As for James Comey, who was head of the FBI, the reason he was fired was that he refused to make a public statement that Trump was not a target in an FBI investigation, according to Rudy Giuliani. Comey had assured Trump privately that he wasn't a target.

Justice under Trump: overrun the Capitol, you're a "Patriot," refuse to defend Trump, "you're fired."

> **TRUMP**: We created a brand-new DOJ task force and anti-Christian bias, and under Director Patel, we're getting the FBI agents out of the headquarters in Washington, DC and back on the streets in pursuit of dangerous criminals where they belong and where they want to be....

Trump then talks about reducing the size of the FBI and putting it in a smaller building.

> **TRUMP**: We're going to have the best staff that you've ever seen, and that's what I need.... And they want to have far fewer people, but we also want to have them in DC. And if for no other reason, we like having law enforcement walking the streets of our capitol because when the bad guys are out there and they see there's an FBI agent, that's the ultimate in law enforcement and they're not going to be acting so bad....

Trump then talks about cleaning up Washington, D.C.

> **TRUMP**: We're going to have a crime-free capital. When people come here, they're not going to be mugged, shot, or raped. They're going to have a crime-free capital again, it's going to be

cleaner and better and safer than it ever was, and it's not going to take us too long....

He talks about Indiana basketball coach Bobby Knight for about three minutes before turning to immigration and foreign affairs.

TRUMP: We have a real big shot at making this country so great, so great. What happened to our country was so sad. What they've done in four years to our country with the borders, with Afghanistan, the embarrassing, most embarrassing period of time, allowing the Russian situation. It was never going to happen with Ukraine; allowing October 7 to happen would've never happened because under me, Iran was totally broke. They had no money. They weren't given any money to Hamas or Hezbollah, was totally broke, but allowing inflation. Look at what inflation's done to people, been so devastating.

Trump is rambling a bit here, wandering among different topics.

He touts "a brand-new DOJ task force and anti-Christian bias under [FBI] Director Patel." Trump has already announced policies that enhance all the traditional American biases against women, Black people, Latinos, Native Americans, other ethnicities, immigrants, LGBTQ+ people, and all the other minorities. Now he embraces the imaginary anti-Christian bias. That should be much easier to fix, since it's so hard to find.

On the other hand, it doesn't address the Christian Nationalism that so many Trump appointees believe in. But that's not bias. That's an ideology for taking over the country.

Trump doesn't say why he thinks it would be a good idea to have FBI agents out on foot patrol.

Trump's summary of the Biden years is as self-serving as it is unreliable.

The borders have been an issue for decades, and Trump made little difference during his first term.

Afghanistan was a two-decade disaster that started under President Bush. Trump made it worse by caving to the Taliban and undercutting the Afghan government. Trump's negotiating with the Taliban, to the exclusion of the Afghan government, foreshadows his negotiating with Russia to the exclusion of Ukraine. In Afghanistan, Trump left Biden with an impossible commitment to pull out, which Biden managed to handle very badly.

The "Russian situation" has been aggravated by Trump since he was campaigning in 2016 and suggested recognizing Russia's occupation of Crimea as legal. That's no way to support Ukraine, a country the U.S. and Europe have claimed to be an ally. But it's wholly consistent with Trump's current position, pushing Ukraine to surrender to every Russian demand and calling it peace.

Saying the October 7 Hamas attack would not have happened in 2023 if he'd been president is pure self-aggrandizement. Israeli intelligence knew it was coming, and it happened anyway. And it served as an excuse for the Israeli genocide in Gaza. And Trump supports that. Israel seeks a final solution for the Palestinian problem, and too many people look away.

What's That Got to Do With the Price of Eggs?

TRUMP: And now, you see that by the way, price of eggs is down 35% of the last week and a half, we're doing a good job. Brooke is doing a good job…. And inflation's down, interest rates are down. Gasoline has come down, down to a level that we haven't seen in a long time. All things that we wanted to do because then everything else is going to be coming down. We want it to come down. We want bacon to come down and groceries. A term I used to use, it's an old-fashioned term, but I used to use it on the campaign trail. Those last 90 perfect beautiful days, we just hit it.

Eggs are not down. Inflation is essentially flat. Interest rates are essentially flat or slightly lower. Gasoline is flat. Bacon is flat. The economy in Trump's first hundred days contracted.

"When I win, I will immediately bring prices down, starting on Day One," Trump promised in August 2024 at a press conference surrounded by groceries as props. He repeated the promise numerous other times. It's nostalgia now.

Trump praises White House chief of staff Susie Wiles and others.

TRUMP: We had an amazing judge in Florida, and her name is Aileen Cannon, and I didn't know her. I still don't know her. I don't believe I ever spoke to her even during the trial, but I did appoint her, federal judge.

And these fake lawyers, these horrible human beings were hitting her so hard public relations-wise, they were playing the ref. I don't think it's legal. I don't think it's legal. They might as well go out and just shout it in a courthouse. They were saying, "She was slow. She wasn't smart. She was totally biased. She loved Trump." I didn't know her other than I saw her the couple of days that I was in court, and I thought her decorum was amazing. Anything bad they could say, though, they were saying about her, it was whatever they could say bad about a human being all made up, because actually she was brilliant. She moved quickly. She was the absolute model of what a judge should be, and she was strong and tough. And how do you get them to stop if you're a judge? How do you get them to stop with the playing the ref? Bobby Knight would play the ref....

Trump talks about Coach Bobby Knight some more, then returns to Cannon.

TRUMP: It's totally illegal what they do. I just hope you can all watch for it. But it's totally illegal. And it was so unfair what they were doing to her, but they do it all the time with judges. But in her case, she was very courageous, and it only made her angry. When you say, it just made her angry. She didn't like it. A lot of them say, "Oh, please don't say that about me. My family. What's my husband going to say? What's my wife going to say, or my kids? Please don't say that." And it had absolutely no impact on her in the case against me, which was a case, I will not use a bad word, I promised my wife, I would never use a bad word, so just a little bad. The case against me was bullshit. And she correctly dismissed it.

Methinks he doth protest too much.

Aileen Cannon Has Much to Answer for, Don't Hold Your Breath
Judge Aileen Cannon did not work quickly. She helped Trump by

slow-walking the case. She took her time getting to the dismissal on July 15, 2024, on grounds that she could have cited months earlier. The dismissal was controversial. It was appealed. It was overturned. But the election was too near, and justice was obstructed.

Cannon surely appeared to be biased. Her handling of the case was consistent with bias. As Pro Publica has reported, Cannon "has repeatedly violated a rule requiring that federal judges disclose their attendance at private seminars.... Cannon's performance during almost four years of a lifetime appointment has drawn criticism from lawyers, former federal judges, and courtroom observers who told ProPublica that she doesn't render timely decisions and has made unpredictable rulings in both civil and criminal matters."

In September 2022, Cannon issued an order to appoint a special master to review the documents the government had seized from Mar-a-Lago in Trump's national security documents case. On December 1, 2022, the Eleventh Circuit Court of Appeals reversed Cannon's order, finding that Cannon "improperly exercised equitable jurisdiction" in hearing the case and that the entire proceeding (filed by Trump) should be dismissed. Notably, the court also found that regardless of the status of a document in question (personal or presidential), the government maintains the authority to seize it under a warrant supported by probable cause.

The panel wrote, "The law is clear. We cannot write a rule that allows any subject of a search warrant to block government investigations after the execution of the warrant. Nor can we write a rule that allows only former presidents to do so."

When she dismissed the case in July 2024, claiming the special prosecutor's appointment was illegal, she ignored the opposite findings by all the other courts that had ruled on the matter.

As former presidential counsel W. Neil Eggleston told the Harvard Gazette:

> Two other district courts and the D.C. Circuit have considered this issue – the legality of the special counsel – and they have all rejected it. Cannon is the only judge to find the appointment invalid. The D.C. Circuit has twice rejected a challenge to the use

of special counsels – during the Iran-Contra investigation and during Special Counsel Robert Mueller's probe of Trump. Judge Dabney Friedrich of the District Court in D.C., who is a Trump appointee, tossed aside a similar challenge without a lot of effort in a fairly short opinion in a case involving Mueller, who oversaw the investigation into Russian interference in the 2016 election. Judge T.S. Ellis of the Eastern District of Virginia similarly tossed this issue aside in a case that also involved Mueller. So, the other courts that have looked at this issue have had no trouble with it and have ruled contrary to Cannon.

Cannon may or may not actually be biased, but her actions were consistent with bias. She indisputably helped Trump avoid accountability for his actions. No wonder he's grateful.

Trump Complains About the Way Some People Treat Supreme Court Justices

TRUMP: They're in a position they can't really fight back really very well. And so, what they do is sometimes they get weak, I would say, a majority maybe of the times. That's why I'm so impressed with Judge Cannon in Florida, how strong she was, how she held up. It actually made her more resolute than anything I've seen. I mean, it was amazing because they were hitting her so hard. It was so sad to watch this, but it's sad what they do to other judges. It's very sad what they do to the Supreme Court. And a lot of the judges that I had, if you look at them, they take tremendous abuse in the New York Times and the Washington Post, all of the different networks, they take such abuse….

They don't want bad publicity, and it's truly interference, in my opinion. And it should be illegal, and it probably is illegal in some form. There's no difference than speaking to a judge or shouting to a judge or doing whatever you have to do in a courthouse….

Trump Behaves in a Courtroom Like Trump

Trump's behavior during his criminal trial in New York (convicted by a jury on 34 counts) exemplified his version of trying to play the ref. As reported by NBC, Trump's behavior was volatile, marked by defiance and a disregard for courtroom norms:

- Manhattan Supreme Court Judge Arthur Engoron reprimanded Trump for inappropriate gestures toward potential jurors during jury selection and for his combative testimony, which included insults directed at the judge and the New York Attorney General.
- After a judge fined him $10,000 for violating a gag order and denied a defense motion for a verdict in his favor, Trump stormed out of the courtroom. The gag order had prohibited him from targeting the judge's staff.
- While testifying, Trump repeatedly insulted the judge and the prosecutor, dismissed the case as a "political witch hunt," and attempted to read from notes, leading to a 15-minute recess for his legal team to coach him on courtroom decorum.
- Outside the courtroom, Trump continued to criticize the trial and its participants. He labeled the trial as "very corrupt," referred to the judge as a "Democrat judge" under pressure, and called the New York Attorney a "political hack."

Trump digresses to criticize some of his critics – attorney Andrew Weissman, special prosecutor Jack Smith, and Norm Eisen of CREW. His sense of being a victim is showing.

> **TRUMP:** We had to take all of that abuse even during the trials. We had to take tremendous abuse, like these wonderful guys. They're not legitimate people there. They're horrible people, they're scum, and you have to know that. You're going to have these cases where you can't allow yourselves to be deflected. You just can't let it happen. You have so many, you have such a higher calling.
>
> I believe that CNN and MSDNC [a derogatory blend of MSNBC and DNC (Democratic National Committee)], who literally write 97.6% bad about me, are political arms of the Democrat party. In my opinion, they're really corrupt and they're illegal. What they do is illegal. It makes no difference

how big a victory I had, I can have the biggest victory in history. It makes no difference what kind of a failure the other side has. These people are going to go after me.

I said it during the other night, during the big speech on Tuesday night. I said about Democrats, and I don't like that. I have great respect, by the way, for what [Democratic Senator] Schumer did today. He went out and he said that I'm going to have to vote with the Republicans because it's the right thing to do. I couldn't believe what I heard, but I think he's going to get some credit for it. I think, let's see what happens tonight with the big vote as it comes…. We're bringing our country back faster than anyone ever thought possible. We're working so hard at doing it and we want fairness in the courts. The courts are a big factor.

The elections which were totally rigged are a big factor. We have to have honest elections, we have to have borders, and we have to have courts and law that's fair or we're not going to have a country.

So, how does that work? If elections "were totally rigged," how is he a legitimate president? Some say he's not, but the evidence isn't there yet.

"We have to have borders," Trump says, reasonably enough. But then he acts as if borders aren't that important for Canada. Or Mexico. Or Greenland. Or Panama. Or Ukraine. Or Gaza.

And he says, "We have to have courts and law that's fair or we're not going to have a country." Who could argue with that? But that doesn't explain – or justify – why his administration is attacking judges. Or threatening judges. Or arresting judges. Or encouraging Congress to reduce judicial authority arbitrarily. Or failing to respond when his supporters threateningly send unordered pizzas to judges at their homes.

"We're not going to have a country," is what he said, and he's working on it.

And attacking First Amendment principles, such as press freedom and free speech, as "illegal" is one more way to destroy the Constitution.

When he's done, he can make the lie "the biggest victory in history" into the only official truth.

Will Ukraine Come Between Trump and Putin?

Trump rambles for a couple of minutes. Then he touches on Ukraine with his usual falsehoods.

> **TRUMP**: I can tell you that there was a case where there would've been no war if I were president, and it's just 100% would not have happened, would never have happened. I used to speak to President Putin a lot about it. I said, "Don't do it. Don't do it." I won't tell you what the consequence was. I won't tell you what, but if he believed even 5% of what I said, then he would say, "I'm not going to do it," and I think he did. We had a good relationship, and we had a professional relationship and his respect for this country, and I think we've had some very good results....
>
> First of all, you don't want to pick on somebody that's a lot larger than you, even with the money. There's a lot of money that we gave them and a lot of equipment. We make the best military equipment in the world, but even with all of that, it's unbelievable. Right now, you have a lot of Ukrainian soldiers that are encircled and in grave danger, and I've asked them not to kill those soldiers please. Not to kill those soldiers. We don't want them killed. It's such a shame to see what's happened. A thing like that would've never happened.

What on earth is he talking about? What does "you don't want to pick on somebody that's a lot larger than you" even mean? He thinks Ukraine is picking on Russia? Is he back to blaming Ukraine for starting the war that began when Russia invaded?

Trump rambles for several minutes. He repeats his claims that, if he had been president, inflation would have never happened, that the October 7 Hamas attack would have never happened, that Afghanistan would have remained stable, and that the U.S. would have remained in control of the Bagram Air Force base in Afghanistan – much of it unintelligible.

> **TRUMP**: I just want to say, God bless America because we

have to say, God bless. We're lucky we're still here, frankly. This whole thing could lead, I think we have it. I think we have it, but this could lead to World War Three very easily. Could very easily lead to World War Three. But I think we're in pretty good shape, a lot better than we were before we got involved.

That I can tell you. It was going, that was heading into World War Three territory. That would've been a war like no other because of nuclear weapons and other types of weapons that you don't even want to know about. But as many of you do know, well, we're focused on persecuting. These people we're really focused on persecuting Republicans.

This borders on incoherent. What could lead to World War III? Maybe he means Ukraine. He doesn't say. But he's in high rant now – in the Great Hall of the Justice Department, with an audience of administration and law enforcement officials. He wants them to believe the country is threatened by immigrants, the unnamed, unidentified, mostly non-existent people he's been threat-mongering for years. He can demagogue it to death, and people – some people – believe him.

OK, Let's Demagogue on Crime for a Bit

TRUMP: The last administration presided over the worst increase in violent crime in our country in many, many decades. We had levels of violence and crime, and a lot of it had to do with the illegal immigrants that came in. Remember when I used to complain about it? Because I knew how tough they were, how mean they were. They said, no, no. People that come into our country are all wonderful people. No, they're not wonderful. These are stone-cold killers. They make our killers look nice by comparison. They make our killers look nice. These are rough, tough people with the tattoos all over their face.

Historically speaking, I don't want to discriminate against anybody, but historically speaking, they're not going to be the head of any major bank that we know of. These are rough people. These are rough, rough killer people and they allowed them in by the millions in major cities like New York, Chicago, and Washington.

Mothers can't walk their children to the park without fear of being shot or killed or raped or anything. Women can't ride the subway without worrying that a hoodlum will shove them onto the train tracks. In New York, it's happened twice in the last couple of weeks. They're standing there, perfect Wall Street gentleman in one case and another person who was a worker, good worker, electrician. Gets pushed into a train going 45 miles an hour just prior to the train, not stopping, going to go through that. I know the stations very well. I used to take the subway. I used to feel safe. When I was young, I'd go to, my parents would drop me off at the subway. I'd take the subway to my school. Can you believe it? Today, they wouldn't be doing that. We want to get a country back maybe where you can do that again, Pam. It's so sad to see what's taking place.

Under the Biden regime, average monthly homicides increased by 14%. Property crime rose tremendously. Violent crime went up at least 37% that they know of. Rape soared by 42%. Car theft rose by 48%, and robbery surged to 63% to 100% percent. They don't even know what the number is. I have no higher mission as President of the United States than to end this killing and stop this law-breaking and to making America safe again. That's what you're all about in this room. We want to protect Americans, and we protect everybody that's in our country, American or not American. We want to have a safe and proud country.

Trump's crime statistics are made up. They are all lies or fantasies, with no basis for rational policy. But they don't need to be rational to be politically successful: if you get people to believe in an imaginary crime wave, and then they see it vanish in reality, you can claim the credit, and who's to call you out?

Here are the facts:

- Homicides in 2020, when Trump was president, increased at the highest rate in history. They declined each year over the next four years when Biden was president.

■ Property crime declined by 8.1% in 2020 under Trump. Property crime declined by about 7% in 2021, under Biden, continuing a decline over the previous decade. The rate continued to decline over the next two years.

■ Violent crime rates (especially homicide) experienced a sharp increase in 2020 under Trump. In 2021, it rose 3% under Biden and continued to rise in 2022. Violent crime rates declined in 2023 and 2024, coming close to returning to 2019 pre-pandemic levels. There is no basis for Trump's claim of a 37% increase.

■ Rape increased slightly in 2021, compared to 2020. The rate declined for the next three years. The rate in 2024 was down 6% and lower than pre-pandemic levels. There is no basis for Trump's claim of a 42% increase.

■ Car theft increased by about 14% in 2021 over 2020, continuing to rise in 2022 and 2023. In 2024, the car theft rate decreased by the greatest amount in 40 years, 17% lower than 2023. In 2020, roughly 810,000 vehicles were stolen. This number rose to over a million in 2023, before dropping to 850,000 in 2024. There is no basis for Trump's claim of a 48% increase.

■ Robbery rates decreased by 13.8% in 2020 and by another 9% in 2021. The rate remained nearly flat for the next two years, then declined another 10% in 2024 under Biden.

The room was full of law enforcement officials who may well have known the actual statistics. None of them spoke up. Why would they?

Don't Forget, It's All Joe Biden's Fault, Whatever It Is

Trump then praises police officers, sheriffs, and sheriff's deputies in the audience. He doesn't refer to the rioters he pardoned for attacking police officers.

> **TRUMP**: On day one, I signed an executive order directing Attorney General to ensure that anyone who murders a police officer, immediately with as fast a trial as we could have, gets the death penalty.
>
> Last month, I fired all the radical left pro-crime U.S. attorneys appointed by Joe Biden. There were so many that were

bad, and I know there were some that were probably very good, but there were so many that were so bad and so evil, so corrupt. Instead of having Marxist prosecutors who want to put police officers in handcuffs and go after a police officer rather than a criminal, I appointed patriotic tough-on-crime warriors who will partner with police to put dangerous offenders behind bars, put them in jail.

We're fully reviving 1033 program to provide state and local law enforcement with surplus military equipment that we have so much of it. I did it in my last administration, and I remember Obama wouldn't do it. He wouldn't do it before me. Would not do it because he thought it made them look too strong, too military. I said, no, that's what I want them to look like. I want them to look strong. It was protective defensive equipment. We had billions of dollars., I gave it out, and now I'm going to have a chance to give it out again....

Trump's riff on firing "radical left pro-crime U.S. attorneys" is so absurd as to be almost funny. These "Marxist" attorneys were not pro-crime. Many of them were involved in pursuing cases against Trump for crimes for which he was serially indicted. They were, in fact, "tough on crime warriors," but in Trump's view, tough on the wrong crimes, the ones he committed.

Why weren't they spending more time going after all the imaginary immigrants committing all the imagined crimes in Trump's fevered demagoguery? Fair question. Part of the answer lies in what the Trump administration has been doing: deporting people with no evidence of wrongdoing, denying them any hearing to argue their innocence. Why would they do that? To pump up the statistics? Because an actual criminal is much harder to find than a graduate student from Turkey who wrote an op ed for her campus newspaper? And employing police state tactics is much less difficult than actually investigating and proving cases.

Repelling an Imaginary Invasion of America

TRUMP: Perhaps most importantly, we're securing our border and repelling the invasion of America....

Over the past four years, other countries emptied out their prisons and jails, mental institutions, and insane asylums and sent the killers, drug smugglers, and bloodthirsty inmates from the filthiest dungeons of the world straight into the USA and open border., We had an open border policy. Anybody could come in. No matter what you were, no matter where you came from, no matter what you looked like, no matter what you were doing, no matter what you did, no matter how many people you murdered, you could come right into our country. We have murderers right now walking the streets.

Trump seizes every opportunity to stir up unfounded fear and resentment toward immigrants. This is his usual, dishonest portrayal of people who are mostly here because where they came from is worse. In many countries, it's worse because of American support for dictatorships.

There's no verified evidence that "other countries emptied their prisons or asylums" and intentionally sent dangerous individuals to the U.S. in an organized way. Overwhelmingly, the evidence shows that immigrants – legal and illegal alike – are law-abiding, productive residents.

Undocumented immigrants pay billions in federal and state taxes every year ($96.7 billion in 2022). They paid $25.7 billion for Social Security in 2022, a program for which they're not eligible.

Based on the limited information available, most of Trump's deportation efforts in 2025 have rounded up innocent people. Maybe 1 in 10 has a serious criminal record. The government asserts that they are all criminals or gang members based on little or no persuasive evidence. The government deprives them of their constitutional right to due process of law. The government deports them, sometimes in defiance of a court order, giving them no chance to contest the charges in a formal hearing before a judge. The government doesn't always deport them to their home countries, but to facilities that are crimes against humanity, like the concentration camp in El Salvador.

The President and government agents break the law, again and again, without consequence. That's the nature of a police state.

Trump then honors Tammy Nobles, whose 20-year-old autistic daughter,

Kayla Hamilton, was murdered in 2022 by Walter Martinez, a 17-year-old MS-13 gang member from El Salvador, in the country illegally. He is now serving a 70-year sentence in prison. Kayla's family has filed a $100 million wrongful death lawsuit against the U.S. Departments of Homeland Security (DHS) and Health and Human Services (DHHS), accusing the agencies of committing "operational negligence" for allowing Martinez into the country.

> **TRUMP:** On day one of my administration, I declared a national emergency on our southern border. In our first full month in office, we achieved the lowest level of illegal border crossings ever recorded. Even lower than four years ago....
>
> All you needed was a new president. I said that the other night. That's all you needed was a new president saying, close the borders because the border patrol is unbelievable. ICE is unbelievable and all of our law enforcement is just incredible. All of you guys are amazing and the people of our country respect you and they love you, and a lot of times you don't hear that because you have to listen to the fake news back there, but they have great respect for you. I just want you to know that ....
>
> And we're ending the migrant occupation of America. And what we're doing now is we're liberating our cities and our suburbs and our towns. And you see a big difference. I'm getting calls all the time from even leaders of other countries saying, "Sir, the whole world feels liberated now. It feels like there's a light over America, but there's a light over the whole world." I hear that so much. It's so nice to hear, too. And I feel it. I feel it. I look at it, I see the polls. I don't know if the polls are right, but they're certainly very good. I'll take them right now....

The statement that President Trump achieved the lowest level of illegal border crossings ever recorded during his first full month back in office is actually supported by recent data.

In February 2025, the U.S. Border Patrol apprehended approximately 8,450 migrants trying to cross the U.S.-Mexico border illegally, the lowest monthly total since at least 2000. The previous low was 11,000 apprehensions in April 2017. This significant decrease follows the implementation of stricter immigration enforcement policies under the Trump administration, including the deployment of U.S. military personnel to the border and the reinstatement of the "Remain in Mexico" policy. Increased collaboration with Mexican authorities has led to more stringent controls on migration routes.

As for the calls Trump is getting "all the time" from foreign leaders, that's probably apocryphal. Or a lie.

His standing in the polls is wishful thinking. He's underwater. He was slightly under water in January, and he's continued to sink slowly ever since. But not that much. In mid-May, his approval was still over 40%. According to Fox News, both Republicans and Democrats had approvals slightly above 40%, with Republicans three points higher. Both parties had greater than 50% disapproval, with Democrats worse. The country doesn't seem to like anyone very much. And why would they?

Here's Some More Made-Up Stuff About Gangs

TRUMP: Last month, we officially designated MS13 in Tren de Aragua. That's the Venezuelan gang, the toughest gang they say, in the world and the Mexican drug cartels as foreign terrorist organizations. That's a big deal. Nobody wanted to do that in the past. And by the way, we've caught hundreds of them, the Venezuelan gang, which is as bad as it gets. And you'll be reading a lot of stories tomorrow about what we've done with them. And you'll be very impressed, and you'll feel a lot safer, too, because they are a vicious group.

They went into Colorado. They took over areas of Colorado. They sort of were like me, they were in the real estate business, but they didn't go out and get financing. They just took over a building and kept it. And they said to the tenants, "Get the hell out of here." One man called the police, and they cut off his fingers and they say, "You call again, your other fingers, and you call a third time and you're dead." These are tough people and bad people, and we're getting them out of our country. And some are so bad we don't want to get them out. We have to put them in jail because we don't want to even take a chance that they can come back.

Trump's version of events in Colorado is unreliable. But the reality is that Aurora, Colorado, has had serious gang issues of some sort since June 2023. The issue is highly politicized since Aurora borders Denver, which is a sanctuary city. Aurora has three conservative city councilors who pushed the gang story beyond reality.

In September 2024, Colorado Newsline reported under the headline, "The Greatest Threat to Aurora Is Not a Gang. It's Dishonest Council Members":

> Aurora was thrust into the national spotlight in recent weeks as right-wing media amplified a false story claiming Venezuelan gang members had taken over apartment buildings in the Colorado city. Former President Donald Trump supercharged this misinformation when he mentioned it last week during a debate with Vice President Kamala Harris, which was viewed by tens of millions of Americans.
>
> The swell of negative attention hurt the city and jeopardized residents. It has given cover to an out-of-state slumlord who's responsible for unbearable conditions at the apartment buildings. And the worst part is that the city's own elected leaders are to blame for so much of the fallout. They propagated bigoted falsehoods in reckless pursuit of partisan advantage and fame. They failed the most basic duty of any public servant – to protect the public.
>
> It is true that about 40,000 migrants from Central and South America, including Venezuela, have arrived in the Denver area since December 2022. And individuals associated with the Venezuelan gang Tren de Aragua have been identified in Aurora. But they number 10 (reported by the Aurora Police Department and posted on X) – the only thing they have taken over in Aurora is the dark imagination of right-wing conspiracy theorists.

Unsafe conditions at the apartment buildings in question predate the uptick in immigration and have nothing to do with gangs. [The] Denver Post reporting establishes that tenants of out-of-state landlord CBZ Management's Aurora properties endured unlivable conditions going back to at least 2020. "The problems have included black mold, water leaks, a lack of hot water, broken appliances, sagging infrastructure, fees for amenities that didn't work or didn't exist, rodent and cockroach infestations, poor building security and slapdash repairs," the Post reported....

Conservative city officials jumped in, none more vocally than City Council member Danielle Jurinsky. She and two other council members in early August pushed the gang-takeover story. In an appearance on Fox, Jurinsky made an incendiary claim:

"This gang, they are marking their territory, they are putting up their gang-related graffiti on the blocks, on the areas they have taken over, and quite frankly, I have heard too many stories from too many property owners, business owners and residents to think this is anything other than a complete gang takeover in parts of our city."

Republican Mayor Mike Coffman, though he often chose more tempered language, in his own appearance on Fox, told a national audience that several buildings in Aurora had "fallen to these Venezuelan gangs."

Aurora, Colorado – They're Not Eating Cats There Either

In 2025, Aurora remains in ferment. It has seen increased immigration enforcement actions, particularly targeting alleged members of the Venezuelan gang Tren de Aragua. These actions have sparked public debate and fear within the city's immigrant population, with some fearing widespread deportations and the disruption of family life. While some claim Aurora is facing an influx of gang members, data indicates a decline in crime rates in the city, according to the Aurora Police Department.

Aurora was not the only false immigration story Trump repeated on the campaign trail. He also lied about Springfield, Ohio, defaming Haitian immigrants there. During the September 10, 2024, presidential debate, he falsely claimed: "In Springfield, they are eating the dogs. The people that came in, they are eating the cats. They're eating – they are eating the pets of the people that live there. This is what's happening in our country." That was an utter lie.

Moderator David Muir immediately fact-checked this: "ABC News did reach out to the city manager there. He told us there have been no credible reports of specific claims of pets being harmed, injured, or abused by individuals within the immigrant community –"

Trump interrupted: "Well, I've seen people on television –"

After they squabbled briefly, Muir turned to Kamala Harris for a response. Trump's brazen lie was a fat target. Maybe Harris didn't know. She missed an opportunity to skewer Trump and show some strength. But she ignored the overt lie and instead talked at length about all the Republicans who had endorsed her. Trump then dismissed all those people, claiming: "I fired them."

The lie about Haitians eating cats remained unrefuted.

> **TRUMP:** Thanks to our efforts, Mexico recently handed over 29 of the biggest cartel leaders, including the depraved kingpin charge with the 1985 murder of DEA agent Kiki Camarena, and that was a big deal. If you know they've been looking for this person for years, many years, and we got him. This evil killer will be now prosecuted to the fullest extent of the law, and we know that, well, let's put it this way. I have to be nice. It's a very strong case.
>
> We're stopping the criminals pouring across our borders at record levels and we're also stopping the massive quantities of deadly drugs. In 2023 alone, drug overdoses killed more Americans in 12 months than they did during the entire decade between 1980 and 1990. So, 10 times more, but it's much higher than that. More Americans died from fentanyl last year than died in the Korean War or the Iraq war, the Afghanistan

war, all of them combined. That's why I've placed large tariffs
on Mexico, Canada, and China, and they will remain in place
until these deadly poisons stop pouring into our country. And I
will tell you, as soon as I put on the tariffs on Mexico, Canada,
and China, unbelievable results have been seen in the last few
weeks. Unbelievable results. They weren't happy about it. You
probably read they weren't happy, but they are working like hell
to end it. And they weren't working very hard before I did that.

On February 27, as Trump said, Mexico extradited 29 drug cartel members, including Rafael Caro Quintero. Once a leader of the Guadalajara Cartel, Caro Quintero was involved in the kidnapping and murder of DEA agent Camarena in 1985. After serving 28 years in a Mexican prison, he was released in 2013 but was recaptured in 2022 for resuming drug trafficking activities.

Mexico's action on cartel members was part of an effort to avoid pending tariffs.

Trump's drug statistics are reliable. Drug overdose deaths in 2023 were about 110,000. According to the DEA, there were 74,702 fentanyl-related deaths in the U.S. in 2023, more than the number of Americans who died in Korea (36,574), Iraq (4,576), and Afghanistan (2,432) combined.

Trump honors Anne Fundner, whose 15-year-old son Weston overdosed on fentanyl. Fundner speaks briefly about her son, "who absolutely loved President Trump." She added, "We knew there was only one person that could save us from the devastation on our American soil, and that was President Trump."

> **TRUMP**: Thank you, Anne, very much. Weston is, I just said
> to Anne, Weston is up in heaven watching his mom and he's
> so proud of you. He's so proud of you. Thank you. We're also
> joined today by a number of other American families who have
> lost loved ones to fentanyl. And I'd love you to just stand up
> for a second, and we want to acknowledge you and also your
> daughters, your sons. They're looking down on you and they're
> loving you like crazy. Thank you very much. Thank you. Thank
> you. Thank you....

I spoke with the president of Mexico, very nice woman, very fine woman. And I said, "Let me ask you. You're sending a lot of drugs into our country. We're not liking it at all. Can't do that." But I said, "Is Mexico, does it have much of a drug?" She said, "No, we're not a consuming nation." I thought it was an interesting term. And I said, "Why?" And which I've heard also, by the way, they're not a consuming nation. They distribute, but they don't consume.

But I said, "Why are you not a consuming?" "Well, we're very close with family." I said, "We're very close with family, too. I mean, our families are being devastated, and we are just as close. Why else?" She said, "Well, we spend a lot of money on advertising saying how bad drugs are. They're very rough ads. They show the skin falling off and the teeth falling out and going blind and losing hair and everything that these things do. You look like you just came out of a horrible concentration camp." And she said it was, they're rough ads....

The Mexico Peace Index (MPI) 2025, published in May by the Institute for Economics and Peace (IEP), reported:

> While Mexico has traditionally been seen as a producer and transit point for drugs destined for the United States, its internal drug market has been growing in recent years. The rate of retail drug crimes... [experienced] by far the largest increase over the past 10 years and was the only sub-indicator to consistently rise each year since 2016. This trend reflects the increasing reliance of Mexican drug traffickers on sales to domestic consumers.

MPI also found that:

> Organized criminal groups remain the primary driver of extreme violence in Mexico, largely due to their efforts to supply the U.S. market with illicit drugs, particularly fentanyl. Illicit trafficking of arms and people along the Mexico-United States border has become a core activity within organized crime, and given its transnational scope, poses a growing challenge to the bilateral relationship.... Meanwhile, the number of missing

people continues to grow. The rising number of mass graves and clandestine burial sites discovered across the country suggests that many of the missing may have been victims of organized crime.

Mexico abolished the death penalty in 2005. The last state executions were in 1961. Mexico is the world's most populous country (almost 130 million people) to have completely abolished the death penalty.

The Death Penalty Cures Drugs

Trump then talks about developing an ad campaign to get drug use down.

TRUMP: And the way you get it down, if you want to get it down to close to a hundred percent, is with the death penalty, but I think maybe America's not ready for that. China has a death penalty. Singapore has the death penalty. Various places have the death penalty.

Wherever you have the death penalty, you don't have drugs, but I just don't know if this country's ready for it. So, I tell people, and it's always an option, but I don't know. I just don't know if you're ready for it. And that's okay. It's nothing you can do, but what we're going to do is we're doing this campaign, and I think we can get it down 50, 5-0 percent, with this campaign because when people see all the horrible things that these drugs do to you, we are especially focused on fentanyl. When they see all of the horrible things that happen when you take drugs, how you look, you lose your look. Everyone's vain. They don't want to lose their look. The look is so important. And I think when they see these things, they may say, "You know what? I'm going to take a pass." But there is big danger….

A lot of people are taking fentanyl and not even knowing. They think they're doing something else or maybe taking another drug, but at a much lower level, and they die. You can put on the pin, think of this, the head of a pin, fentanyl, and it's too much and it will kill the strongest person in the room. And it's amazing, but we're going to do this campaign. It's going to be launched fairly soon, and I think it's going to have a big impact. I think if we got it down by another 30, 35 points. And I really believe we can. I think that's an incredible idea.

I thank the president of Mexico actually. It was a call on tariffs, and we talked about drugs. And she gave me an idea that I think we'll be very successful. And based on what I saw, it's going to be amazing. Under our leadership, this department is once again laser focused on protecting the American people. We're defending our borders, our streets, our children, and our God-given, this is God-given rights and liberties once and for all.

We're going to defend our country and we're going to defend our rights. Etched onto the walls of this building are the words, English philosopher John Locke said, "Where law ends, tyranny begins."

And I see that, and I saw it over the last four years when somebody was allowed to attack viciously with this department and the FBI, his political opponent. How did that work out? Didn't work out too well, but it wasn't pleasant. It wasn't pleasant. I was attacked by a political opponent, and probably it helped that I was attacked more than anybody in the history of our country. Alphonse Capone, the great Alphonse Capone, legendary Scarface, was attacked only a tiny fraction of what Trump was attacked. And maybe it worked out well. I don't know. If I had to give it up, I probably wouldn't. But only because I've gone through it, but I wonder what the difference would be. Maybe they helped get me elected by those margins, the big margins, the big mandate that we received. But you can't go after your political opponent.

After meandering through drug issues, Trump gets back to one of his favorite self-pitying themes – the way people persecute him. It goes way back. At a summit in 2018, when he was President, he asked, "Who gets attacked more than me?" In a speech in 2022, he said, "A friend of mine once said that I was the most persecuted person in the history of our country."

These assertions are subjective. They are not supported by objective historical evidence. Trump has spent his adult life being a deliberately confrontational public figure. Unsurprisingly, he has faced significant public scrutiny, legal challenges, and political opposition. He's even been indicted several times – and convicted on 34 felony counts. At what point does the treatment of a felon and adjudicated finger rapist stop being persecution and just become justice?

He feels "persecuted?" Compared to what? Compared to the Rev. Martin Luther King, Jr., or any other Black person in America? More than the innocent immigrants he demonizes and sends to a concentration camp in El Salvador? Is he more persecuted than anyone in America's underclasses?

Trump's persecution is pretty much as imaginary as "those margins, the big margins, the big mandate that we received" in the election. Less than a majority is not a big margin. Winning by 1.5% is winning with one of the smallest margins in modern presidential elections. In 2016, Trump won with an even smaller margin (less than zero), losing the popular vote by 2% to Hillary Clinton. In 2000, George W. Bush also won by a negative margin, losing the popular vote. In 1968, Richard Nixon won with a 0.7% margin in the popular vote. No one else has won by a smaller margin than Trump's 1.5% in 2024 since Benjamin Harrison's minority vote win in 1888.

Trump's mandate is a self-perpetuated illusion. It's a deliberate lie to attempt to justify policies most voters reject.

'The Return of Law and Order'

TRUMP: Nobody's ever seen anything like it actually. And hopefully, they won't see anything like it. But now, with the return of law and order, the entire world is witnessing the triumph of American justice and American freedom. That's why we're here today, gathered with people that have love for our country. In the coming years, we will revive the storied legacy of this department. And it's happening right now.

You can feel it and rekindle the spirit of the great lawmen and legal lions of the past. Americans like Wyatt Earp, Elliot Ness, Frank Hammer, Rudy Giuliani. Rudy Giuliani had to suffer greatly. Greatly. The greatest mayor in the history of our country had to suffer greatly. Ed Meese, Antonin Scalia, Robert Jackson, and Robert F. Kennedy. We will rebuild pride in our institutions. We will restore the prestige of this great department, and we will bring back faith in our justice system for the citizens of every race, religion, color, and creed.

There is no "return of law and order." Most of Trump's executive orders are illegal. Most of Trump's deportations are illegal. Most of Trump's graft, meme coins, and crypto grift is illegal.

Trump promises to "bring back faith in our justice system for the citizens of every race, religion, color, and creed." It took him almost no time to fail to meet this promise, deporting thousands of immigrants of a variety of races, colors, and creeds with absolutely no due process of law. Arrests by unidentified agents with no warrants. Making arrests with no provable evidence. Holding prisoners in custody with no access to family or an attorney. Shipping hostages to a foreign concentration camp with no hearing. All of this has undermined Americans' confidence in the justice system.

Oh, wait, Trump said "citizens." Not every one of the people abused by the Trump justice system is a citizen. But they all have rights that have been ignored. Even the citizens. Even a two-year-old citizen. Even a four-year-old citizen with stage 4 cancer, shipped out of the country without medication, without consultation with doctors.

Tom Homan, Trump's border czar, was all heart on these deportations:

We're keeping families together. What we did was remove children with their mothers who requested the children depart with them. There's a parental decision.... They weren't deported. We don't deport U.S. citizens. Their parents made that decision, not the United States government.... Having a U.S. citizen child does not make you immune from our laws.

Homan did not address the likelihood that, in one instance, deporting a very sick child was tantamount to a death sentence.

According to Trump, Rudy Giuliani is "a legal lion of the past." On January 6, 2025, Giuliani was held in contempt of court because he "willfully violated a clear and unambiguous order of this court" in the case of a

$148 million defamation suit that he lost to Georgia election workers. On January 10, he was again found in contempt of court, in a different federal court, for continuing to spread lies about the Georgia election workers.

As the Guardian reported, Giuliani reacted to the second contempt finding in a Trumpian manner: "Shortly before Friday's hearing began, Giuliani slammed the judge in a social media post, calling her 'bloodthirsty' and biased against him and the proceeding a 'hypocritical waste of time.'"

Ed Meese? Another "lion?" He was a champion of "constitutional originalism," the idea that you have to assess contemporary legal problems as if you didn't know anything more than you could have known in 1789. It requires mind-reading at a distance of more than 200 years. This irrational argument is one of the great legal "triumphs" of right-wing jurists of our time. Meese is also known for his prudery, requiring the naked statue of Justice in the DOJ to have her naked marble breasts covered.

Antonin Scalia? He was a constitutional originalist on the Supreme Court who thought it was a good idea to award the presidential election of 2000 to George Bush (who lost the popular vote) rather than making sure all the votes were counted in Florida. Scalia was in the majority of a 5-4 decision. Asked about that by a reporter, Scalia responded, "Get over it."

Maybe, someday, we will.

'You're Going to Win, Win, Win and Fight, Fight, Fight'

TRUMP: And I want to just tell you that this has been a great honor. I was asked to do it, and I said, "Is it appropriate that I do it?" And then I realized, it's not only appropriate, I think it's really important, and I may never do it again. I may never have another chance to do it again because this is something that I'm leaving to the greatest people I know, the best people, the smartest people, the toughest people I know, and they're going to do an incredible job. And it's an honor for me to have won this election so that I can appoint these people to do their job. And they're going to do it like you have never seen. I just want to wish all of you good luck. It's going to be an interesting journey. Not going to be easy, but you're going to win. You're going to win, win, win, and fight, fight, fight, and it's going to end up being a tremendous result for this country. Thank you all very much. God bless America. God bless you all. Thank you.

Assuring the audience of law enforcement officials that they're "going to win" is Trump's valedictory note. What does it mean for them "to win"? And what will it take? The administration has weaponized the Department of Justice. It has weaponized the FBI. It has weaponized the Department of Homeland Security. It has weaponized ICE and the DEA. The traditional rule of law is no longer secure in the United States. It is becoming a tool to control a formerly free people.

Trump Invokes Alien Enemies Act of 1798

On March 14, the same day as this speech, the Trump White House issued an executive order titled: "Invocation of the Alien Enemies Act [AEA] Regarding the Invasion of the United States by Tren de Aragua." This is a direct attack on due process of law by using a rarely invoked statute with unfounded applicability. The claimed "invasion" is imaginary. The impact of this dishonest proclamation continues to be felt.

The Alien Enemies Act is one of the laws enacted as part of the Alien and Sedition Acts in 1798 under President John Adams and the Federalist-controlled Congress. At the time, the U.S. was anticipating a war with France. Legally, invocation of the Alien Enemies Act requires a declared war or an "invasion or predatory incursion [that] is perpetrated, attempted, or threatened against the territory of the United States by any foreign nation or government." The law was last invoked in World War II as the legal authority for interning U.S. citizens and noncitizens of Japanese, German, and Italian descent during a declared war. Congress in 1988 recognized these internments as rooted in "racial prejudice" and "wartime hysteria," not valid security concerns.

Despite its abuse, the Alien Enemies Act has not been repealed or amended. It has not been substantially modified since its adoption. If the United States were to declare war, the president would be able to invoke the Alien Enemies Act's vast detention and deportation power. Worse still, the language of the law is broad enough that a president might be able to wield the authority in peacetime as an end run around the requirements of criminal and immigration law. That's where we are now with Trump's unprecedented peacetime invocation of a wartime law.

Lacking any declaration of war to justify invoking the Alien Enemies Act, Trump asserts in his five-page executive order:

I find and declare that TdA [Tren de Aragua] is perpetrating, attempting, and threatening an invasion or predatory incursion against the territory of the United States. TdA is undertaking hostile actions and conducting irregular warfare against the territory of the United States, both directly and at the direction, clandestine or otherwise, of the Maduro regime in Venezuela.

There is no evidence that any of this is true.

Trump's executive further states:

Pursuant to the Alien Enemies Act, the Attorney General and the Secretary of Homeland Security shall, consistent with applicable law, apprehend, restrain, secure, and remove every Alien Enemy described in section 1 of this proclamation. The Secretary of Homeland Security retains discretion to apprehend and remove any Alien Enemy under any separate authority.

The next day, March 15, the Brennan Center for Justice challenged the legality of Trump's executive order:

Tren de Aragua is a dangerous Venezuelan criminal gang, but immigration law already gives the president ample authority to deport Tren de Aragua members.... There's no need to abuse a wartime authority when immigration and criminal law provide such powerful tools. The president is invoking the Alien Enemies Act to try to dispense with due process. He wants to bypass any need to provide evidence or to convince a judge that someone is actually a gang member before deporting them. The only reason to invoke such a power is to try to enable sweeping detentions and deportations of Venezuelans based on their ancestry, not on any gang activity that could be proved in immigration proceedings.

This power grab is flagrantly illegal. The Alien Enemies Act may be used only during declared wars or armed attacks on the United States by foreign governments. The president has falsely proclaimed an invasion and predatory incursion to use a law written for wartime for peacetime immigration enforcement. The courts should shut this down. If the courts allow it to stand, this move could pave the way for abuses against any group of immigrants the president decides to target – not just Venezuelans – even if they are lawfully present in the U.S. and have no criminal history.

Also on March 15, the ACLU and Democracy Forward filed a class action lawsuit in the District Court for the District of Columbia, *J.G.G. v. Trump*, on behalf of five detained Venezuelan men, challenging their detention and potential deportation under this act. U.S. District Judge James Boasberg issued a temporary restraining order, halting the deportations and requiring the government to provide detainees with due process, including hearings and notifications in a language they understand.

Trump Officials Try to Politicize the Law

Attorney General Pam Bondi criticized the court's decision with high demagoguery:

> Tonight, a DC trial judge supported Tren de Aragua terrorists over the safety of Americans. TdA is represented by the ACLU. This order disregards well-established authority regarding President Trump's power, and it puts the public and law enforcement at risk. The Department of Justice is undeterred in its efforts to work with the White House, the Department of Homeland Security, and all of our partners to stop this invasion and Make America Safe Again.

The Trump administration defied Judge Boasberg's restraining order. Although Boasberg specifically ordered that any planes in the air carrying those covered by his order be turned back and those individuals returned to the U.S., the Trump administration allowed the flights to proceed. Over 260 men were flown to El Salvador, where the migrants were taken into custody and sent to the concentration camp known as the Terrorism Confinement

Center (CECOT).

On March 15, the Trump administration appealed the temporary re-straining order to the Court of Appeals for the District of Columbia. Trump called Judge Boasberg a "Radical Left Lunatic Judge" and called for his impeachment.

On March 17, White House Executive Associate Director of Enforcement and Removal Operations Tom Homan told Fox News, "I don't care what the judges think."

In court, the administration continued to stonewall Judge Boasberg's effort to discover what actually happened when the administration failed to return the places to the U.S. and who was responsible for ignoring the court's order and sending some 260 people to a concentration camp in El Salvador without a shred of due process of law.

On March 18, Representative Brandon Gill of Texas filed articles of im-peachment against Boasberg, alleging "abuse of power." U.S. Supreme Court Chief Justice John Roberts issued a "rare public rebuke," saying rather meek-ly: "For more than two centuries it has been established that impeachment is not an appropriate response to disagreements concerning a judicial decision. The normal appellate review process exists for that purpose."

At a hearing on March 21, Judge Boasberg vowed: "I will get to the bottom of whether they violated my order – who ordered this and what the consequences will be." He told DOJ attorney Drew Ensign that the govern-ment had used "intemperate and disrespectful" language that he's "never seen before from the United States." The DOJ is arguing that Boasberg exceeded his authority in blocking the removals because, they say, Trump's use of the act is unreviewable by federal courts.

The same day, Trump distanced himself from invoking the Alien Enemies Act, claiming he hadn't signed the proclamation that appears in the Federal Register with his signature. He told reporters:

> We want to get criminals out of our country, number one, and
> I don't know when it was signed, because I didn't sign it....
> Other people handled it, but [Secretary of State] Marco Rubio
> has done a great job, and he wanted them out, and we go along
> with that. We want to get criminals out of our country.

Trump is lying. Some of the prisoners taken illegally to El Salvador are likely criminals of some unknown sort, but none has been adjudicated. According to available evidence, the vast majority may have violated an immigration rule or may have done nothing wrong at all. None of them has been adjudicated.

On March 24, Judge Boasberg ruled that the government cannot deport anyone under the AEA without a hearing.

On March 26, in a 2-1 ruling, the appeals court affirmed Judge Boasberg and denied the administration's appeal. The appeals court left Judge Boasberg's restraining order in force. During the hearing on the case, Appellate Judge Patricia Millett observed that "Nazis got better treatment under the Alien Enemies Act."

On March 28, the administration filed an emergency appeal with the U.S. Supreme Court, asking it to vacate Judge Boasberg's restraining order. As of April 3, he was considering initiating contempt of court proceedings against the Trump administration, with a hearing scheduled for April 8. The day before that hearing, the Supreme Court, on its own initiative, intervened to make matters muddier and worse for those illegally detained.

Supreme Court 'Decides' Trump v. J. G.G.

On April 7, in a brief, 5-4 per curiam ([unsigned) decision in the case – *Trump v. J.G.G.* – the court vacated Boasberg's orders, stating that any challenges to removal under the Alien Enemies Act (AEA) must be brought as a habeas corpus petition, which requires that the petition be filed in the district where a petitioner is detained. (How a petitioner in a maximum-security El Salvador prison was supposed to do that went unaddressed.)

The Supreme Court wrote that "the [Venezuelan] detainees subject to removal orders under the AEA are entitled to notice and an opportunity to challenge their removal. The only question is which court will resolve that challenge."

Since the petitioners were detained in Texas, their petition in the District of Columbia had been filed in the wrong jurisdiction. The court did not "reach" any decision as to whether the use of the AEA to deport the men was constitutional, nor whether it applied to the plaintiffs. It added that the government had to give anyone it sought to deport under the AEA enough notice so that they could file habeas complaints challenging their removal. In other words, the administration had acted illegally, but the Supreme Court was unwilling to do anything to hold it to account for its actions. Thomas and Alito dissented.

The majority issued its rushed decision on April 7, even though it knew Judge Boasberg had scheduled a hearing on a permanent injunction for the very next day. The Supreme Court's decision put an end to the class action suit and left every present and future detainee to fend as best they could, in whatever jurisdiction they happened to find themselves, against a hostile government and an unreliable judiciary. It was a decision with no conscience and less respect for any realistic due process of law.

This is the sort of decision a court makes when it doesn't want to make a decision that actually follows the law but would be contrary to the court's majority politics. It is shameful. It turns a blind eye to the reality that customs officials can transport detainees to the prison of their choice with no due process of law. The prison of their choice is – no surprise – in a friendly judicial district such as Texas or Louisiana. In effect, the Supreme Court issued an order that said, "You can have your due process, but not anywhere it will do you any good."

Justice Sotomayor Issues a Powerful Dissent

There were four dissenters to the majority ruling on April 7. Justices Sonia Sotomayor wrote the dissenting opinion, joined in whole or in part by Justices Elena Kagan, Ketanji Brown Jackson, and Amy Coney Barrett. In her dissent, Justice Sotomayor wrote:

> Three weeks ago, the Federal Government started sending scores of Venezuelan immigrants detained in the United States to a foreign prison in El Salvador. It did so without any due process of law, under the auspices of the Alien Enemies Act, a 1798 law designed for times of war....
>
> Critically, even the majority today agrees, and the Federal Government now admits, that individuals subject to removal under the Alien Enemies Act are entitled to adequate notice and

judicial review before they can be removed. That should have been the end of the matter. Yet, with "barebones briefing, no argument, and scarce time for reflection," this Court announces that legal challenges to an individual's removal under the Alien Enemies Act must be brought in habeas petitions in the district where they are detained.

The Court's legal conclusion is suspect. The Court intervenes anyway, granting the Government extraordinary relief and vacating the District Court's order on that basis alone. It does so without mention of the grave harm Plaintiffs will face if they are erroneously removed to El Salvador or regard for the Government's attempts to subvert the judicial process throughout this litigation. Because the Court should not reward the Government's efforts to erode the rule of law with discretionary equitable relief, I respectfully dissent....

Congress requires the President to "make public proclamation" of his intention to invoke the Alien Enemies Act. President Trump did just the opposite. In what can be understood only as covert preparation to skirt both the requirements of the Act and the Constitution's guarantee of due process, the Department of Homeland Security (DHS) began moving Venezuelan migrants from Immigration and Customs Enforcement detention centers across the country to the El Valle Detention Facility in South Texas before the President had even signed the Proclamation. The transferred detainees, most of whom denied past or present affiliation with any gang, did not know the reason for their transfer until the evening of Friday, March 14, when they were apparently "pulled from their cells and told that they would be deported the next day to an unknown destination."...

[Several lawyers] asserted that it would violate the Due Process Clause to deport their clients before they had any chance to challenge the Government's allegations of gang membership. The plaintiffs did not seek release from custody, but asked the court only to restrain the Government's planned deportations under the Proclamation....

Despite knowing of plaintiffs' claim that it would be unlawful to remove them under the Proclamation, the Government ushered the named plaintiffs onto planes along with dozens of other detainees, all without any opportunity to contact their lawyers, much less notice or opportunity to be heard. The Government's plan, it appeared, was to rush plaintiffs out of the country before a court could decide whether the President's invocation of the Alien Enemies Act was lawful or whether these individuals were, in fact, members of Tren de Aragua....

Recognizing the emergency the Government had created by deporting plaintiffs without due process, the District Court issued a temporary restraining order that same morning. The order prohibited the Government from removing the five named plaintiffs, including J.G.G. and G.F.F., pending ongoing litigation. G.F.F., who had been on a plane for about forty minutes to an hour," as "'crying and frightened'" individuals were forced on board, was subsequently retrieved from the plane by a guard who told him he "just won the lottery."

The [District] Court then set an emergency hearing for 5 p.m. that same day.... Despite notice to the Government of the Court's scheduled hearing, DHS continued to load up the two planes with detainees and scheduled their immediate departure. (Government counsel [agreed] that DHS was acting in preparation for the proclamation before it was posted.) Not until an hour before the District Court's scheduled hearing, and only moments before the Government planned to send its planes off to El Salvador, did the White House finally publish the Proclamation on its website....

[The District Court] issued an oral temporary restraining order prohibiting the Government from removing all members of the class pursuant to the Proclamation for 14 days. The order did not disturb the Government's ability to apprehend or detain individuals pursuant to the Proclamation or its authority to deport any individual under the Immigration and Naturalization Act. All it required of the Government was a pause in deportations pursuant to the Proclamation until the court had a chance to review their legality.... The court further directed that "any plane containing" individuals subject to the Proclamation "that is going to take off or is in the air needs to be returned to the United States."

Concerns about the Government's compliance with the order quickly followed. Even now, the District Court continues to investigate what happened via show-cause proceedings. In those proceedings, the Government took the position that it had no legal obligation to obey the District Court's orders directing the return of planes in flight because they were issued from the bench.... Of course, as the Government well knows, courts routinely issue rulings from the bench, and those rulings can be appealed, including to this Court, in appropriate circumstances.

The District Court, for its part, has surmised that "the Government knew as of 10 a.m. on March 15 that the Court would hold a hearing later that day," yet it "hustled people onto those planes in hopes of evading an injunction or perhaps preventing [individuals] from requesting the habeas hearing to which the Government now acknowledges they are entitled." Rather than turning around the planes that were in the air when the Court issued its order, the Federal Government landed the planes full of alleged Venezuelan nationals in El Salvador and transferred them directly into El Salvador's Center for Terrorism Confinement (CECOT).

Deportation directly into CECOT presented a risk of extraordinary harm to these Plaintiffs. The record reflects that inmates in Salvadoran prisons are "highly likely to face immediate and intentional life-threatening harm at the hands of state actors." CECOT detainees are frequently "denied communication with their relatives and lawyers, and only appear before courts in online hearings, often in groups of several hundred detainees at the same time." El Salvador has boasted that inmates in CECOT "will never leave," and plaintiffs present evidence that "inmates are rarely allowed to leave their cells, have no regular access to drinking water or adequate food, sleep standing up because of overcrowding, and are held in cells where they do not see sunlight for days." One scholar attests that an estimated 375 detainees have died in Salvadoran prisons since March 2022.

What if the Government later determines that it sent one of these detainees to CECOT in error?... The Government takes the position that, even when it makes a mistake, it cannot retrieve individuals from the Salvadoran prisons to which it has sent them. The implication of the Government's position is that not only non-citizens but also United States citizens could be taken off the streets, forced onto planes, and confined to foreign prisons with no opportunity for redress if judicial review is denied unlawfully before removal. History is no stranger to such lawless regimes, but this Nation's system of laws is designed to prevent, not enable, their rise....

The D.C. Circuit [Court of Appeals] denied the Government a requested stay and kept in place the District Court's pause on deportations under the Alien Enemies Act pending further proceedings.

It is only this Court that sees reason to vacate, for the second time this week, a temporary restraining order standing "on its last legs." Not content to wait until tomorrow, when the District Court will have a chance to consider full preliminary injunction briefing at a scheduled hearing, this Court intervenes to relieve the Government of its obligation under the order....

The Court's order today dictates, in no uncertain terms, that "individual[s] subject to detention and removal under the [Alien Enemies Act are] entitled to "judicial review as to questions of interpretation and constitutionality" of the Act as well as whether he or she "is in fact an alien enemy fourteen years of age or older."

...So too do we all agree with the per curiam's command that the Fifth Amendment requires the Government to afford plaintiffs "notice after the date of this order that they are subject to removal under the Act. . . within reasonable time and in such a manner as will allow them to actually seek habeas relief in the proper venue before such removal occurs." That means, of course, that the Government cannot usher any detainees, including plaintiffs, onto planes in a shroud of secrecy, as it did on March 15, 2025.... To the extent the Government removes even one individual without affording him notice and a meaningful opportunity to file and pursue habeas relief, it does so in direct contravention of an edict by the United States Supreme Court.

In light of this agreement, the Court's decision to intervene in this litigation is as inexplicable as it is dangerous. Recall that, when the District Court issued its temporary restraining order on March 15, 2025, the Government was engaged in a covert operation to deport dozens of immigrants without notice or an opportunity for hearings. The Court's ruling today means that those deportations violated the Due Process Clause's most fundamental protections....

Against the backdrop of the U. S. Government's unprecedented deportation of dozens of immigrants to a foreign prison without due process, a majority of this Court sees fit to vacate the District Court's order. The reason apparently, is that the majority thinks plaintiffs' claims should have been styled as habeas actions and filed in the districts of their detention. In reaching that result, the majority flouts well-established limits on its jurisdiction, creates new law on the emergency docket, and elides the serious threat our intervention poses to the lives of individual detainees....

Also troubling is this Court's decision to vacate summarily the District Court's order on the novel ground that an individual's challenge to his removal under the Alien Enemies Act "fall[s] within the 'core' of the writ of habeas corpus" and must therefore be filed where the plaintiffs are detained. The Court reaches that conclusion without oral argument or the benefit of percolation in the lower courts, and with just a few days of deliberation based on bare-bones briefing.

This conclusion is dubious…. There is every reason to question the majority's hurried conclusion that habeas relief supplies the exclusive means to challenge removal under the Alien Enemies Act. At the very least, the question is a thorny one, and this emergency application was not the place to resolve it. Nor was it the Court's last chance to weigh in…. If the District Court were to resolve the question in plaintiffs' favor, the Government could have appealed to this Court in the ordinary course, and we could have decided it after thorough briefing and oral argument. In its rush to decide the issue now, the Court halts the lower court's work and forces us to decide the matter after mere days of deliberation and without adequate time to weigh the parties' arguments or the full record of the District Court's proceedings.

The majority's rush to resolve the question is all the more troubling because this is not one of those rare cases in which the Court must immediately intervene despite the risk of error attendant in deciding novel legal questions on the emergency docket. Recall that the dispute has now narrowed into a debate about "which procedural vehicle is best situated for the Plaintiffs' injunctive and declaratory claims": individual habeas petitions filed in district courts across the country, or a class action filed in the District of Columbia. The Government may well prefer to defend against "300 or more individual habeas petitions" than face this class APA case in Washington, D. C. That is especially so because the Government can transfer detainees to particular locations in an attempt to secure a more hospitable judicial forum.

Meanwhile, funneling plaintiffs' claims into individual habeas actions across the Nation risks exposing them to severe and irreparable harm. Rather than seeking to enjoin implementation of the President's Proclamation against all Venezuelan nationals in immigration detention, detainees scattered across the country must each obtain counsel and file habeas petitions on their own accord, all without knowing whether they will remain in detention where they were arrested or be secretly transferred to an alternative location. ("One great advantage of class action treatment... is the opportunity to save the enormous transaction costs of piecemeal litigation.")

That requirement may have life or death consequences.... Anyone the Government mistakenly deports in its piecemeal and rushed implementation of the challenged Proclamation will face grave risks. The stakes are all the more obvious in light of the Government's insistence that, once it sends someone to CECOT, it cannot be made to retrieve them. The Government is at this very moment seeking emergency relief from an order requiring it to facilitate the return of an individual [Abrego Garcia] the Government concededly removed to CECOT "because of an administrative error." The Government's resistance to facilitating the return of individuals erroneously removed to CECOT only amplifies the specter that, even if this Court someday declares the President's Proclamation unlawful, scores of individual lives may be irretrievably lost.

More fundamentally, this Court exercises its equitable discretion to intervene without accounting for the Government noncompliance that has permeated this litigation to date.... While "equity does not demand that its suitors shall have led blameless lives" as to other matters, "it does require that they shall have acted fairly and without fraud or deceit as to the controversy in issue."

Far from acting "fairly" as to the controversy in District Court, the Government has largely ignored its obligations to the rule of law. From the start, the Government sought to avoid judicial review, 'hustling people onto those planes' without notice or public Proclamation…. That the District Court is engaged in a sincere inquiry into whether the Government willfully violated its March 15, 2025, order to turn around the planes should be reason enough to doubt that the Government appears before this Court with clean hands. That is all the more true because the Government has persistently stonewalled the District Court's efforts to find out whether the Government in fact flouted its express order.

The Government's conduct in this litigation poses an extraordinary threat to the rule of law. That a majority of this Court now rewards the Government for its behavior with discretionary equitable relief is indefensible. We, as a Nation and a court of law, should be better than this. I respectfully dissent.

U.S. Government Continues to Batter the Rule of Law

On April 17, alleging government bad faith, the ACLU sought a new restraining order, asserting:

Plaintiffs learned that the government has begun giving notices of removal to class members, in English only, which do not say how much time individuals have to contest their removal or even how to do so. A copy of the notice is attached. And officers last night told class members that they will be removed within 24 hours, which expires as early as this afternoon. Upon information and belief, individuals have already been loaded on to buses.

On April 19, the Supreme Court issued an unsigned order blocking the Trump administration from deporting the Venezuelans held at the Bluebonnet facility in Texas "until further order of this court." Alito and Thomas dissented. According to the ACLU, the Venezuelans were returned to the Bluebonnet facility.

Litigation continued through May and June, as the Trump administration continued to deport Venezuelans to the terrorist prison in El Salvador, without providing any due process of law, without offering any evidence of guilt. The process has been grim and intractable, with the U.S. government continuously acting in bad faith and in defiance of the law. One judge called the situation Kafkaesque.

On June 4, Federal District Judge James Boasberg issued a 69-page order in *J.G.G. v. Trump* that began with a lengthy quotation from Franz Kafka's The Trial, using it as a metaphor for the legal nightmare the plaintiffs had found themselves in since March 15. In one aspect of the legal morass, Judge Boasberg recognizes that the plaintiffs, with few if any resources, are required to post a bond in order to have their habeas corpus claims heard by a court. The judge set the bond at one dollar. He also granted a temporary restraining order and gave the government a week to show how they would give the detainees already shipped to El Salvador some reasonable opportunity to exercise their constitutionally protected habeas corpus rights.

Trump Administration Starts Arresting Judges

On April 25, FBI director Kash Patel posted an incendiary note on social media:

> Just NOW, the FBI arrested Judge Hannah Dugan out of Milwaukee, Wisconsin, on charges of obstruction – after evidence of Judge Dugan obstructing an immigration arrest operation last week. We believe Judge Dugan intentionally misdirected federal agents away from the subject to be arrested in her courthouse, Eduardo Flores-Ruiz, allowing the subject – an illegal alien – to evade arrest. Thankfully, our agents chased down the perp on foot and he's been in custody since, but the Judge's obstruction created increased danger to the public. We will have more to share soon. Excellent work.

Patel's post is a clear violation of professional and legal rules of protocol. Law enforcement agencies are bound by longstanding norms that prohibit public officials from making statements that could influence ongoing legal matters. Announcing an arrest, particularly of a sitting judge, in a celebratory tone on a public social media platform undermines the appearance of judicial impartiality, disregards the presumption of innocence, and threatens the integrity of any future proceedings. Patel effectively pronounces guilt before any trial has occurred. Before any grand jury has heard any evidence.

His commentary could severely prejudice the case, it violates due process rights, and it compromises public confidence in the fairness of the judicial system. And perhaps that's the point.

The DOJ issued an equally fanatic press release the same day, headed: "Justice Department Announces Two Cases Involving Judicial Misconduct and Obstruction of Law Enforcement." The sub-head reads: "Ex-Judge of Dona Ana County Charged with Evidence Tampering and Milwaukee County Circuit Court Judge Charged with Unlawful Obstruction and Concealment."

These two cases in Arizona and Wisconsin are the first judicial arrests under the second Trump administration. They came after weeks of Trump officials criticizing judges, calling them names, and threatening to impeach them. Both of the charged judges are state judges in their 60s. One is retired, and the other is a highly esteemed elected judge. Both are accused of interfering with immigration deportations. Trump's immigration policy encourages arrests in courthouses and other controversial locations, including churches, schools, and hospitals. Courts across the country have barred such arrests.

The DOJ turned the Wisconsin arrest into a full-blown media circus, including Patel's social media posts and Attorney General Pam Bondi promoting it on Fox News. FBI agents arrested Milwaukee County Circuit Judge Dugan, 65, in the parking lot of her courthouse when she came to work on a Friday morning. Media were alerted so that TV cameras could cover her perp walk in handcuffs to a waiting cop car. FBI director Kash Patel posted a photo of Dugan's arrest on X – even though DOJ policy prohibits disclosing a photograph of a defendant unless it "serves a law enforcement function" or is already part of the public record. Neither exception applied.

Judge Dugan later appeared in U.S. District Court for the Eastern District of Wisconsin, but did not enter a plea. She was released on her own recognizance.

As an attorney and later as a judge, Dugan has been a lifelong advocate for judicial integrity, democratic values, and the advancement of women. She has spent much of her career advocating for poor people, specializing in housing and public benefits. In 1995, she represented people who panhandled on downtown sidewalks, arguing that barring them from doing so was unconstitutional. In 2016, she was elected county judge. In 2022, she won re-election, unopposed.

Since her arrest, she has received widespread public and political support in Wisconsin. Her attorney released the following statement:

> Judge Hannah C. Dugan has committed herself to the rule of law and the principles of due process for her entire career as a lawyer and a judge. She has retained former United States Attorney Steven Biskupic to represent her. Judge Dugan will defend herself vigorously and looks forward to being exonerated. This will be the extent of any statements or interviews at this time.

Meanwhile, the Wisconsin Supreme Court suspended her, with pay, during the legal process and transferred her docket to other judges.

Commenting on Dugan's arrest, Attorney General Pam Bondi ranted to Fox News:

> What has happened to our judiciary is beyond me. They're deranged. I think some of these judges think they are beyond and above the law, and they are not. We are sending a very strong message today: If you are harboring a fugitive, we don't care who you are. If you are helping hide one, if you are giving a [gang] member guns, anyone who is illegally in this country, we will come after you, and we will prosecute you. We will find you.

Milwaukee Mayor Cavalier Johnson told reporters: "They're just trying to have this show of force and in the process of a courthouse where people need to go for court proceedings, they're scaring away people from participating in the court process."

Wisconsin Gov. Tony Evers, in a statement, criticized President Trump and the White House for what he said were efforts "to attack and attempt to undermine our judiciary at every level."

So, what did Judge Hannah Dugan do on April 18 to cause such a stir a week later? If it was significant, why did it take the government a week to respond? Accounts, including an FBI affidavit and a DOJ press release, vary considerably. Judge Dugan has not spoken publicly. What happened was something like the following.

On April 18, Judge Dugan was hearing cases in her courtroom, including a pre-trial conference involving Eduardo Flores-Ruiz on three misdemeanor counts of battery/domestic abuse. Flores-Ruiz is an undocumented Mexican immigrant who had previously been deported in 2013. To arrest him at the courthouse on immigration charges, the government sent six plainclothes agents, two each from ICE, the FBI, and the DEA. Ruiz-Flores had not been indicted. The agents had an administrative warrant signed by an ICE administrator. After making their presence known to the court deputy, they were waiting for Ruiz-Flores in the hallway outside Judge Dugan's courtroom.

Before the hearing on April 18, when the judge learned the six agents were there, she confronted them in the hallway. She told them they needed a judicial warrant signed by a judge to make an arrest in the courthouse. (The DOJ claims she "ordered federal agents to leave the courthouse".) Making arrests inside a courthouse disrupts the judicial process. Such arrests have been barred in jurisdictions across the country, but the Milwaukee courthouse was still in the process of determining its policy.

Judge Dugan directed the six agents to consult with the Chief Judge. Two agents talked to the Chief Judge on the phone. The others remained in public areas outside the courtroom. Judge Dugan returned to her courtroom and adjourned the pre-trial conference. (The DOJ claims the Judge "allegedly elected not to conduct a hearing on Flores-Ruiz's case, despite the fact that the victims of his offence were present.") When the Judge concluded the Flores-Ruiz matter, she ushered him and his attorney out a side door of the courtroom. (The DOJ claims that "this doorway led to a non-public hallway," but omits the fact that the only way out from there was the public hallway, where the six agents were waiting.)

Flores-Ruiz and his attorney entered the public hallway, in full view of at least four of the agents. Flores-Lopez and his attorney walked to a bank of elevators that would take them to the main entrance of the courthouse. One of the DEA agents rode down in the elevator with them, but did not engage or arrest Flores-Ruiz. Flores-Ruiz and his attorney were speaking Spanish, and the agent didn't understand what they were saying. Other agents took other elevators to the main entrance. They discovered Flores-Ruiz standing outside. When he saw them, he ran. They caught him a block away and took him into custody. Two agents were still on the phone with the chief judge.

That scenario is now the basis for a federal case for "obstructing a proceeding" and "concealing an individual." Although federal law permits prosecutors to bring initial felony charges through a criminal complaint without a grand jury indictment, the choice to use that shortcut against a sitting judge is also deeply irregular. Under standard practice, and out of respect for judicial independence, felony charges against a member of the judiciary are typically presented to a grand jury first, ensuring public legitimacy and procedural integrity. Trump's weaponized Justice Department bypassed this safeguard to arrest Judge Dugan, just in time to dominate the morning media cycle on rightwing outlets like FOX News.

"This is a drastic escalation and dangerous new front in Trump's authoritarian campaign of trying to bully, intimidate, and impeach judges who won't follow his dictates," said Rep. Jamie Raskin, the ranking Democratic member of the House Judiciary Committee. "It is remarkable that the Administration would dare to start arresting state court judges. It's a whole new descent into government chaos."

On April 29, acting on its own motion, the Wisconsin Supreme Court entered a brief order suspending Judge Dugan with pay:

> In the exercise of [our] constitutional authority and in order to
> uphold the public's confidence in the courts of this state during
> the pendency of the criminal proceeding against Judge Dugan,
> we conclude, on our own motion, that it is in the public interest
> that she be temporarily relieved of her official duties.

On May 13, Judge Dugan's case went before a federal grand jury, and she was indicted the same day. She was charged with obstructing a U.S. agency and concealing an individual to prevent an arrest. She has pleaded not guilty, and her trial is scheduled for July 21.

In a motion to dismiss the charges, Judge Dugan's lawyers wrote:

> The problems with this prosecution are legion, but most immediately, the government cannot prosecute Judge Dugan because she is entitled to judicial immunity for her official acts.

Immunity is not a defense to the prosecution to be determined later by a jury or court; it is an absolute bar to the prosecution at the outset. The prosecution against her is barred. The Court should dismiss the indictment.

On June 9, the prosecution filed a motion opposing dismissal:

Dugan asks this court for an unprecedented dismissal on grounds of judicial immunity, ignoring well-established law that has long permitted judges to be prosecuted for crimes they commit. Combined with Dugan's attempt to define "judicial acts" expansively, such a ruling would give state court judges carte blanche to interfere with valid law enforcement actions by federal agents in public hallways of a courthouse, and perhaps even beyond.

On May 6, more than 150 former state and federal judges had written to Attorney General Pam Bondi to tell her that:

We unequivocally reject your and the Trump Administration's assault on the judiciary, the Rule of Law and those who administer it, including Judge Dugan. This does not make us 'deranged' [in Bondi's claim]. It's what makes us Americans.

The letter said:

This latest action is yet another attempt to intimidate and threaten the judiciary after a series of rulings by judges appointed by presidents of both parties holding the Trump Administration accountable for its countless violations of the Constitution and laws of the United States. On April 25, you called judges "deranged" and said that "[the Administration is] sending a very strong message" and that "we will come after you and we will prosecute you." On April 28, White House Press Secretary Karoline Leavitt went so far as to say that the Trump Administration will not rule out arresting members of the United States Supreme Court.

The intent to intimidate Judge Dugan and the judiciary is clear from the circumstances of Judge Dugan's arrest which took place seven days after the alleged offense. There was no emergency whatsoever; the administration could have easily issued a summons for Judge Dugan to appear before a court, as they would have done in other white collar cases. There is not an ounce of doubt that Judge Dugan would have appeared in court in response to a summons. Instead, the United States Department of Justice at your direction decided to create an embarrassing spectacle that included the FBI's arrest and hand-cuffing of Judge Dugan and the Director of the FBI, Kash Patel, posting a photo of the perp walk on X. As you know well, the Confidentiality and Media Contacts Policy that appears on the Justice Department's website directs that DOJ personnel "should not voluntarily disclose a photograph of a defendant unless it serves a law enforcement function or unless the photo-graph is already part of the public record in the case." The cir-cumstances of Judge Dugan's arrest make it clear that it was nothing but an effort to threaten and intimidate the state and federal judiciaries into submitting to the Administration....

End Notes

Why Democrats and Kamala Harris Lost in 2024

Vice President Kamala Harris was a perfectly reasonable choice for president. She seemed as capable of fulfilling the role at least as well as any of her half-dozen or more predecessors. So why did she lose? There are myriad reasons, each of which cost her a significant tranche of votes in the American electorate:

- Misogyny. She was a woman. Too many Americans hate women.
- Race. She was not white. Too many Americans hate non-whites.
- Immigrant. She's a natural-born citizen of immigrant parents.
- Biden. She chose to carry the burden of Biden. Separating herself from the Biden administration was probably too hard. Especially in a short campaign. It was a dead weight.
- Split staff. She kept too many Biden staffers, not enough of her own. This made campaign coherence a challenge.
- Gaza. She never objected to the Israeli genocide.
- War criminals. She said she was "honored" to be supported by Dick Cheney and other Iraq War perpetrators.
- Charisma. She never showed any. She was too programmed.
- Change. She was not inspiring and didn't seem to try to be. She failed to offer change to an electorate clamoring for it.

■ Trump. She never effectively engaged him for who he is. Calling him "weird" is not an argument. Failing to challenge his lie about Haitians eating neighborhood cats didn't help.

■ Appointed. She ran in no primaries, won the nomination by diktat, giving her an aura of illegitimacy.

■ Old Democrat. She represented the traditional Democratic party that has been failing America's majority for decades. She had no compelling vision of a better future.

■ Timing. All of the factors above were made worse by the forced timing of her run for the presidency. Absent some miracle, she didn't have time to mount an effective campaign.

Are there more reasons? Probably. These are more than enough. Given her inability (gender) or unwillingness (genocide) to change the conditions of her candidacy, it's something of a small miracle that she almost won. She lost by less than 1.5% of the popular vote, which is almost a credit to the American electorate.

The election was duly certified on January 6, 2025, by a joint session of Congress, presided over by Vice President Kamala Harris. There were no serious objections. There was no riot. The election was over.

But did Trump actually win? Why would anyone think otherwise? Former CIA officer Michael D. Sellers has explored multiple election fraud theories on his Substack page DEEPER LOOK and come up with nothing he found meaningful. According to Sellers, other fact-checking organizations – including Snopes, PolitiFact, FactCheck.org, AP, Wired, and Al Jazeera – have also come up empty.

Sellers didn't mention Greg Palast. Palast is an investigative journalist who has worked on voting issues for years. On June 16, Palast posted a piece on his website gregpalast.com with the headline: "Trump Lost. Suppression Won." His argument was simple and direct: "Trump lost. That is, if all legal voters were allowed to vote, if all legal ballots were counted, Trump would have lost the states of Wisconsin, Michigan, Pennsylvania, and Georgia. Vice-President Kamala Harris would have won the Presidency with 286 electoral votes."

In the words of Antonin Scalia, "Get over it." We'll see.

Ensuring Accountability for All Agencies

This is the unintendedly ironic title of Trump's executive order #14215 of February 18, in which he seeks total presidential control over all federal agencies, including congressionally created independent agencies such as the Federal Election Commission (FEC). The executive order's Section 7 states:

> The President and the Attorney General, subject to the President's supervision and control, shall provide authoritative interpretations of law for the executive branch. The President and the Attorney General's opinions on questions of law are controlling on all employees in the conduct of their official duties. No employee of the executive branch acting in their official capacity may advance an interpretation of the law as the position of the United States that contravenes the President or the Attorney General's opinion on a matter of law, including but not limited to the issuance of regulations, guidance, and positions advanced in litigation, unless authorized to do so by the President or in writing by the Attorney General.

This is a bald assertion by Trump that the president's opinion is law.

The Democratic National Committee (DNC) and others immediately took issue and on March 11 filed in federal court, seeking a preliminary injunction to block enforcement of the executive order (*DNC v. Trump*, 25-cv-587-AHA). The plaintiffs contended that this executive order gave the president and attorney general unilateral authority to interpret and enforce federal election laws, effectively stripping the bipartisan FEC of its independent decision-making powers. The lawsuit challenged the order's constitutionality, arguing that it endangered the neutrality of campaign finance regulation by allowing the president to dictate legal interpretations that could disadvantage political opponents.

Additionally, the plaintiffs alleged immediate harm to their operations, as the order threatened their ability to receive impartial guidance from the FEC and defend themselves in election-related legal matters. They cited a pending FEC complaint against DSCC, alleging campaign finance violations, which could now be resolved under legal interpretations dictated by the president rather than bipartisan commissioners.

Trump and the FEC filed motions to dismiss the case.

On June 3, Judge Amir Ali dismissed the Democrats' lawsuit, saying the case was simply too speculative to justify emergency intervention from the court at this time. He noted that the FEC had pledged to remain independent, had received no directive from the White House to change its practices, and had vowed to abide by the law. Without evidence to the contrary, he said he was compelled to dismiss the suit, while leaving it open to renewal under changed circumstances.

In recent months, Judge Ali has been vilified by Trump and his allies for his February 13 ruling that ordered the Trump administration to honor some $2 billion in USAID debt for work already done on Congress-approved contracts that were in place before Trump took office. With the government failing to pay anyone, Judge Ali issued an order to pay by February 26. Supreme Court Chief Justice John Roberts promptly put a stay on Judge Ali's order. On March 5, the Supreme Court issued an unsigned 5-4 ruling reinstating Judge Ali's order and directed him to clarify the government's obligations, since the judge's earlier deadline of February 26 had already passed. According to Reuters on March 20, quoting a court filing, the Trump administration "expects to finish paying about $671 million owed for completed work to foreign aid organizations suing it over its sweeping shutdown of most U.S. foreign aid work by [March 21], nearly two weeks after a court-ordered deadline."

Judge Ali has ruled that the Constitution requires the administration ultimately to spend all of the money appropriated by Congress for foreign aid. The administration turned to Congress for help. On June 12, the House voted 214-212 to allow the administration to rescind $8.3 billion in funds previously allocated for foreign aid.

'We're Not Monsters,' Ice Agent Claims

In one of those widely circulating videos showing ICE agents (and other federal agents) detaining people with blatantly illegal and violent methods, one ICE agent, standing to the side, says to bystanders, "We're not monsters." No one responds.

The ICE agent is wrong. They are monsters.

All the federal agents engaged in this lawless roundup of alleged undocumented immigrants are monsters. They are trained to be monsters. Their superiors are monsters. ICE (Immigration and Customs Enforcement) has been a monstrous agency for years.

- Illegally detaining people without a judicial warrant is monstrous.
- Illegally detaining people without showing any identification is monstrous.
- Using violence on unresisting detainees is monstrous.
- Separating a migrant mother from her nursing infant is monstrous.
- Illegally treating people with a presumption of guilt is monstrous.
- Illegally incarcerating people with no due process of law is monstrous.
- Illegally detaining people in conditions with too little food or water is monstrous.
- Illegally deporting people in violation of court orders is monstrous.
- Illegally deporting children who are U.S. citizens is monstrous.
- Illegally deporting adults who are U.S. citizens is monstrous.
- Continuing to violate the law, defying court orders is monstrous.
- Violating your oath to defend the Constitution is monstrous.
- Dishonestly claiming to be "just following orders" is monstrous.
- "Just following orders" was the Nazi defense. They were monsters.

During the first Trump administration, things were bad with ICE and other agencies involved with immigration. In an article published in the July 24, 2017, issue of The New Yorker under the headline, "A Veteran ICE Agent, disillusioned with the Trump Era, Speaks Out," the agent was quoted as saying:

> You have guys who are doing whatever they want in the field, going after whoever they want.... We used to look at things through the totality of the circumstances when it came to a removal order – that's out the window.... It all adds up to contempt that I've never seen so rampant towards the aliens.... We seem to be targeting the most vulnerable people, not the worst.

That was 2017. Federal law enforcement, especially ICE, has only gotten worse: defiantly illegal, recklessly violent, totally disconnected from anything like justice or the rule of law – a nascent police state. Monstrous.

They wear masks. They don't wear badges. They don't show credentials. They don't have warrants. They rely on fear, intimidation, and brute force.

They are monsters. They are our monsters. And they will own us if we are unable to own them.

U.S. Intelligence Report Contradicts Trump

When Trump invoked the Alien Enemies Act of 1798 to deport immigrants in 2025, he claimed in his executive order of March 15 that the gang Tren de Aragua (TdA) was conducting "irregular warfare" in the U.S. and was controlled by the Venezuelan government of Nicolas Maduro. These conditions were necessary to invoke the act. The claims were false.

Several federal judges have ruled that Trump had unlawfully invoked the act and imposed temporary restraining orders against the government's use of it.

On April 7, the National Intelligence Council (NIC) produced a six-page report that contradicted the President's claim. The NIC found that Maduro's "regime probably does not have a policy of cooperating with TdA and is not directing TdA movement to and operations in the United States." This was the shared assessment of 18 U.S. intelligence agencies.

This was first reported by The Washington Post on April 17 and vehemently denied by Director of National Intelligence, Tulsi Gabbard. She released the report on May 5 in response to a Freedom of Information request.

The report confirmed the Post's reporting. The president was wrong. His executive order was unlawful.

On May 14, Gabbard fired the top two NIC officials, acting NIC chair Mike Collins and his deputy Maria Langan-Riekhof. Each of them has more than 25 years of intelligence experience. They had each served presidents of both parties since the 1990s.

In an email, Gabbard said they were fired for opposing Trump, without offering any examples. Her office issued a statement claiming, without apparent irony, that "The director is working alongside President Trump to end the weaponization and politicization of the intelligence community." No facts, please, just political alignment.

Rep. Jim Himes (D-CT), ranking member of the House Select

Committee on Intelligence, said in a statement: "Absent evidence to justify the firings, the workforce can only conclude that their jobs are contingent on producing analysis that is aligned with the President's political agenda, rather than truthful and apolitical."

Former CIA Director John Brennan told MSNBC that Collins and Langan-Riekhof "are two of the most experienced, accomplished, and talented analysts in the entire U.S. intelligence community."

Brennan assessed their firing as an exercise in political correctness, at the expense of reliable intelligence: "It's clearly a signal to tell analysts throughout the intelligence community: 'You tell the truth, you provide objective analysis, as you're supposed to be doing, you are running the risk of getting fired.'"

All of this was a sideshow, albeit useful for maintaining Trumpian political correctness in the intelligence agencies.

The main event was taking place at the Supreme Court and lower courts all over the country. On April 7, in a strange non-decision decision, the Supreme Court ruled 5-4 that Trump could use the Alien Enemies Act, but that he had to honor the habeas corpus rights of detainees wherever they happened to be (some were imprisoned in El Salvador). It was a decision that imposed chaos that was still roiling the courts two months later. Justice Sonia Sotomayor dissented. [See subsection "Justice Sotomayor Issues a Powerful Dissent" on page 193.]

As Maine Goes, So Should the Nation

On February 21, at the White House, Trump called out Maine Governor Janet Mills, a lawyer and former Maine attorney general. Trump wanted to know whether Maine was going to comply with his (illegal and totally unscientific) executive order #14201 of February 5 titled "Keeping Men Out of Women's Sports," which directs federal agencies to withhold funding from states whose schools and colleges fail to comply.

Trump asked the Maine governor, "Are you not going to comply with that?"

Governor Mills replied, "I'm complying with the state and federal laws."

Trump responded, "We are the federal law…. You better comply, you better comply, because otherwise you're not getting any federal funding."

"We're going to follow the law, sir. We'll see you in court," Mills answered.

To the best of anyone's knowledge, Maine has exactly two transgender women athletes who would fall under Trump's ban. The state has done nothing to prevent them from competing, as allowed by state and federal law.

At some time in February, Republican state legislator Laurel Libby of Auburn shared an online post that called attention to a transgender athlete who placed first in the girls' pole vault at the state's track-and-field championship. Her post included photos and the name of the athlete, who is a minor. Her post blurred the faces of other athletes, for the sake of their privacy. The post went viral. The athlete's school needed increased security. Libby refused to remove the post, despite warnings that it was endangering the athlete.

Maine House Censures Transphobic Rep

On February 25, the Maine House of Representatives voted 75-70 to censure Libby and required her to apologize. The Censure Resolution said, in part:

- Representative Libby's post has received national attention that she has amplified by appearing on national television and radio broadcasts to discuss;
- Numerous replies to Representative Libby's post suggested that harm should come to the young athlete;
- Representative Libby's post named the minor and used photos of the minor without that minor's consent, in an effort to advance her political agenda;
- When it was brought to her attention that her post may endanger the minor, Representative Libby refused to take down the post and instead continued to bring media attention to the minor;
- It is a basic tenet of politics and good moral character that children should not be targeted by adult politicians, especially when that targeting could result in serious harm;
- The Legislative Code of Ethics expressly states that "a Legislator is entrusted with the security, safety, health, prosperity, respect and general

well-being of those the Legislator serves and with whom the Legislator serves" and that "The Maine Legislator will be ever mindful of the ordinary citizen who might otherwise be unrepresented and will endeavor conscientiously to pursue the highest standards of legislative conduct inside and outside of the State House."

The resolution found "the conduct of Representative Laurel D. Libby to be reprehensible and in direct violation of our code of ethics," for which she should be censured. The resolution further held that "Representative Laurel D. Libby must accept full responsibility for the incident and publicly apologize to the House and to the people of the State of Maine."

Libby was brought to the well of the House, where she refused to apologize. House Speaker Ryan Fecteau then found her in violation of a Maine House rule that prohibits a member guilty of a violation of the legislature's rules and orders from voting or speaking "until the member has made satisfaction." Libby has not been allowed to speak or vote since then. She took her case to federal district court, which declined to intervene in a "legislative act." The First Circuit Court of Appeals upheld the district court. On April 28, Libby filed with the U.S. Supreme Court – *Libby v. Fecteau* – for emergency relief.

On May 6, Libby told Fox News:

> I, along with two-thirds of my fellow Mainers, agree that it's absolutely not fair, that biological males are dominating in women's sports, are pushing girls aside. And consider this, for a state where we're told this isn't happening, it's not a big deal, stop making an issue of it, this same athlete has been dominating in girls' cross-country running, in Nordic skiing, and now in track.

She's objecting to one transgender athlete. Maine has two. The other is apparently not as successful. Sometime in late April, the successful transgender athlete won both the 800- and 1600-meter girls' cross-country races at a high school track meet. According to Fox News, "The athlete has been making national headlines in Maine dating back [to October 2023] after jumping to 4th place in the 5k division in the girls' category after previously finishing 172nd among boys. The athlete again made national headlines for competing in Nordic skiing and taking a podium spot in Maine's High School State Nordic Skiing Championships this past February."

Ninth Grader Puts Transphobe to Shame

Libby got some surprising pushback from Anelise Feldman, a ninth-grader at Yarmouth High School. She came in second behind the transgender runner in the 1600-meter race. Feldman wrote a public letter addressing Libby's bigotry:

> Rep. Laurel Libby, R-Auburn, recently used my second-place finish in the 1600-meter run, and that of my teammate in the 800-meter run, to malign Soren Stark-Chessa, the trans-identified athlete who finished first.
>
> One of the reasons I chose to run cross-country and track is the community: Teammates cheering each other on, athletes from different schools coming together, and the fact that personal improvement is valued as much as, if not more than, the place we finish.
>
> Last Friday, I ran the fastest 1600-meter race I have ever run in middle school or high school track and earned varsity status by my school's standards. I am extremely proud of the effort I put into the race and the time that I achieved. The fact that someone else finished in front of me didn't diminish the happiness I felt after finishing that race. I don't feel like first place was taken from me. Instead, I feel like a happy day was turned ugly by a bully who is using children to make political points.
>
> We are all just kids trying to make our way through high school. Participating in sports is the highlight of high school for some kids. No one was harmed by Soren's participation in the girls' track meet, but we are all harmed by the hateful rhetoric of bullies, like Rep. Libby, who want to take sports away from some kids just because of who they are.

Meanwhile, Maine is seeing a lot of the Trump administration in court and other venues.

On March 23, on Truth Social, Trump demanded a "full-throated apology" from Governor Mills for their spat over transgender athletes at the White House the month before.

The next day, Governor Mills responded to Trump's demand that she apologize, telling reporters:

> I don't communicate with public officials by tweet or Instagram or social media....[A]ll of my issues are about the rule of law pure and simple. It's not about transgender sports; it is about who makes the laws and who enforces the laws. I read the Constitution. The Constitution says the president, the chief executive, shall take care that the law be faithfully executed. It doesn't allow him to make laws out of whole cloth by tweet or Instagram post or press release or executive order. That is fundamental law, and I stand for the rule of law and the separation of powers.

Mills added that "if the current occupant of the White House wants to protect women and girls, he should start by protecting the women and teenage girls who are suffering miscarriages and dying because they can't get basic, life-saving health care in states across this country."

DOJ Weaponizes Funds for Helping Prisoners

On April 8, Attorney General Pam Bondi announced that the Justice Department was terminating funding programs for the Maine Department of Corrections because a transgender woman was incarcerated in a women's prison. The terminated grants help pay for drug treatment for adults in re-entry programs that foster engagement between incarcerated parents and their children, and resources for corrections agencies to improve post-release supervision in order to prevent recidivism and reduce crime.

On April 16, Attorney General Pam Bondi announced a federal suit to force Maine to comply with the administration's ban on transgender women from women's sports, based on Trump's arbitrary order claiming there are only two sexes. Bondi was joined at the announcement by professional transgender hater Riley Gaines, who was "robbed" of a fourth-place finish in a 2022 NCAA swim meet.

Maine's attorney general, Aaron Frey, said on April 16 that he is confident

Maine was acting in accordance with state and federal law: "Our position is further bolstered by the complete lack of any legal citation supporting the Administration's position in its own complaint. While the President issued an executive order that reflects his own interpretation of the law, anyone with the most basic understanding of American civics understands the president does not create law nor interpret law."

On May 2, the Trump administration gave up efforts to freeze funds intended for a Maine child nutrition program. The U.S. Department of Agriculture initially suspended funding because of the dispute over transgender athletes. In return, Maine will drop its lawsuit against the Department of Agriculture. In April, a federal judge had ordered the Trump administration to unfreeze funds after finding that Maine was likely to succeed in its legal challenge.

Maine Attorney General Aaron Frey said in a statement: "It's unfortunate that my office had to resort to federal court just to get USDA to comply with the law and its own regulations. But we are pleased that the lawsuit has now been resolved and that Maine will continue to receive funds as directed by Congress to feed children and vulnerable adults."

On May 20, in a "shadow docket" ruling with no written opinion, the Supreme Court issued an injunction overruling the Maine House of Representatives' decision to block Maine Rep. Laurel Libby from voting or speaking on the chamber floor. She had been censured for posting personal information about a transgender student on her legislative Facebook page.

Libby called the decision "a victory not just for my constituents, but for the Constitution itself. The Supreme Court has affirmed what should never have been in question – that no state legislature has the power to silence an elected official simply for speaking truthfully about issues that matter."

Justice Ketanji Brown Jackson dissented, arguing that the case raised important questions about the rights of state legislatures to enforce their rules that the court "neither addressed nor answered." She also questioned whether Libby's appeal warranted emergency relief:

> Not very long ago, this Court treaded carefully with respect to exercising its equitable power to issue injunctive relief at the request of a party claiming an emergency. Those days are no more.

Today's Court barely pauses to acknowledge these important threshold limitations on the exercise of its own authority. It opts instead to dole out error correction as it sees fit, regardless of the lack of any exigency and even when the applicants' claims raise significant legal issues that warrant thorough evaluation by the lower courts that are dutifully considering them.

What Kind of Schools Does America Need?

White House Deputy Chief of Staff Stephen Miller has an answer: we will have school where:

Children will be taught to love America. Children will be taught to be patriots. Children will be taught civic values for schools that want federal taxpayer funding. So, as we close the Dept of Education and provide funding to states, we're going to make sure these funds are not being used to promote communist ideology.

Trump Officials Defy Judge's Due Process Orders

On March 23, detainees in the custody of the Department of Homeland Security (DHS) filed a federal class action suit against DHS (#1:25-cv-10676-BEM). The detainees are noncitizens with final removal orders, but DHS is not sending them to their home countries. DHS intends to send them to South Sudan, which is in a state of virtual civil war. The detainees are demanding their due process rights to challenge deportation to a third country where they would face persecution, torture, or death. DHS has no written policy for deporting detainees to third countries that are not their home countries.

The detainees have had no opportunity to challenge their deportation orders. They argue that this violates the Immigration and Nationality Act, the due process clause of the Fifth Amendment, and treaty obligations of the United States.

It is unchallenged that the plaintiffs in this case are criminals convicted of violent crimes that make them suitable for detention and deportation. The Trump administration released a 70-page document describing their criminal records. Their convictions, however, do not deprive them of their constitutional right to due process of law.

On March 28, Federal District Judge Brian E. Murphy granted a temporary restraining order (TRO) prohibiting DHS from removing the detainees as well as any other individuals subject to a final order of removal to a third country until they are provided with written notice of the third country to which they may be removed and given a "meaningful opportunity" to submit an application under the Convention Against Torture (CAT), an international agreement prohibiting the deportation of people to a country where they would likely be tortured. The government promptly appealed to stay the TRO.

On April 7, the U.S. Court of Appeals for the First Circuit denied the government's appeal, finding that "the temporary restraining order was not appealable."

On April 18, Judge Murphy issued a preliminary injunction that required the government to inform all detainees included in the class action suit about their third-country removals in advance and to give them a "meaningful opportunity" to show or explain why they qualify for CAT protection.

On May 20, in violation of the federal court order, DHS put the plaintiff detainees, along with other detainees who were not part of the suit, on a plane leaving Harlingen, Texas. ICE had told the Court its standard practice was to give 24 hours' notice. The detainees had less than 16 hours' notice, none of it during business hours. The detainees denied the means to exercise their due process rights and had no access to counsel. The plane arrived the next day in Djibouti, where the detainees were held at an American military base.

DHS originally intended to send the detainees to South Sudan, a nation suffering more than a decade of murderous chaos that has uprooted thousands of Sudanese. The detainees had no opportunity to learn anything about South Sudan.

In early April, South Sudan rejected a non-Sudanese detainee from the U.S. The next day, Secretary of State Marco Rubio cancelled all visas for South Sudanese citizens, claiming falsely that officials would not "accept repatriation of their own nationals." The man rejected by South Sudan was from the Democratic Republic of Congo. South Sudan later accepted the man, but the U.S. left the visa ban in place. South Sudan has been heavily reliant on U.S. financial and humanitarian aid, now threatened by Trump's cuts to foreign aid.

ICE Violates Judicial Injunction

On May 21, the detainees again moved for a restraining order, alleging the government was violating the prior TRO by attempting to remove detainees to South Sudan without advanced notice or an opportunity to demonstrate CAT (Convention Against Torture) eligibility. During the hearing on the motion, the court ordered the government "to maintain custody of the individuals while everybody figured out what was happening." The court found that DHS had violated the court's preliminary injunction. To remedy that violation, the court issued a written order that said:

> Each of the six individuals must be given a reasonable fear interview in private, with the opportunity for the individual to have counsel of their choosing present during the interview, either in-person or remotely, at the individual's choosing. Each individual must be afforded access to counsel that is commensurate with the access that they would have received had these procedures occurred within the United States prior to their deportation, including remote access where in-person access would otherwise be available. Each individual must also be afforded the name and telephone number of class counsel, as well as access to a phone, interpreter, and technology for the confidential transfer of documents that is commensurate with the access they would receive were they in DHS custody within United States borders. Each individual, along with class counsel, must be given no fewer than 72-hours' notice of the scheduled time for each reasonable fear interview.

> Should any individual raise a fear with respect to deportation to the third country that DHS determines falls short of "reasonable fear," the individual must be provided meaningful

opportunity, and a minimum of 15 days, to seek to move to reopen immigration proceedings to challenge the potential third-country removal. During that 15-day period, the individual must remain within the custody or control of DHS, and must be afforded access to counsel that is commensurate with the access they would be afforded if they were seeking to move to reopen from within the United States' borders.

Judge Murphy's order also described the chaotic circumstances created by the government:

Sometime on May 19, 2025, Defendants [DHS] informed eight individuals in I.C.E. detention that they were being removed to South Africa. Later that day, [DHA] told them instead that they were being removed to South Sudan.

The U.S. Government has issued stark warnings regarding South Sudan, advising [U.S.] citizens not to travel to there because of "crime, kidnapping, and armed conflict." South Sudan Travel Advisory, U.S. DEPARTMENT OF STATE, Mar. 8, 2025. The U.S. Department of State further warns that "violent crime, such as carjackings, shootings, ambushes, assaults, robberies, and kidnappings are common throughout South Sudan, including Juba [its capital]. Foreign nationals have been the victims of rape, sexual assault, armed robberies, and other violent crimes."

... An elementary and fundamental requirement of due process in any proceeding which is to be accorded finality is notice reasonably calculated, under all the circumstances, to apprise interested parties of the pendency of the action and afford them an opportunity to present their objections.... Given the totality of the circumstances, it is hard to take seriously the idea that [DHS] intended these individuals to have any real opportunity to make a valid claim.

On May 22, an hour before a scheduled court hearing, DHS held a press conference where they revealed the names and criminal histories of the individuals on the plane to Djibouti, at least six of whom were among the plaintiffs. Based on the government's removal of detainees to Djibouti without due process, the court ruled that the government had violated the court's preliminary injunction. Nevertheless, the court, in its own words, "crafted a remedy based on [the government's] requests made during the hearing." This was consistent with Judge Murphy's conscientious effort to avoid the court's interference with the government's prerogatives in foreign affairs.

Judge Takes ICE Lawyers to Task

On May 23, the government filed motions asking the court to reconsider its injunction and, in the alternative, to order a stay while the government appealed. In response, on May 26, the court issued a 17-page order, not only denying the government's motions but taking the government ("Defendants") to task for its behavior:

> [DHS has] mischaracterized this Court's order, while at the same time manufacturing the very chaos they decry. By racing to get six class members onto a plane to unstable South Sudan, clearly in breach of the law and this Court's order, [DHS] gave this Court no choice but to find that they were in violation of the Preliminary Injunction.
>
> Even after finding that violation, however, the Court stayed its hand and did not require [DHS] to bring the individuals back to the United States, as requested by [the detainees]. Instead, the Court accepted [DHS's] own suggestion that they be allowed to keep the individuals out of the country and finish their process abroad ....
>
> Since that hearing [on May 21], merely five days ago, [DHS has] changed their tune. It turns out that having immigration proceedings on another continent is harder and more logistically cumbersome than [DHS] anticipated. However, the Court never said that [DHS] had to convert their foreign military base into an immigration facility; it only left that as an option, again, at [DHS] request.
>
> The other option, of course, has always been to simply return to the status quo of roughly one week ago, or else choose any

other location to complete the required process. To be clear, the Court recognizes that the [detainees] at issue here have criminal histories. But that does not change due process.....

"The history of American freedom is, in no small measure, the history of procedure." [*Malinski v. New York* (1945)]
"It is procedure that spells much of the difference between rule by law and rule by whim or caprice. Steadfast adherence to strict procedural safeguards is our main assurance that there will be equal justice under law." [*Joint Anti-Fascist Refugee Comm. v. McGrath*, (1951)]

The Court treats its obligation to these principles with the seriousness that anyone committed to the rule of law should understand. It continues to be this Court's sincere hope that reason can get the better of rhetoric. The orders put in place here are sensible and conservative. Accordingly, and for the reasons stated herein, [DHS] motions for reconsideration and for stay pending appeal are DENIED.

This action concerns the procedures that the Government must take before removing non-citizens to "third" countries.... In the first instance, the Government generally must remove a non-citizen to their country of origin or to the country designated on their Order of Removal. If those options prove "impracticable, inadvisable, or impossible," the Government may remove the non-citizen to any other country whose government will accept them, i.e., to a "third" country.

The Government's power to designate third countries for removal is subject to certain limitations set by Congress. In particular, the Government may not remove a non-citizen to a country where they are likely to be tortured. A non-citizen's claim that he or she qualifies for this type of protection is called a "CAT" claim, referring to the Convention Against Torture, an international agreement implemented by Congress....
Twice, well-founded allegations of non-compliance or imminent non-compliance led this Court to amend or clarify the

Preliminary Injunction. Neither of those changed the substance of the Preliminary Injunction, which continued to require [DHS] to give written notice of the third-country removal and a meaningful opportunity to make a CAT claim....

[DHS] effectively tell[s] this Court that it should have at least tried to micromanage the Department of Homeland Security as it fulfills its required obligations, but that is not the role of the courts..... See *Martinez v. Bondi*, (2025) (explaining that the appropriate remedy for improper agency action, "except in rare circumstances, is to remand to the agency for additional investigation or explanation").

Rather, this Court has strived to give [DHS] as much flexibility as possible within legal bounds....

Consistent with this approach, the Court has repeatedly asked [DHS] to weigh in on the particulars of its remedies, and [DHS has] consistently refused. The Court has been forced to decide on an appropriate time limit because [DHS was] unable, unwilling, or incapable of meaningfully engaging in a discussion about what process was required to provide aliens with a meaningful opportunity to contest a finding that their fear was reasonable.

Even in this latest round of back-and-forth, nearly two months later, the Court again asked [DHS] for input on the appropriate length of time to raise a fear-based claim – [DHS] again refused to engage.... The Court then suggested that [DHS] could provide additional authority after the hearing. [DHS] did not. From this course of conduct, it is hard to come to any conclusion other than that [DHS] invites lack of clarity as a means of evasion....

All of this is to say that the Court has reviewed the totality of the situation, including the criminal histories of the individuals and the undoubted operational costs, and has weighed those factors in ordering as narrow relief as the Constitution will tolerate.

Trump Lies, Takes Federal Judge to Task

Trump promptly went bananas on Truth Social, posting what Judge Murphy called a complete lie:

> A Federal Judge in Boston, who knew absolutely nothing about the situation, or anything else, has ordered that EIGHT of the most violent criminals on Earth curtail their journey to South Sudan, and instead remain in Djibouti. He would not allow these monsters to proceed to their final destination. This is not the premise under which I was elected President, which was to PROTECT our Nation. The Judges are absolutely out of control, they're hurting our Country, and they know nothing about particular situations, or what they are doing—And this must change, IMMEDIATELY!

Also on May 26, the same day Judge Murphy's order was issued, U.S. Solicitor General D. John Sauer filed an emergency appeal to the Supreme Court that was inherently political demagoguery. Picking up on Trump's tone, Sauer wrote, falsely characterizing the legal issues in the case: "This case addresses the government's ability to remove some of the worst of the worst illegal immigrants. The United States is facing a crisis of illegal immigration, in no small part because many aliens most deserving of removal are often the hardest to remove."

The immigrants in question have been in U.S. custody for some time. On May 26, they were in a U.S. military facility in Djibouti. Of the eight, only one is from Sudan. The others are from Cuba, Laos, Mexico, Myanmar, and Vietnam. This case is not about the crimes these men have been convicted of committing; it is about the due process required when DHS decides to change plans and send them to a third country.

The Trump administration has cut deals with several third countries to take in deported migrants, including El Salvador, Costa Rica, and Panama. Deportations to all three countries face current, ongoing legal challenges.

In Panama, legal and political action led to the release of dozens of detainees, including families with children, mostly from Asia. They were given 30 days to leave Panama, regardless of whether they had anywhere else to go. Human Rights Watch has published a 36-page report documenting the inhumanity and illegality of American immigration practices.

In Costa Rica, deportation flights from the U.S. had delivered migrants from as far away as Afghanistan, Russia, Iran, China, and other Asian countries. Some had been separated from their families, who were still in the U.S. Most had no idea where they were being sent. All were locked up in CATEM (Temporary Migrant Care Center) against their will. In early May, the Costa Rican government granted temporary humanitarian status to all who were detained at CATEM. Authorities have returned their documents and are now allowing them to move freely in the country. The government's decision came after collective advocacy by human rights organizations, including AFSC (American Friends Service Committee), the Jesuit Service for Migrants, and the Center for Justice and International Law. Other organizations—like Refugees International, Global Strategic Litigation Council, Amnesty International, and Human Rights Watch—have also pressured the government to uphold migrants' rights.

In the Supreme Court, Solicitor General Sauer referred to his ad hominem argument about the men's character, which is not in dispute, while ignoring the Constitution that the administration is violating:

> Just last week, the government was in the process of removing a group of criminal aliens who had been in the country for years or decades after receiving final orders of removal, despite having committed horrific crimes. These aliens include one who was convicted of sexually abusing a child victim for the better part of a decade, beginning when the victim was seven years old. Another was convicted of sexually abusing a mentally handicapped woman with the mental capacity of a three-year-old. At least two others were convicted of murder.
>
> All these aliens have already received extensive legal process. All were tried and convicted in a criminal court, with all the process and protections afforded to criminal defendants. All were adjudicated removable by an immigration judge. A single federal district court, however, has stalled these efforts nationwide.

Hard to see that as a bad thing, given the inhumanity and illegality of

American immigration practices.

ICE Complains About Conditions ICE Created

On June 4, Melissa Harper, the Acting Deputy Executive Associate Director for the United States Department of Homeland Security (DHS), Immigration and Customs Enforcement (ICE), Enforcement and Removal Operations (ERO) since May 29, filed a sworn affidavit designed to blame the court for the conditions that DHS had created by holding detainees in Djibouti:

> The aliens are currently being held in a conference room in a converted Conex shipping container on the U.S. Naval base in Camp Lemonnier, Djibouti. This has been identified as the only viable place to house the aliens.… There are currently eleven ICE officers assigned to guard and maintain custody of the aliens and two ICE officers assigned support the medical staff. The eleven ICE officers are divided into groups of two and work twelve-hour shifts. Five officers are assigned to the day shift, and six officers are assigned to the night shift.… ICE officers do not have the capacity to maintain constant surveillance, custody, and care of the aliens for prolonged periods of time.…
>
> The alien-designated restroom has sinks, six toilet stalls, and six showers. The designated restrooms are located in a separate trailer, which is forty to fifty yards from the unit in which the aliens are housed. The ICE officers conduct pat-downs and searches for contraband during movements to the restroom, or for any other outside activity. Only one alien is allowed to use the toilet or shower at a time, and one officer is required to escort the alien. Aliens are permitted to shower every other day, and showers occur at night due to the heat. From the onset of these ICE operations, the daily temperature outside has exceeded 100 degrees Fahrenheit during the day.
>
> The conference room in which the aliens are housed is not equipped nor suitable for detention of any length, let alone for the detention of high-risk individuals. Notably, the room has

none of the security apparatus necessary for the detention of criminal aliens. If an altercation were to occur, there is no other location on site available to separate the aliens, which further compromises the officers' safety.

ICE officers are currently sharing very limited sleeping quarters, consisting of a trailer with three sets of bunk beds and six beds in total…. ICE medical staff has also received limited medication and medical supplies for both officers and the aliens from DOD. ICE personnel had to interrupt the flight and disembark in Djibouti without being on anti-malaria medication for at least 48-72 hours prior to arrival, as recommended by medical professionals. They were not able to start taking anti-malarials until after arrival in Djibouti. There continues to be an unknown degree of exposure despite taking the antimalarial as full efficacy of the medication is unknown currently….

Djibouti utilizes burn pits as a way disposing of trash and human waste. The burn pits are located within five miles outside the base and turned on at night. These pits create a smog cloud in the vicinity of Camp Lemonnier, making it difficult to breathe and requiring medical treatment for the officers, who have experienced throat irritation. Some officers have taken extra precaution by sleeping with N-95 masks…. Due to the temperature in Djibouti being over 100 degrees Fahrenheit during the day and in the 90s at night with usually no breeze, the smoke from the burn pits lingers.

Within 72 hours of landing in Djibouti, the officers and detainees began to feel ill. The medical staff did not have immediate access to medication necessary to treat their symptoms…. ICE officers continue to feel ill with symptoms such as coughing, difficulty breathing, fever, and achy joints. These symptoms align with bacterial upper respiratory infection, but ICE officers are unable to obtain proper testing for a diagnosis….

[DOD officials warned] of imminent danger of rocket attacks from terrorist groups in Yemen. The ICE officers lack body armor or other gear that would be appropriate in the case of an attack.

All this is concerning to be sure, but DHS created the condition without any help. DHS violated a restraining order to send the detainees to Djibouti. DHS had full control of whatever planning was needed. The court has given DHS the option of bringing the detainees back to the U.S. DHS prefers the conditions in Djibouti. These horrendous conditions are marginally better than the subhuman conditions reported at other ICE detention centers including Miami, Los Angeles, Alligator Alcatraz and Jena, LA.

On June 23, the Supreme Court ruled 6-3 in an unsigned order to stay Judge Murphy's ruling. The ruling facilitates the government's ability to deport detainees to third countries while its appeal moves forward, but provides no reasoning for the decision. In a 19-page dissent, Justice Sonia Sotomayor, joined by Justices Kagan and Jackson, rejected the court's willingness "to grant the Government emergency relief from an order it has repeatedly defied." Sotomayor argued that even if Judge Murphy's injunction order was wrong, the government was still required to follow it while it was in effect:

> That principle is a bedrock of the rule of law.... The Government's misconduct threatens it to its core.... each time this Court rewards noncompliance with discretionary relief, it further erodes respect for courts and for the rule of law.... Apparently the Court finds the idea that thousands will suffer violence in far-flung locales more palatable than the remote possibility that a District Court exceeded its remedial powers when it ordered the Government to provide notice and process to which the plaintiffs are constitutionally and statutorily entitled.

On June 30, the Global Detention Project reported that the situation in Djibouti remains largely unchanged. Judge Murphy, while acknowledging that the Supreme Court had stayed his broader order on sending detainees to third countries, ruled that his narrower order in the case of the detainees headed for South Sudan remained in effect. On July 3, the Supreme Court stayed that order as well, freeing the government to send its detainees to

South Sudan without providing constitutionally required due process of law.

Trump's Fight With Harvard — It Matters Who Wins

Harvard is a private institution, founded in 1636 in Cambridge, Massachusetts. It is the oldest university in the U.S. It's not clear exactly when Harvard became a target for the Trump administration. During the 2024 presidential campaign, Trump promised to punish universities in general over alleged "antisemitism" claims.

On January 21, 2025, Harvard settled two civil rights lawsuits filed in 2024 by two groups of students, accusing the university of mishandling antisemitism on campus. Under the settlement, Harvard will clarify that its non-discrimination policies protect Israeli and Jewish students. and it will adopt the widely used but controversial International Holocaust Remembrance Association definition of antisemitism. Harvard explicitly stated it will adopt the definition's "accompanying examples," which state that it is antisemitic to describe Israel's existence as a "racist endeavor" or compare its contemporary policies to those of the Nazis. Two of the plaintiffs rejected the settlement and planned to continue their suits. Harvard's settlement was among several such settlements by universities, including Brown and the University of California, accused of failing to respond to "antisemitism."

On January 29, Trump issued an executive order #14188 titled "Additional Measures to Combat Anti-Semitism," expanding on his executive order in December 2019 on combating antisemitism. The new order asserts that, since the Hamas attack on October 7, 2023, "Jewish students have faced an unrelenting barrage of discrimination; denial of access to campus common areas and facilities, including libraries and classrooms; and intimidation, harassment, and physical threats and assault…." The order provides no supporting evidence. The order directs various federal agencies to gather information about antisemitism and invites recommendations for **familiarizing institutions of higher education with the grounds for inadmissibility [of aliens]** under 8 U.S.C. 1182(a)(3) so that such institutions may monitor for and report activities by alien students and staff relevant to those grounds and for ensuring that such reports about aliens lead, as appropriate and consistent with applicable law, to investigations and, if warranted, actions to remove such aliens. [Emphasis added.]

GSA Targets Harvard for Antisemitism

This implicitly included Harvard, along with every other American institution of higher education. The targeting moved closer to home on March 31 with a one-page memo from Commissioner Josh Gruenbaum of the General Services Administration (GSA) titled "Review of Federal Government Contracts," which began:

> Pursuant to President Trump's Executive Order, "Additional Measures to Combat Anti-Semitism," on January 29, 2025, a multi-agency Task Force to Combat Anti-Semitism was created, consisting of the Departments of Justice, Education, Health and Human Services, and the General Services Administration. GSA is leading a Task Force comprehensive review of Federal contracts with certain institutions of higher education that are being investigated for potential infractions and dereliction of duties to curb or combat anti-Semitic harassment, including Harvard University....
>
> Please be advised that alongside our fellow agencies, we will also be reviewing the greater than $8.7 billion of multi-year grant commitments between Harvard University, its affiliates and the Federal Government for potential compliance concerns, false claims or other infractions."

On April 3, in a follow-up to his March 31 memo, Commissioner Grauenbaum and his task force members at the Department of Education and the Department of Health and Human Services sent a two-page letter to Harvard's president, Dr. Alan M. Garber, and to Lead Member of the Harvard Corporation, Penny Pritzker, striking an initially friendly tone:

> ...Harvard has asked for a dialogue with the Task Force to discuss this ongoing review. Below, you will find several broad, non-exhaustive areas of reform that the government views as necessary for Harvard to implement to remain a responsible recipient of federal taxpayer dollars. We look forward to a meaningful

dialogue focused on lasting, structural reforms at Harvard....

So far, so good. But near the end of the second paragraph, the task force enters its verdict without the benefit of anything like a trial:

Harvard University, however, has fundamentally failed to protect American students and faculty from antisemitic violence and harassment in addition to other alleged violations of the Civil Rights Act of 1964. This letter outlines immediate next steps that we regard as necessary for Harvard University's continued financial relationship with the United States government.

The balance of the letter outlines nine areas of compliance that Harvard must meet to keep its federal funding. The "reforms" listed cover virtually the entire operation of the university: admissions, student discipline, faculty hiring, governance, elimination of DEI (diversity, equity, inclusion), cooperation with law enforcement, and transparency in federal reporting.

In effect, the federal task force is pressing for changes that will allow the federal government to run Harvard. This is a demand letter, and the demands are backed by a threat, deemed necessary for a "continued financial relationship" with the federal government.

A similar demand letter to Columbia University on March 13 prompted Columbia to make substantive changes in its operations under the threat of billions of dollars in cuts. Harvard had almost $9 billion in federal grants and contracts at stake.

Harvard was the fifth private Ivy League school targeted in a pressure campaign by the administration, which has also paused federal funding for the University of Pennsylvania, Brown, Princeton, and Columbia to force compliance with its political agenda. In April, the Department of Education sent similar demand letters to more than 60 universities across the U.S.

Antisemitism Is Real, Not Rampant

The Trump pretext of an investigation into campus antisemitism is transparently bogus. It has always been a dishonest wedge issue. The task force letter offers no evidence to support its demands. The antisemitism trope presently raging through political culture is pure dishonesty. There is only limited evidence of any increase in antisemitism in recent years, especially at universities where antisemitism is rare and not tolerated.

There has been considerable increase in hostility to Israel and its Zionist-minded assault on Gaza. There is vastly more bigotry toward Palestinians and Arabs generally. Higher education institutions like Columbia have cracked down hard even on peaceful protesters who object to the mass killings of Palestinians in Gaza. The fraud at the heart of the "antisemitism" campaign is that it requires one to affirm an absurdity: that it's antisemitic to oppose genocide. This political reality was illustrated on May 22 at Trump's $148 million meme coin dinner that included cryptocurrency investors whose coins are named things like "F*CK THE JEWS."

Reacting to the Trump letter of April 3, Harvard history professor Kirsten Weld, president of the campus chapter of the American Association of University Professors, called it a "dominance test" and called for resistance:

> If Harvard, the wealthiest university on the planet, accedes to these demands, the [government] task force won't go away – it will simply return with additional demands, just like a schoolyard bully. Harvard must contest this patently unlawful attack in the courts.

On April 11, the Harvard chapter of the American Association of University Professors sued the Trump administration in federal district court (#1:25-cv-10910) over an "unlawful and unprecedented" attempt to use federal funding cuts to restrict free speech. This was the second suit that the Harvard AAUP chapter had filed against the Trump administration this year. The first was a joint suit with other chapters in federal court (#1:25-cv-10685) on March 25, including one from Columbia, over federal efforts to deport Mahmoud Khalil and students who engaged in pro-Palestinian activism.

Harvard alumni also supported resistance in a letter calling for Harvard to "legally contest and refuse to comply with unlawful demands that threaten academic freedom and university self-governance." Anurima Bhargava, one of the alumni behind the letter said: "It's a time for courage, not capitulation. This is an unlawful attack and an attempt to coerce Harvard by threatening the very lifeblood of the institution, which its researchers, innovators, entrepreneurs, and scholars."

U.S. Task Force Issues Harvard Takeover Memo

On April 11, the task force sent Harvard a five-page, single-spaced letter expanding its demands as to how the university should be run. The letter gave Harvard just four months to comply with what amounted to a complete re-structuring of a university with more than 24,000 students and more than 20,000 faculty. The letter asserted government oversight of Harvard through 2028. The letter demanded an investigation of events in 2023-2024. The letter demanded that Harvard report on these mandated changes quarterly, the first report due on June 30 (before the August deadline for implementation).

The April 11 letter, again without evidence, asserted:

> Harvard has in recent years failed to live up to both the intellectual and civil rights conditions that justify federal investment. But we appreciate your expression of commitment to repairing those failures and welcome your collaboration in restoring the University to its promise.

In an April 14 letter (in response to the task force letter of April 11), Harvard wrote:

> Harvard is committed to fighting antisemitism and other forms of bigotry in its community. Antisemitism and discrimination of any kind not only are abhorrent and antithetical to Harvard's values but also threaten its academic mission.
>
> To that end, Harvard has made, and will continue to make, lasting and robust structural, policy, and programmatic changes to ensure that the university is a welcoming and supportive learning environment for all students and continues to abide in all respects with federal law across its academic programs and operations, while fostering open inquiry in a pluralistic community free from intimidation and open to challenging orthodoxies, whatever their source....
>
> As a result, Harvard is in a very different place today from where it was a year ago. These efforts, and additional measures the university will be taking against antisemitism, not only are the right thing to do but also are critical to strengthening

Harvard's community as a place in which everyone can thrive. It is unfortunate, then, that your letter disregards Harvard's efforts and instead presents demands that, in contravention of the First Amendment, invade university freedoms long recognized by the Supreme Court. The government's terms also circumvent Harvard's statutory rights by requiring unsupported and disruptive remedies for alleged harms that the government has not proven through mandatory processes established by Congress and required by law.

No less objectionable is the condition, first made explicit in the letter of March 31, 2025, that Harvard accede to these terms or risk the loss of billions of dollars in federal funding critical to vital research and innovation that has saved and improved lives and allowed Harvard to play a central role in making our country's scientific, medical, and other research communities the standard-bearers for the world....

The university will not surrender its independence or relinquish its constitutional rights. Neither Harvard nor any other private university can allow itself to be taken over by the federal government.... Harvard remains open to dialogue about what the university has done, and is planning to do, to improve the experience of every member of its community. But Harvard is not prepared to agree to demands that go beyond the lawful authority of this or any administration.

Trump Freezes $2.2 Billion in Harvard Grants

Within hours after receiving this letter, the Trump administration announced that it was moving to freeze $2.2 billion in grants and $60 million in contracts to Harvard. The task force issued a false and demagogic statement, claiming: "Harvard's statement today reinforces the troubling entitlement mindset that is endemic in our nation's most prestigious universities and colleges – that federal investment does not come with the responsibility to uphold civil rights laws."

On April 15, 2025, a PBS NewsHour story said: "The hold on Harvard's funding marks the seventh time President Trump's administration has taken the step at one of the nation's most elite colleges, in an attempt to force compliance with Trump's political agenda. Six of the seven schools are in the Ivy League."

On April 16, DHS Secretary Kristi Noem sent Harvard a rather strident, hostile letter that began:

> It is a privilege to have foreign students attend Harvard University, not a guarantee. The United States Government understands that Harvard University relies heavily on foreign student funding from over 10,000 [actually less than 7,000] foreign students to build and maintain their substantial endowment. At the same time, your institution has created a hostile learning environment for Jewish students due to Harvard's failure to condemn antisemitism.

Noem offered no basis for the false accusation. She simply referred to Trump's executive order 14188 of January 29, making it U.S. policy "to combat anti-Semitism vigorously, using all available and appropriate legal tools, to prosecute, remove, or otherwise hold to account the perpetrators of unlawful anti-Semitic harassment and violence." She then cited the Student and Exchange Visitor Program (SEVP) as the basis for demanding that Harvard provide, for each student visa holder, such information as "known illegal activity," "known dangerous or violent activity," "known threats to other(s)," and so on, through eight categories, none of which is inherently antisemitic.

Noem demanded that Harvard provide the information no later than April 30. Harvard has roughly 6,800 foreign students from 140 countries. They represent about 27% of Harvard's total student population of 24,596 (including 7,000 undergraduates).

Also on April 16, according to a vitriolic DHS press release, "Secretary Noem announced the cancelation of two DHS grants totaling over $2.7 million to Harvard University, declaring it unfit to be entrusted with taxpayer dollars."

The DHS press release continued that, "The Secretary also wrote a scathing letter demanding detailed records on Harvard's foreign student visa holders' illegal and violent activities by April 30, 2025...."

And it quoted Noem as saying:

> Harvard bending the knee to antisemitism – driven by its spine-less leadership – fuels a cesspool of extremist riots and threatens our national security. With anti-American, pro-Hamas ideology poisoning its campus and classrooms, Harvard's position as a top institution of higher learning is a distant memory. America demands more from universities entrusted with taxpayer dollars.

Harvard responded to DHS by April 30 as required, but Noem claimed that the school had not satisfied the agency's demands. Harvard's response included identifying three international students who were "subject to discipline that resulted in a change of academic status" as defined by regulation. Forbes magazine speculated: "It is possible no reply or records provided would have satisfied DHS because the Trump administration had decided to remove Harvard's ability to enroll international students to punish it for not submitting to its other demands."

On April 17, Trump called for eliminating Harvard's tax-exempt status. That would require action by the Internal Revenue Service (IRS). In 1983, the IRS denied tax-exempt status to Bob Jones University, a private Christian university that banned interracial dating and marriage on campus, a decision upheld by the Supreme Court. In 1998, Congress passed a law that forbade federal officials from telling the IRS to investigate any taxpayer in an effort to increase trust in tax enforcement. Congress also passed legislation barring the IRS "from targeting individuals and organizations for ideological reasons," after a controversy over how it treated Tea Party groups in 2013.

Harvard Takes Government to Court

On April 21, Harvard announced that it had filed suit in federal district court (#1:25-cv-11048) to halt a federal freeze on more than $2.2 billion in grants. Harvard President Alan Garber had said that the university would not bend to the government's demands. The Harvard lawsuit called the government freeze "arbitrary and capricious" as well as a violation of both the First Amendment and the Civil Rights Act:

> The Government has not – and cannot – identify any rational

connection between antisemitism concerns and the medical, scientific, technological, and other research it has frozen that aims to save American lives, foster American success, preserve American security, and maintain America's position as a global leader in innovation.

Nor has the Government acknowledged the significant consequences that the indefinite freeze of billions of dollars in federal research funding will have on Harvard's research programs, the beneficiaries of that research, and the national interest in furthering American innovation and progress....

Defendants' actions are unlawful. The First Amendment does not permit the Government to "interfere with private actors' speech to advance its own vision of ideological balance."

The email response to the lawsuit by White House spokesman Harrison Fields was Trumpian in its evidence-free political venom:

The gravy train of federal assistance to institutions like Harvard, which enrich their grossly overpaid bureaucrats with tax dollars from struggling American families is coming to an end. Taxpayer funds are a privilege, and Harvard fails to meet the basic conditions required to access that privilege.

Harvard was the first American university to stand up to the Trump administration, and the first to go to court to defend its independence.

Harvard Releases Self-Study

On April 29, Harvard released a 300-page final report of its Presidential Task Force Combating Antisemitism and Anti-Israeli Bias, after more than a year of work. The task force was established in January 2024 by Harvard's then-interim President Alan Garber to address the political turmoil sparked by the October 7, 2023, Hamas attack on Israel and Israel's ongoing genocidal response. Garber charged the Harvard task force to:

Examine the recent history of antisemitism and its current manifestations on the Harvard campus. It will identify causes of and contributing factors to anti-Jewish behaviors on campus; evaluate evidence regarding the characteristics and frequency of these behaviors; and recommend approaches to combat anti-semitism and its impact on campus.

The Hamas attack in October 2023 turned out to be an earth-shaking event. Harvard was no more prepared for the attack, the hostage-taking, or the genocidal Israeli response than anyone else. In the aftermath, as Israeli forces dominated a battlefield in a conflict that hardly qualified as a "war," emotions ran high and positions hardened. Peaceful demonstrations turned violent, often because of police overreaction. Jewish students were on both sides, supporting Israel's right to defend itself and opposing the genocidal assault on Palestinian civilians. Support for either side was morally compromised. As the final report wrote:

> Harvard, like other elite universities, has faced a profound crisis. Since Fall 2023, different factions at Harvard have fought to force various University leaders to make statements, invest, divest, hire, fire, doxx, un-doxx, discipline students and undiscipline them. Without a doubt, the 2023-24 academic year was one of the most challenging years in recent history in American higher education. Campuses found themselves struggling to understand how to handle wide differences of opinion across and within educational communities.

> By January 2024, the situation at Harvard was particularly difficult, as the institution contended with the sudden departure of its recently installed president and faced legal challenges alleging systematic antisemitism and anti-Arab bias within the University. This current crisis would have been unimaginable just a few years ago.

Institutionally, Harvard made many efforts to cope with the multi-faceted crisis, including the creation of this task force that has now made sweeping recommendations for institutional changes. Some, no doubt, reflect things the Trump administration wants, but without the venom or the demand for outside control. The final report noted this added difficulty:

> We recognize that we are releasing this report at a particularly challenging time, and we have significant concerns that the important work that was entrusted to us will be undermined.

We want to be clear. The adoption of the recommendations of this report, born of the experiences of our Jewish and Israeli community, are of the utmost importance to us. So is the way they are adopted.

These significant reforms must be adopted through internal processes that have widespread buy-in within the Harvard community. We are concerned that external parties, even if well-intentioned, will seek to compel adoption of some of our proposed reforms. If they do so, they will make it more difficult for Harvard to fix itself.

Harvard has expressed the determination to fix itself, and has acknowledged that that will prove difficult. Government supervision is not likely to make it easier to improve Harvard, especially if it costs the university its academic freedom and institutional integrity. As the final report argues:

Our Task Force, comprised of [15] faculty and students, views this report as a starting point rather than a definitive conclusion, laying the groundwork for wide-ranging recommendations essential in our view for the future of our campus community. We each come to this work with our own experiences here at Harvard, and while those may inform our individual perspectives, our work over the past year relies principally on the experiences of others.

We are not dispassionate in these efforts. We have found many of the narratives we heard upsetting, at times deplorable, often heartbreaking, but we have sought in this report to share what we were told generally without overlay or gloss, leaving to the readers of this report their own conclusions about what has transpired over the past year at a university we cherish.

Despite national media coverage, the Trump administration has taken no public notice of Harvard's self-analysis or of the 16-month process that produced the study, started on Harvard's own initiative under the Biden administration. The Trump administration has demonstrated no detailed understanding of America's oldest university and even less willingness to support its efforts to continue running itself after almost 400 years of self-governance.

DHS Decertifies Harvard's Right to Host Foreign Students

On May 22, DHS secretary Kristi Noem wrote Harvard to inform the university that DHS had decertified Harvard's participation in the Student and Exchange Visitor Program (SEVP) for the academic year 2025-26. This ruling would require all of Harvard's 6,800 foreign students to transfer to other institutions if they wanted to continue to study in the United States Noem wrote:

> I am writing to inform you that effective immediately, Harvard University's Student and Exchange Visitor Program is revoked....
>
> As a result of your refusal to comply with multiple requests to provide the Department of Homeland Security pertinent information while perpetuating an unsafe campus environment that is hostile to Jewish students, promotes pro-Hamas sympathies, and employs racist "diversity, equity, and inclusion" policies, you have lost this privilege.... The Trump administration will enforce the law and root out the evils of anti-Americanism and antisemitism in society and campuses.

Noem's letter then listed six categories about which she required "full and complete responses" within 72 hours. All six categories involved "nonimmigrant students enrolled in Harvard University in the last five years." Nonimmigrant students are foreign nationals studying in the U.S. on student visas. Noem demanded to know such things as any and all records regarding "illegal activity," "dangerous or violent activity," "threats to others," "disciplinary records," or "protest activity."

In conjunction with this letter, DHS issued a press release announcing the decertification and including a full page of links to alleged Harvard misdeeds (including a link to Harvard's April 29 Final Report), under the headline: "Harvard University Loses Student and Exchange Visitor Program Certification for Pro-Terrorist Conduct."

The press release quoted Noem as dishonestly saying:

> This administration is holding Harvard accountable for

fostering violence, antisemitism, and coordinating with the Chinese Communist Party on its campus.... It is a privilege, not a right, for universities to enroll foreign students and benefit from their higher tuition payments to help pad their multibillion-dollar endowments. Harvard had plenty of opportunity to do the right thing. It refused. They have lost their Student and Exchange Visitor Program certification as a result of their failure to adhere to the law. Let this serve as a warning to all universities and academic institutions across the country.

The next day, the Wall Street Journal asked in an editorial headlined, "Is Trump Trying to Destroy Harvard?":

The Trump Administration has frozen billions in federal grants to Harvard University, threatened its tax-exempt status and sought to dictate its curriculum and hiring. Now the government seems bent on destroying the school for the offense of fighting back. And for what purpose? That's how we read the Department of Homeland Security's move Thursday [May 22] to bar foreign students from attending the world-renowned institution.

Harvard Gets Temporary Restraining Order Against DHS

On May 23, less than 24 hours after Noem's letter, Harvard filed a 72-page complaint to "enjoin the government's unlawful acts" in revoking its foreign student certification "without process or cause." Harvard (case # 1:25-cv-11472) argued that:

This revocation is a blatant violation of the First Amendment, the Due Process Clause, and the Administrative Procedures Act. It is the latest act by the government in clear retaliation for Harvard exercising its First Amendment rights to reject government's demands to control Harvard's governance, curriculum, and the "ideology" of its faculty and students.

The government's actions are unlawful for other equally clear and pernicious reasons. They disregard the government's own regulations – under which Harvard should remain certified to host F-1 and J-1 visa holders. They depart from decades of settled practice and come without rational explanation. And they were carried out abruptly without any of the robust procedures the government has established to prevent just this type of upheaval to thousands of students' lives.

With the stroke of a pen, the government has sought to erase a quarter of Harvard's student body, international students who contribute significantly to the University and its mission.

Within hours of Harvard's filing, federal district judge Allison D. Burroughs issued an order granting Harvard's motion for a temporary restraining order. She found that unless a TRO was granted, Harvard "will sustain immediate and irreparable injury before there is an opportunity to hear from all parties." The judge ordered:

Accordingly, Defendants, their agents, and anyone acting in concert or participation with Defendants are hereby enjoined from:

A. Implementing, instituting, maintaining, or giving effect to the revocation of Plaintiff's SEVP certification;

B. Giving any force or effect to the Department of Homeland Security's May 22, 2025 Revocation Notice.

Foreign students who qualified remained eligible to graduate on May 29. The thousands of others had their futures in limbo at least till the court case played out, which could go as far as the Supreme Court. Among those remaining at risk was Belgium's Princess Elizabeth, who had just finished her first year in a Harvard graduate program.

On May 26, Nobel laureate economist Paul Krugman posted on Substack that the Trumpist effort to destroy Harvard and other elite universities "will do vast damage to our nation's future." He described Harvard as "a major U.S. exporter," since foreign students mostly pay full tuition, which is a plus in the U.S. trade balance. Additionally, Harvard is a critical element in Boston's regional economy, "one of the crown jewels of the U.S. economy, one of the most important generators of high incomes, specialized knowledge and innovation," which would be threatened with collapse without Harvard. Krugman added:

So, destroying Harvard... would be like pulling a crucial piece out of a Jenga tower. The odds are that the whole structure of the Greater Boston education and innovation ecosystem would collapse. Consequently, America would lose all that Greater Boston does to advance and enrich our nation.

Do MAGA types understand how much damage their campaign against universities will do to American prosperity and power? Probably not. But I suspect that it wouldn't matter if they did. From their point of view, making America poorer, weaker and sicker is an acceptable price for keeping the nation suitably ignorant.

Trump Raises Stakes Again Against Harvard

On May 27, the GSA (General Services Administration) directed federal agencies to review and replace about 30 contracts across nine agencies with Harvard worth about $100 million. The contracts include executive training for Department of Homeland Security officials, research on health outcomes related to energy drinks, and graduate student research services. This action is in addition to more than $2.6 billion in grants and contracts to Harvard, cancelled by the Trump administration and contested in court by Harvard.

Trump accused Harvard of refusing to release the names of its foreign students. They are not secret. They all have visas granted by the State Department.

At a rally outside Harvard Yard on May 27, Jacob Miller, a former president of Harvard Hillel, a Jewish campus organization, told the gathering that the ban on international students has "nothing to do with combating antisemitism." He added:

Antisemitism is a real problem. It's a problem at Harvard. It's a problem in our country. These [Trump administration] policies will do nothing to combat this age-old hatred. Instead, they are designed to divide us.... The Jewish community rejects this administration's narrative. We will not allow our identities to be invoked to destroy Harvard.

Miller graduated from Harvard College on May 29, earning a bachelor's degree in math with a concurrent master's degree in statistics.

On May 28, the Commonwealth of Massachusetts filed a 24-page amicus curiae brief in support of Harvard's certification to host foreign students. Massachusetts asserted that the Trump administration is weaponizing immigration-related enforcement to retaliate against international students and academics. The state said that it benefits from international students attending colleges and universities in Massachusetts and will suffer irreparable harm from the student revocation.

Also on May 28, Trump falsely claimed that Harvard offers "remedial mathematics" on topics such as simple addition. Harvard does not offer a remedial math class covering basic arithmetic. A White House spokesperson provided information about Mathematics MA5, which was introduced in the fall of 2024 to offer extra support in calculus. What Trump had falsely claimed was:

> Harvard announced two weeks ago that they're going to teach remedial mathematics, remedial, meaning they're going to teach low grade mathematics like two plus two is four. How did these people get into Harvard? If they can't, if they can't do basic mathematics, how did they do it?

Harvard responded with detailed information, including that the median math score for the most recently admitted class at Harvard College was 790 out of 800 on the SATs and 35 out of 36 on the ACTs. The average high school GPA was 4.2.

Judge Burroughs Maintains TRO Against DHS

On May 28, the DHS attempted to modify its position before the court in order to make the TRO go away. The DHS filed a five-page letter to Harvard, purporting to be a compromise position. The letter reiterates the government's intent to decertify Harvard from the Student and Exchange Visitor Program (SEVP) "for failing to comply with the federal regulations" required. (Harvard says it has complied twice, DHS says it hasn't, and there is no objective third-party assessment, which is why the issue is in court.) The DHS letter goes on to rehash the history of the dispute, emphasizing what it considers Harvard's multiple shortcomings.

The "compromise" offered is to give Harvard 30 days to respond (implying but not stating that the SEVP decertification is suspended). There is nothing in the letter to persuade a neutral reader that Harvard has an actual opportunity to reverse the previous SEVP decertification decision. The letter looks like a ploy to distract the court. Or possibly to entice Harvard to give up gracefully, as suggested in the final paragraph: "your school has the option to voluntarily withdraw its SEVP certification by submitting a letter on official letterhead…."

Judge Burroughs wasn't persuaded that the DHS offer was meaningful. On May 29, at the end of a 20-minute hearing, she maintained the restraining order against the Department of Homeland Security and said that she intends to grant a preliminary injunction prohibiting the Trump administration from revoking Harvard's ability to have international students. Both Harvard and the Trump administration will submit proposals for a permanent injunction that would block DHS from immediately revoking the school's SEVP certification. Under the current TRO, Harvard will continue to be able to enroll international students.

Regardless of the TRO, DHS said it would continue to pursue the administrative avenue to revoke Harvard's SEVP certification.

Judge Burroughs suggested she would allow that administrative process to play out, with Harvard submitting evidence to rebut the allegations made by DHS that they allowed antisemitism on campus and failed to provide information on international students. Judge Burroughs explained:

> I do think an order is necessary. It doesn't need to be draconian, but I want to make sure nothing changes. I want to maintain the status quo. I would feel more comfortable given what has preceded this. It gives some protection to international students who are anxious about coming here.

Maybe. And for how long?

Trump Attacks Harvard's Accreditation

On July 9, whatever talks there were between Harvard and the Trump administration apparently broke down, as Trump officials launched a pair of surprise legal attacks, targeting both Harvard's international student community and its academic accreditation.

The Department of Homeland Security (DHS) issued administrative subpoenas demanding data about Harvard's international students, including "relevant records, communications and other documents relevant to the enforcement of immigration laws since Jan. 1, 2020." An administrative subpoena ordered by a bureaucrat lacks the force of a judicial subpoena ordered by a judge. DHS appears to be demanding more or less the same information it demanded earlier. DHS Secretary Kristi Noem postured that she was defending the interests of Harvard's students, without explaining how.

In a separate quasi-legal assault, the Departments of Education (DOE) and Health and Human Services (HHS) challenged Harvard's accreditation, claiming that the university had violated federal civil rights law. According to DOE Secretary Linda McMahon:

> By allowing antisemitic harassment and discrimination to persist unchecked on its campus, Harvard University has failed in its obligation to students, educators and American taxpayers. The Department of Education expects the New England Commission of Higher Education to enforce its policies and practices, and to keep the department fully informed of its efforts to ensure that Harvard is in compliance with federal law and accreditor standards.

This is little more than harassment of Harvard. The New England Commission has not found Harvard to be out of compliance. Even if the commission were to find against Harvard, which is unlikely, Harvard would have years to come into compliance before losing its accreditation.

At a hearing on July 23, a skeptical Judge Burroughs called the Trump administration's arguments "a little mind-boggling."

This is all part of the Trump administration's extra-legal effort to take control of American higher education, as DHS made clear in a statement: "Other universities and academic institutions that are asked to submit similar information should take note of Harvard's actions, and the repercussions, when considering whether or not to comply with similar requests."

Outrage Over Trump's Trip to Saudi Arabia

Political strategist Steve Schmidt is best known for his work on the campaigns of George W. Bush, Arnold Schwarzenegger, and John McCain, so he has plenty to regret. He now identifies as a Democrat. He helped start The Lincoln Project, a political action committee founded in December 2019 by moderate conservatives and former Republican Party members who oppose Trump and Trumpism. In his newsletter, The Warning, posted on Substack on May 13, Schmidt wrote:

> The images of Donald Trump's arrival in Saudi Arabia are disgraceful and without precedent. What the American people are witnessing is an "Eras" tour of corruption and crony capitalism that beggars belief and description, while being broadcast in the plain light of day.
>
> It is a death march and a celebration of decay, collapse, and the shattering of free market capitalism in favor of a new Trump gangsterism that picks winners and losers. Trump will be joined on his gilded journey by dozens of business leaders, including:
>
> Elon Musk, chief executive of Tesla and SpaceX
> Stephen A. Schwarzman, chief executive of the Blackstone Group
> Larry Fink, chief executive of BlackRock
> Arvind Krishna, chairman and chief executive of IBM
> Jane Fraser, chief executive of Citigroup
> Kelly Ortberg, chief executive of Boeing
> Ruth Porat, chief investment officer of Google
> Andy Jassy, chief executive of Amazon
> Sam Altman, chief executive of OpenAI
> Jensen Huang, chief executive of Nvidia
> Alex Karp, chief executive of Palantir
> Jeff Miller, chief executive of Halliburton
> Travis Kalanick, former chief executive of Uber and founder of Cloud Kitchens
> Kathy Warden, chief executive of Northrop Grumman
> James Quincey, chief executive of Coca-Cola

Dara Khosrowshahi, chief executive of Uber
Francis Suarez, mayor of Miami
Reid Hoffman, executive chairman of LinkedIn
Gianni Infantino, president of FIFA Patrick Soon-Shiong,
executive chairman of Immunity Bio and owner of The
Los Angeles Times

Trump is center stage and fully naked, starring in a type of corruption pornography to which the American fascist has no living peer. Trump has come to the Arab thugs, hat in one hand, with weapons systems dangling from the other, looking for more for Trump, while telling the American people that they must have less for America. When historians look back at this era, there will never be a lack of fascination over our anesthetized culture and indifferent population that was the frog in the pot for 10 long years before the water boiled....

America's politicians, billionaires, and CEOs have turned aggressive against the American people, the U.S. Constitution, free market capitalism, the rule of law, personal liberty, and democracy.... There has never been a worse lot of Americans who have ever gathered together with temporary power, and more profoundly betrayed the interests of the people who gave it to them in the entire history of America.

Who's Weaponizing Whom?

Trump chronically whines about Biden and others "weaponizing" government against him. This is more than just self-pity, though it is that. He might well have felt like government was weaponized against him as he faced multiple indictments and one conviction on 34 felony counts. But the cases were all fact-based, they all followed due process of law, and the justice system still failed to hold him to account for his actions. What he should be feeling is grateful.

He makes no substantive, evidence-based case to support his claim that Biden weaponized government. But the claim does another job rather well. By crying "weaponization" over and over, he diverts attention from the very real weaponization of government agencies currently going on under the Trump administration.

"It is Trump who is actually weaponizing the federal government against both his political enemies and countless other American citizens today," said retired federal judge J. Michael Luttig in a piece in The Atlantic. Luttig is a Republican and former general counsel for the Boeing Corp.

In his article, as summarized by Heather Cox Richardson:

> Luttig warned that Trump is trying to end the rule of law in the United States, recreating the sort of monarchy against which the nation's founders rebelled. [Among Trump's affronts to the law] he lists Trump's pardoning of the convicted January 6 rioters (which he did with the collusion of Ed Martin), the arrest of Judge Dugan, which Luttig calls 'appalling,' the deportation of a U.S. citizen with the child's mother, and the 'investigation' of private citizen Christopher Krebs.

Krebs is an attorney who served as head of the Cybersecurity and Infrastructure Security Agency during Trump's first term. After Trump started lying about how the 2020 election was stolen, Krebs stated officially that the 2020 election was the "most secure in American history."

Then Trump fired him.

In his article, Luttig stated unequivocally: "For not one of his signature initiatives during his first 100 days in office does Trump have the authority under the Constitution and laws of the United States that he claims."

Not for tariffs, not for unlawful deportations, not for attacks on colleges and law firms, not for his attacks on birthright citizenship, not for handing power to billionaire Elon Musk and the Department of Government Efficiency, not for trying to end due process, not for his attempts to starve government agencies by impounding their funding, not for his vow to regulate federal elections, not for his attacks on the media.

According to Judge Luttig, the courts are holding, and will continue to hold, but Trump "will continue his assault on America, its democracy, and rule of law until the American people finally rise up and say, 'No more.'"

Who will weaponize the people against their government?

Federal Courts Rule Against Trump Over 160 Times

According to The New York Times on May 18, "there are new lawsuits and fresh rulings emerging day and night.... [A]t least 160 of those rulings have at least temporarily paused some of the administration's initiatives." The lawsuits keep coming. Among those initiatives found illegal by the courts so far are:

> Firing government personnel
> Freezing budgets approved by Congress
> Cancelling birthright citizenship
> Creating DOGE without Congressional action
> Deporting immigrants without due process of law
> Infringing on the rights of transgender people
> Offering reparations to convicted January 6 rioters
> Challenging New York City's congestion pricing
> Denying climate change or global warming
> Destroying or falsifying public health data
> Barring reporters, lawyers, and others from public spaces
> Censoring the Federal Elections Commission
> Imposing tariffs without Congressional approval

Trump has responded angrily to various judicial orders. In March, he called for the impeachment of a federal judge who ruled against his deportation flights. This moved John Roberts, the usually passive Supreme Court Chief Justice, to offer a mild, implied rebuke in a public statement: "For more than two centuries, it has been established that impeachment is not an appropriate response to disagreement concerning a judicial decision. The normal appellate review process exists for that purpose."

Supreme Court Upholds Constitutional Right

On May 16, in an unsigned decision in the case of *A.A.R.P. v. Trump* (# 24A1007), the Supreme Court ruled 7-2 that immigration officials must give detainees due process of law before deporting them, as provided in the Constitution's Fifth and Fourteenth Amendments. The ruling blocked the administration from using the Alien Enemies Act, a 1798 wartime law, to deport a group of Venezuelan migrants, who argued they had a right to a fair opportunity to contest their deportation order. The migrants, being held in Texas, have had no hearings to determine their guilt or innocence.

The underlying case arose in Texas in mid-April when the government was preparing to deport Venezuelan migrants, apparently to El Salvador, without having provided any due process of law. The migrants sought an injunction to prevent their deportation. The injunction was denied by the federal district court and subsequently by the Fifth Circuit Court of Appeals, leading to the appeal to the Supreme Court.

The Government's view was draconian and unreasonable, as it argued that deporting the migrants as soon as the next day would be consistent with its due process obligations, and it reserved the right to take such action.

The Supreme Court slapped the government down, noting government bad faith in a different case: "Had the detainees been removed from the United States to the custody of a foreign sovereign on April 19 [the next day], the Government may have argued, as it has previously argued, that no U.S. court had jurisdiction to order relief."

This referred to the earlier case of Abrego Garcia, who, as the government acknowledged, had been deported in error, in violation of a lower court order. On appeal, the Supreme Court ruled 9-0 that the government had to "facilitate" Abrego Garcia's return to the U.S. Returning the case to the district court for further proceedings, the court noted distrustfully: "In the proceedings on remand, the District Court should continue to ensure that the Government lives up to its obligations to follow the law." Despite the Supreme Court's admonition, the government defied the court's order to facilitate Abrego Garcia's return and initiated a campaign to defame him with new, unsubstantiated accusations, while he is illegally held in an El Salvador gulag.

All Justices Agree: Due Process Is Required

The court's *A.A.R.P. v. Trump* opinion pointed out that:

> The Fifth Amendment entitles aliens to due process of law in the context of removal proceedings. Procedural due process rules are meant to protect against the mistaken or unjustified deprivation of life, liberty, or property. We have long held that no person shall be removed from the United States without opportunity, at some time, to be heard. Due process requires notice

that is reasonably calculated, under all the circumstances, to apprise interested parties and that afford[s] a reasonable time... to make [an] appearance.

The court continued:

> In J.G.G., this Court explained – with all nine Justices agreeing – that AEA [Alien Enemies Act] detainees must receive notice... that they are subject to removal under the Act... within a reasonable time and in such a manner as will allow them to actually seek habeas relief before removal. In order to actually seek habeas relief, a detainee must have sufficient time and information to reasonably be able to contact counsel, file a petition, and pursue appropriate relief. The Government does not contest before this Court the applicants' description of the notice afforded to AEA detainees in the Northern District of Texas, nor the assertion that the Government was poised to carry out removals imminently. The Government has represented elsewhere that it is unable to provide for the return of an individual deported in error to a prison in El Salvador, see *Abrego Garcia v. Noem*, where it is alleged that detainees face indefinite detention.... The detainees' interests at stake are accordingly particularly weighty. Under these circumstances, notice roughly 24 hours before removal, devoid of information about how to exercise due process rights to contest that removal, surely does not pass muster. But it is not optimal for this Court, far removed from the circumstances on the ground, to determine in the first instance the precise process necessary to satisfy the Constitution in this case. We remand the case to the Fifth Circuit for that purpose. To be clear, we decide today only that the detainees are entitled to more notice than was given on April 18, and we grant temporary injunctive relief to preserve our jurisdiction while the question of what notice is due is adjudicated.

Sadly, the court ducks the question of what would constitute sufficient notice to satisfy constitutional due process. It does not even suggest a minimum level of compliance. This leaves vast leeway for government bad faith, of which the court is keenly aware. Why leave the government more running room to defy the Constitution?

Court Leaves Fundamental Issues Unaddressed

The court's opinion continues:

> We did not on April 9 – and do not now – address the underlying merits of the parties' claims regarding the legality of removals under the AEA. We recognize the significance of the Government's national security interests as well as the necessity that such interests be pursued in a manner consistent with the Constitution. In light of the foregoing, lower courts should address AEA cases expeditiously.

Such is "the law's delay, the insolence of office" lamented by Hamlet. Trump's invocation of the Alien Enemies Act is lawless on its face. To invoke the act legitimately, the U.S. must be at war or be facing an invasion. There is no war. There is no apparent invasion. Trump will argue there's an "invasion" by the Venezuelan-backed gang Tren de Aragua, but U.S. intelligence agencies say that's not true. But for the Supreme Court, the issue is not ripe, and we must wait for the poisoned tree to deliver its fruit in a timely manner. Different federal courts have ruled differently on the AEA – three decided Trump's action was illegal, one didn't. So, it's on track for coming before the Supreme Court sooner or later.

The court's opinion concludes:

> The judgment of the Fifth Circuit is vacated, and the case is remanded to the Fifth Circuit…. The Government is enjoined from removing the named plaintiffs or putative class members in this action under the AEA pending order by the Fifth Circuit and disposition of the petition for a writ of certiorari…. The Government may remove the named plaintiffs or putative class members under other lawful authorities. It is so ordered.

The penultimate sentence looks like a loophole big enough to drive thousands of migrants through, unless the government acts within the legal confines of the Constitution. Any bets?

Dissenting from this opinion were Justices Sam Alito and Clarence

Thomas, arguing that the court didn't have the authority to weigh in at this stage.

Posting on Truth Social, Trump said the court's decision limiting his ability to deport immigrants without a court hearing represents "a bad and dangerous day for America." Invoking his standard, unsubstantiated trope about immigrants, Trump complained that: "The result of this decision will let more CRIMINALS pour into our Country, doing great harm to our cherished American public. The Supreme Court of the United States is not allowing me to do what I was elected to do."

Later, Trump posted falsely: "THE SUPREME COURT WON'T ALLOW US TO GET CRIMINALS OUT OF OUR COUNTRY!"

Actually, the Supreme Court will let him deport as many migrants as he wants, regardless of their guilt, so long as he follows due process and the rule of law. Does Trump really believe he was elected to run roughshod over the Constitution?

Abrego Garcia 'Freed' From El Salvador Gulag

The Trump administration spent months lying about its inability to secure the return of Kilmar Abrego Garcia, 29, illegally deported to El Salvador without a shred of due process. Trump people admitted that Albrego Garcia was supposed to be protected by an administrative judge's 2019 order preventing his deportation to his home country of El Salvador, where he was likely to be persecuted, tortured, or killed. The government did not appeal that ruling. Abrego Garcia was living in the U.S. legally.

Abrego Garcia is a Salvadoran national who entered the U.S. illegally in March 2012, when he was a teenager. He is married to a U.S. citizen and is the father of three children. Court documents indicate he is a union member who is employed full-time in Baltimore as a sheet metal apprentice and has been pursuing his own license at the University of Maryland.

In 2019, he was adjudged to be an MS-13 member, based on a confidential informant. He was later adjudged to be in danger of persecution if deported to El Salvador, and an immigration judge issued an order barring his deportation there. ICE did not appeal. Since 2019, Abrego Garcia has been fully compliant with the court order that he check in regularly with

ICE, as required.

In April 2025, DHS released his wife's 2021 request for a temporary protective order that was granted, but never finalized, as the parties settled out of court. DHS used the document to imply that Abrego Garcia was guilty of spousal abuse, an MS-13 gang member, and "not a sympathetic figure."

On April 18, DHS released a report and a press release describing a vehicle stop by a Tennessee Highway Patrol officer on December 1, 2022, alleging Abrego Garcia was speeding. According to DHS, none of the eight other people in the vehicle had luggage, while they listed the same home address as Abrego Garcia, and that he was traveling from Texas to Maryland, via Missouri, to bring in people to perform construction work. He said the vehicle belonged to his boss and that he worked in construction. According to DHS, the Tennessee Highway Patrol officer suspected him of human trafficking and took the names of the occupants. Abrego Garcia was never charged with a crime and the officer allowed him to drive on with only a warning about an expired driver's license. In December 2022, the Biden White House accused Abrego Garcia of human trafficking, based on his Tennessee traffic stop that resulted in no charges.

Based on this report, DHS spokesperson Tricia McLaughlin stated in her prejudicial press release:

> Kilmar Abrego Garcia is a MS-13 gang member, illegal alien from El Salvador, and suspected human trafficker. The facts reveal he was pulled over with eight individuals in a car on an admitted three-day journey from Texas to Maryland with no luggage. The facts speak for themselves, and they reek of human trafficking. The media's sympathetic narrative about this criminal illegal gang member has completely fallen apart. We hear far too much about the gang members and criminals' false sob stories and not enough about their victims.

Supreme Court Rules 9–0 to 'Facilitate' His Release

Trump people called Abrego Garcia's illegal deportation on March 15, 2025, an "administrative error." In a Supreme Court filing, the DHS admitted that his removal to El Salvador was "illegal." On April 4, a federal district court ordered the U.S. to "facilitate" Abrego Garcia's return. On April 10, the Supreme Court ruled 9-0 that the U.S. was obligated to "facilitate" Abrego Garcia's return.

The Trump administration defied the Supreme Court, saying it didn't understand what "facilitate" meant. And then they lied, claiming there was nothing they could do since he was in a foreign country. Attorney General Pam Bondi lied when she said of Abrego Garcia's return, "That's up to El Salvador, if they want to return him. That's not up to us."

Despite the Supreme Court ruling, the Trump administration spent almost three months doing nothing to "facilitate" Abrego Garcia's release. During that time, Trump and his functionaries spent a lot of time publicly trying to destroy Abrego Garcia's reputation – calling him a wife beater, human trafficker, gang member, and such, with little or no credible evidence. Trump even showed reporters a photograph purporting to be Abrego Garcia's hand with MS-13 tattoos on his knuckles – although "MS-13" clearly appeared to be photoshopped.

Previously, Bondi had said about Abrego Garcia: "He is not coming back to our country. There was no situation ever where he was going to stay in this country. None. None."

Suddenly It's Convenient to Return Abrego Garcia to the U.S.

On June 6, El Salvador returned Abrego Garcia to the United States. All it took was a phone call from the U.S. saying they had a warrant for his arrest and asking for his return. The U.S. immediately took him into custody. His release from a terrorist prison was little more than a cynical trap. The Trump administration had set him up for a show trial.

Also on June 6, concurrent with Abrego Garcia's return, Attorney General Pam Bondi held a press conference at which she sprang the trap. At this point, Abrego Garcia had not been allowed contact with his lawyers or family. Asked directly, Bondi did not say when the investigation of Abrego Garcia began, but she said the warrant was based on "recently found facts." She made a brief, politically loaded statement of decreasing credibility that went like this:

We're here today to announce an important update in an

important case. Abrego Garcia has landed in the United States to face justice.

On May 21, a grand jury in the middle district of Tennessee returned a sealed indictment charging Abrego Garcia with alien smuggling and conspiracy to commit alien smuggling in violation of Title 8. U.S. Code 1324…. This is what American justice looks like.

Upon completion of his sentence, we anticipate that he will be returned to his home country of El Salvador. The grand jury found that over the past nine years Abrego Garcia has played a significant role in an alien smuggling ring. They found this was his fulltime job, not a contractor. He was a smuggler of humans and children and women. He made over a hundred trips, the grand jury found, smuggling people throughout our country, MS-13 members, violent gang terrorist organization members, throughout our country. Thousands of illegal aliens were smuggled.

This is especially disturbing because Abrego Garcia is also alleged with transporting minor children. The defendant traded the innocence of minor children for profit. There are even more disturbing facts that the grand jury uncovered. It is alleged this defendant is part of the same smuggling ring responsible for the deaths of more than 50 migrants in 2021 after the tractor-trailer overturned in Mexico. This is part of that same ring.

The defendant abused undocumented alien females, according to co-conspirators, who were under his control while transporting them throughout our country. This defendant trafficked firearms and narcotics throughout our country on multiple occasions. They were using vehicles – SUVs – with added seats in the back, floors that had been ripped out, guns, narcotics, children, women, MS-13 members – that is what the grand jury found.

A co-conspirator alleged that the defendant solicited nude photographs and videos of a minor. A co-conspirator also alleges the defendant played a role in the murder of a rival gang member's mother. These facts demonstrated Abrego Garcia is a danger to our community.

Justice Department's Strict Rules on Prejudicial Comment

By speaking publicly about an accused individual, Bondi violated strict Justice Department guidelines created to ensure fair trials and avoid prejudicing legal proceedings. In particular, DOJ personnel are prohibited from making statements or releasing information that they know or reasonably should know would have a "substantial likelihood of materially prejudicing an adjudicative proceeding."

None of the reporters asked Bondi what would happen if Abrego Garcia is not convicted. Would he still be sent back to El Salvador? What are the odds?

Adding to pre-trial prejudice against an accused, on June 6, Trump told reporters that the Justice Department made a decision "to bring him back, show everybody how horrible this guy is." Trump added:

> He should've never had to be returned. Either way it's a total disaster – this is a pretty bad guy…. The man has a horrible past, and I can see a decision being made. I could see it either way, bringing him back or not bringing him back but bringing him back you can show how bad he is. He's a bad guy.

Also on June 6, DHS Secretary Kristi Noem took her own pre-trial prejudice to X, where she posted:

> For the past two months, the media and Democrats have burnt to the ground any last shred of credibility they had left by glorifying Kilmar Abrego Garcia – a known MS-13 gang member, human trafficker, and serial domestic abuser. Today, the United States of America confronts Kilmar Abrego Garcia with overwhelming evidence – he is being indicted by a grand jury for human smuggling, including children, and conspiracy. Justice awaits this Salvadoran man.

And in Nashville on June 6, Assistant United States Attorney Ben Schrader resigned, posting on social media:

Earlier today, after nearly 15 years as an Assistant United States Attorney, I resigned as Chief of the Criminal Division at the U.S. Attorney's Office for the Middle District of Tennessee. It has been an incredible privilege to serve as a prosecutor with the Department of Justice, where the only job description I've ever known is to do the right thing, in the right way, for the right reasons. I wish all of my colleagues at the U.S. Attorney's Office in Nashville and across the Department the best as they seek to do justice on behalf of the American people.

Schrader made no further public comment, but ABC News reported that sources said that "the decision to pursue the indictment against Abrego Garcia led to the abrupt departure of Ben Schrader, a high-ranking federal prosecutor in Tennessee. Schrader's resignation was prompted by concerns that the case was being pursued for political reasons." You think?

As Pam Bondi observed, "This is what American justice looks like."

On July 23, in a coordinated effort, judges in Tennessee and Maryland issued orders rejecting government orders and mocking government arguments. The orders thereby set Abrego Garcia free in his home state of Maryland, with conditions of release, at least for the time being. As Tennessee Judge Waverly Crenshaw wrote: the government failed to show that Abrego Garcia was a danger to others or the community.

Pope Snubs JD Vance After Inaugural Mass

In an interview on Fox News on January 29, recently converted Catholic JD Vance said:

There is a Christian concept that you love your family and then you love your neighbor, and then you love your community, and then you love your fellow citizens, and then after that, prioritize the rest of the world. A lot of the far left has completely inverted that.

This caused a stir, with significant pushback. The Gospel of Matthew, verse 44, quotes Jesus saying:

Love your enemies and pray for those who persecute you.... If you love those who love you, what reward will you get? Are not even the tax collectors doing that? And if you greet only your own people, what are you doing more than others? Do not even pagans do that?

Responding to Vance's Fox interview, Cardinal Robert Prevost posted on X: "JD Vance is wrong: Jesus doesn't ask us to rank our love for others."

Then the cardinal became Pope Leo XIV. Fast forward to May 18, 2025, when the Pope gave his inaugural mass at St. Peter's Cathedral, with Vance in attendance. In his sermon, Pope Leo condemned nationalism, environmental destruction, and cruelty toward migrants – pretty much the heart of Trump policy, with no names mentioned.

The Pope said:

> In this our time, we still see too much discord, too many wounds caused by hatred, violence, prejudice, the fear of difference, and an economic paradigm that exploits the Earth's resources and marginalizes the poorest. For our part, we want to be a small leaven of unity, communion, and fraternity within the world…. This is the path to follow together, among ourselves but also with our sister Christian churches, with those who follow other religious paths, with those who are searching for God, with all women and men of goodwill, in order to build a new world where peace reigns!

During the meet-and-greet after the mass, the Pope shook Vance's hand and spent 17 seconds with him. The Pope spent over 75 minutes in the receiving line and later met privately with others, including Ukraine's President Volodymyr Zelensky.

What's Going On With FEMA – Anything Good?

FEMA is the acronym for the Federal Emergency Management Agency. That name is curiously absent from the official FEMA website, managed by its parent agency, the Department of Homeland Security (DHS).

President Carter established FEMA by Executive Order 12127 in April 1979. Congress has expanded FEMA several times, providing clear direction for emergency management and disaster response. Congress designated the FEMA Administrator as the principal advisor to the President, the

Homeland Security Council, and the Secretary of Homeland Security for all matters relating to emergency management in the United States.

In 2018, Congress provided the agency with expanded authorities in the Disaster Recovery Reform Act. The legislation is a landmark law that highlights the federal government's commitment to increasing investments in mitigation and building the capabilities of state, local, tribal, and territorial partners. Under the Constitution, Trump is legally obligated to run FEMA as Congress intended – in the words of the Constitution, the president "shall take Care that the Laws be faithfully executed."

That's not what's happening in 2025. Since January, the Trump administration has been cutting or freezing FEMA funding, cutting over 2,000 FEMA personnel, and redefining FEMA's mission such that it's uncertain how effective FEMA can be.

There's unintended irony running all through this. Homeland Security is allowing the homeland to become increasingly insecure. FEMA has failed to respond to recent emergencies in 2025, such as tornadoes in May that killed at least 27 people in Missouri and Kentucky. Another two died in Virginia, where FEMA was also AWOL. And FEMA denied aid to Arkansas after it was hit by tornadoes. FEMA's absence before, during, and after weather disasters has become the new normal under DHS Director Kristi Noem, as per Trump policy.

Trump has called FEMA "a disaster" and said it might "go away" entirely, something of a self-fulfilling prophecy.

"I say you don't need FEMA, you need a good state government," Trump said while visiting the Los Angeles fires in January. "FEMA is a very expensive, in my opinion, mostly failed situation."

Emergency Management is a Management Emergency

Based on a January 20 memo from DHS, Trump officials illegally disbanded FEMA advisory councils critical to collecting unbiased, science-based analysis and recommendations on policies and programs. Each of the advisory councils was established by an act of Congress. Trump did not consult Congress before eliminating the following:

- The National Advisory Committee (NAC), established to help address needs and gaps in disaster assistance and planning. The Trump administration has taken previous NAC reports off the FEMA website (they are only available by email request).

■ The Technical Mapping Advisory Council (TMAC), established in 2012 to help improve and review FEMA's National Flood Insurance Program (NFIP) and incorporate climate change science to help communities plan for climate change-related impacts into the future.

■ The National Dam Safety Review Board, established in 1996 to help ensure that states are in federal compliance with safety standards. Dam failures can be deadly and are critical given the number of dams across the U.S. From January 2005 through June 2013, there were 173 dam failures and 587 episodes that would have become failures if not for state intervention.

In January, Trump appointed Cameron Hamilton as acting director of FEMA. Hamilton, a former Navy SEAL, had worked for five years as a supervisory emergency management specialist for the State Department. He also spent a couple of years overseeing 4,000 emergency medical technicians on the southern border for the Department of Homeland Security.

In 2006, Congress enacted the Post-Katrina Emergency Management Reform Act to ensure that future administrators demonstrate emergency management and homeland security knowledge and background, and have a minimum of five years of executive leadership and management experience in the public or private sector. Members of Congress have requested the Government Accountability Office to determine whether Cameron Hamilton legally meets these requirements.

Given all that, POLITICO predicted Hamilton's appointment would be a disaster, based on his posts on X:

> Besides promoting inaccurate criticisms of the agency he's now in charge of, Hamilton's many posts about politics, international affairs and national security included slams on diversity, equity and inclusion; his dismissal of Trump's hush-money conviction as a "sham"; an unflattering photograph of former U.S. health official Rachel Levine, who is transgender....

One post repeated misinformation that FEMA had diverted

$1 billion in disaster aid to help "illegals" entering the U.S. from Mexico. As FEMA itself notes, Congress gave the agency $1 billion specifically to help detained migrants.

According to Wonkette, Hamilton evolved in his new role at FEMA, "When he threatened to quit a couple of months ago over his clashes with the administration, senior staff even talked him out of it."

FEMA Head Takes Orders From Trump and Noem

On February 11, a FEMA official ordered a freeze on federal grant programs, and in March, FEMA blocked $10 million in disaster aid on the pretext of immigration concerns. The result is chaos with states and jurisdictions scrambling to recover or replace the funds they were promised.

On February 21, Trump fired 200 FEMA staff. By May 1, FEMA staff was down by about 2,000 workers. In 2022, the GAO and Congressional Research Service agreed FEMA was already understaffed by 35% or more.

On March 19, Trump signed an executive order calling for "State and local governments and individuals [to] play a more active and significant role in national resilience and preparedness," without addressing the contradiction in asking localities to address national needs. When it comes to handling catastrophic disasters, even larger states such as California don't have the same resources as the federal government. If Trump gets his way, disaster response and recovery will be more chaotic and ineffective, endangering more lives. The order called for agencies to study the issue.

On April 4, the Trump administration ended one of FEMA's most effective and popular grant programs, the Building Resilient Infrastructure and Communities (BRIC) program, which President Trump originally signed into law in 2018. The cancellation of BRIC leaves communities less prepared, even as disasters are mounting and as the Atlantic hurricane season approaches. For 2025, this puts $3.3 billion into jeopardy for projects across the U.S. that would help mitigate heat, wildfires, floods, and other extreme weather and natural hazards. On average, every $1 invested in federal mitigation grants saves $6 in avoided losses while also saving lives. FEMA mitigation projects save approximately $700 million annually.

On April 12, FEMA head Cameron Hamilton and 50 FEMA staff were given lie detector tests for allegedly leaking "national security information" after taking part in a meeting with top DHS officials. While Hamilton was cleared, some officials "failed" the polygraph test and were escorted out of the building, instilling a culture of fear at FEMA.

FEMA Head Tries to Defend FEMA, Sort Of

On May 7, in a Congressional hearing, Hamilton actually objected to plans to eliminate FEMA. He testified that he was pushing for changes to FEMA and was committed to finding ways that the agency could be more efficient and focus on priorities, even if he also wanted to reduce the scope of FEMA's mission. Hamilton was asked if he agreed with Noem and Trump that FEMA has failed the American people and needs to be eliminated. Hamilton answered:

> As the senior adviser to the president on disasters and emergency management and to the secretary of Homeland Security, I do not believe it is in the best interest of the American people to eliminate the Federal Emergency Management Agency....
>
> Having said that, I'm not in a position to make decisions and impact outcomes on whether or not a determination as consequential as that should be made. That is a conversation that should be had between the president of the United States and this governing body.

On May 8, DHS fired Hamilton without explanation. DHS replaced him with David Richardson, assistant secretary for the DHS Countering Weapons of Mass Destruction Office and a former Marine with zero experience in emergency management. On the day he was appointed, Richardson told staff in a phone call across the agency that he would "run right over" anyone who resists changes and that all decisions must now go through him:

> I, and I alone in FEMA, speak for FEMA. I'm here to carry out the president's intent for FEMA.... Obfuscation, delay, undermining. If you're one of those 20% of people and you think those tactics and techniques are going to help you, they will not, because I will run right over you.... I am as bent on achieving the president's intent as I was on making sure that I did my duty

when I took my Marines to Iraq.

FEMA became increasingly dysfunctional as hurricane season approached. This is not a good sign. The Trump administration has been denying help to more and more places hit by natural disasters. Mississippi is one of the latest. Trump thinks, according to his executive order, that states and localities, and even individuals, are best suited to cope with natural disasters. His thinking is supported by no facts and no cogent arguments. And he ignores the reality that in 1979, Congress created FEMA in the first place because individual states don't have the disaster relief infrastructure to handle the ever-larger natural disasters that keep hitting America. And they don't have the money to build that sort of infrastructure.

Trump's policy, which has no basis in factual argument or reasoned analysis, appears to be totally at odds with reality.

This was underlined on July 4, when disastrous flooding hit the Guadalupe River in central Texas. More than a hundred people died, with another 170 or so missing. Rescue workers from Mexico showed up almost at once. There was no FEMA presence for three days, prolonged by DHS Secretary Noem's failure to authorize funding promptly.

Trump's War on Reality Includes Weather

NOAA is the acronym for the National Oceanic and Atmospheric Administration, a scientific and regulatory agency within the Department of Commerce. NOAA is responsible for providing weather, climate, ocean, and coastal information as well as managing fisheries and other marine resources. NOAA's mission involves understanding and predicting changes in the Earth's environment, sharing knowledge, and conserving and managing coastal resources.

NOAA's workforce exceeded 12,000 worldwide in 2024. Trump's DOGE-inspired personnel cuts have illegally removed more than 1,000 people. Courts have reversed some dismissals. But experts and employees express concerns that the cuts could negatively impact NOAA's ability to forecast weather, track hurricanes, and provide warnings for public safety.

Trump is proposing to cut NOAA's annual budget by $1.7 billion, from $6.1 billion to $4.45 billion, as proposed by the Office of Management and Budget (OMB), whose director, Russell Vought, is an author of Project 2025. Among the programs targeted for reduction or elimination are climate research, oceanic and atmospheric research, tornado research, and ocean acidification research. The OMB's 922-page proposal calls for NOAA to "be broken up because it's one of the main drivers of the climate change alarm industry."

On April 8, Commerce Secretary Howard Lutnick cancelled almost $4 million in funding from NOAA to Princeton University. The decision was openly made based on climate change denial. This is how the Commerce press release described two of the programs defunded:

> Cooperative Institute for Modeling the Earth System I: This cooperative agreement promotes exaggerated and implausible climate threats, contributing to a phenomenon known as "climate anxiety," which has increased significantly among America's youth. Its focus on alarming climate scenarios fosters fear rather than rational, balanced discussion. Additionally, the use of federal funds to support these narratives, including educational initiatives aimed at K-12 students, is misaligned with the administration's priorities. NOAA will no longer fund these initiatives.
>
> Climate Risks & Interactive Sub-seasonal to Seasonal Predictability: This cooperative agreement suggests that the Earth will have a significant fluctuation in its water availability as a result of global warming. Using federal funds to perpetuate these narratives does not align with the priorities of this Administration and such time and resources can be better utilized elsewhere.

The National Weather Service (NWS) is a separate agency within NOAA. Its stated mission is to "Provide weather, water and climate data, forecasts, warnings, and impact-based decision support services for the protection of life and property and enhancement of the national economy." In simpler terms, NWS strives to provide reliable weather forecasts.

Trump has eliminated more than 550 of the weather service's 4,800 employees. Many of the nation's 122 local weather service forecast offices, typically staffed 24/7, are now shorthanded. NWS has eliminated or cut back on weather balloon releases. As the Scientific American observed on May 12:

> Ultimately, storm experts say, disruption caused by existing and proposed cuts will hit multiple fronts. An understaffed and underfunded NWS could mean that a tornado warning doesn't come in time, that a hurricane forecast is off just enough so that the wrong coastal areas are evacuated or that flights are less likely to be routed around turbulence.
>
> "The net result is going to be massive economic harm," said climate scientist Daniel Swain. "As we break these things, eventually it will become painfully and unignorably obvious what we've broken and how important it was. And it's going to be unbelievably expensive in the scramble to try and get it back – and we might not be able to get it back."

Why Did Trump's DOJ Charge a Congresswoman?

It's a long story. And annoyingly complicated. But essential to our reality. Article I, Section 6 of the Constitution states:

> The Senators and Representatives… shall in all Cases, except Treason, Felony and Breach of the Peace, be privileged from Arrest during their Attendance at the Session of their respective Houses, and in going to and returning from the same….

When it comes to ICE, lawful behavior is not always the rule. In this case, in Newark, New Jersey, there's an ICE detention facility that was under reconstruction by the country's second-largest private prison company, GEO Group, a top ICE contractor poised to profit from Trump's immigration crusade. The facility, known as Delaney Hall, had previously operated as an immigration detention center until 2017, when it closed and was converted into a drug treatment center and halfway house.

In 2021, New Jersey Governor Phil Murphy signed a law that barred public and private entities from entering contracts to house immigrant detainees. The move came after years of protests by immigrant advocates who called on Democratic leaders to sever their contracts with ICE, which housed immigrant detainees in county jails.

In February 2023, CoreCivic, America's largest private prison company, sued the state of New Jersey, challenging the law controlling detention centers. In April 2023, CoreCivic won a federal court judgment that it was unconstitutional for New Jersey to prohibit private immigration detention facilities. The Biden administration sided with CoreCivic. New Jersey appealed that ruling to the U.S. Third District Court of Appeals in September 2023 (case #23–2598, pending). At the time, CoreCivic ran New Jersey's only detention site, in Elizabeth, with about 300 beds.

On January 23, 2025, Newark made national headlines when ICE agents detained several undocumented workers and U.S. citizens, including a military veteran, at a warehouse in the city. The veteran showed his military ID but was still detained and questioned. Some citizens were fingerprinted and had photos of their faces and IDs taken. ICE agents reportedly blocked exits and banged on bathroom doors before questioning at least eight people and taking three into custody.

In response, Newark Mayor Ras Baraka said agents did not show the store owner a warrant, nor has ICE produced one. He argued that people can disagree on politics, but there shouldn't be disagreements about the U.S. Constitution and rights of due process. Baraka, a Democrat who ran for governor this year, said: "This egregious act is in plain violation of the Fourth Amendment of the U.S. Constitution. Newark will not stand by idly while people are being unlawfully terrorized."

Reportedly, New Jersey is home to more than 400,000 undocumented immigrants. Newark is about a 30-minute drive from New York City, where there are an estimated 400,000 more undocumented immigrants.

Baraka also condemned ICE plans to reopen Delaney Hall as "nothing short of lawlessness." Baraka said the city would not let the federal government trample on people's constitutional rights. Even after President Donald Trump threatened to prosecute city and state officials who resist immigration enforcement, Baraka vowed not to stand down: "They threaten democracy, they threaten us individually, they say they're going to arrest us if we stand up and uphold these rights. I'm not afraid of that, and if he thinks we're gonna just go to jail quietly, he's got another thing coming."

"Private detention facilities threaten the public health and safety of New Jerseyans, including when used for immigration purposes," said Michael Symons, a spokesman for Attorney General Matt Platkin.

ICE Signs Billion-Dollar Contract with GEO Group

On February 27, the Trump administration announced plans for its first new detention center to hold immigrants prior to deportation. ICE announced that it had awarded a $1.2 billion, 15-year contract to GEO Group to re-open the company-owned Delaney Hall in Newark to house roughly 1,000 immigrants at a cost of $60 million annually. Within hours, the company's stock price had risen by about 6%. GEO Group's support services include the exclusive use of the facility by ICE, along with security, maintenance, and food services, as well as access to recreational amenities, medical care, and legal counsel.

GEO Group CEO George Zoley told shareholders that the company anticipated that President Trump's mass-deportation agenda would lead to a massive increase in the number of ICE detention beds, to as many as 160,000 from the current 41,000 – along with a surge in deportation flights and electronic monitoring.

"We believe the scale of the opportunity before our company is unlike any we've previously experienced," Zoley said, adding that the company currently projects $2.42 billion in revenue, with the potential for another $1 billion from ICE deportation activity.

Zoley described Delaney Hall as "brand-new inside, and it's all ready to go. All we need to do is the recruitment, the hiring, the background screening, and the training."

GEO Group spent about $5 million upgrading Delaney Hall in 2024, after the Biden administration sought to expand ICE's detention capacity in the Newark area and issued a call for potential contractors. Delaney Hall is located in an industrial stretch of the city near Newark Liberty International Airport.

In early March 2025, prompted by ICE's plans for Newark, the New Jersey Attorney General's Office asked the Third Circuit Court of Appeals to finally hear the state's appeal, stressing that while the appeal is active, the state cannot enforce the 2021 law as it pertains to private companies. In hearings on May 1, 2025, the appellate judges appeared skeptical of CoreCivic's position.

Amy Torres, executive director for the New Jersey Alliance for Immigrant Justice, has criticized lawmakers for not acting sooner on the Trump administration's touted plans of mass deportation:

> I think what's really surprising here is not that the site is opening. It's that we've waited this long and still have done nothing.... The truth is, as soon as the first ruling was laid down, New Jersey should have gotten to acting on protecting immigrant communities, and they just, frankly, haven't.

Torres said critical protections could be put in place through the proposed Immigrant Trust Act, which has stalled in the statehouse since September 30, 2024. The bill would bar public schools, healthcare facilities, shelters, and libraries from collecting data on immigration status and codify bans on local law enforcement from working with federal immigration authorities.

At a March protest, Newark Mayor Ras Baraka vowed he'd "padlock" the facility if necessary to keep immigration detention out of the state's largest city. Like any other business in Newark, health and safety officials are obligated to inspect Delaney Hall and make sure it's up to code for its purpose, in this case, warehousing humans. And the mayor had reason to be concerned, as immigrants in ICE facilities have been dying in custody from a lack of medical care, and there have been reports from all over of horrors like ankle-deep sewage backups in cells and food shortages.

Newark Takes GEO Group to Court Over Permits

On April 1, Newark officials filed suit in state Superior Court in Essex County claiming that GEO Group was renovating the building without proper city permits and had barred city inspectors from accessing the building. The city alleged that without proper inspections, it could not know whether the building is safe to open.

GEO Group's attorneys alleged that city officials who came to inspect the site were told to coordinate with ICE, but the city refused to do so.

ICE has sole control over the facility's secure areas, and ICE required the city to make that appointment, the company said. The prison company also referenced Baraka's threat to "padlock" the building, claiming that the "conclusions and findings of any sham 'inspections' performed have already been clearly telegraphed" by the mayor. On a motion by GEO Group, the case (2:25-cv-02225) was moved to federal district court.

"There can be no question that ICE has an interest in Newark's attempts to force entry into a federal detention facility so that Newark can ostensibly conduct inspections of a federal facility under state and local codes," the filing states.

Eric Pennington, the city's business administrator, said Newark officials will work with the company to make sure that the facility complies with all city and state laws, rules, and regulations: "The city wants to ensure that the facility is safe for occupation by employees and proposed residents."

DOJ Announces Investigation of New Jersey Governor

On April 10, acting U.S. Attorney for New Jersey, Alina Habba, formerly Trump's personal attorney, announced on Fox News that her office was investigating Governor Phil Murphy and state Attorney General Matt Platkin for not cooperating with federal immigration authorities:

> I want it to be a warning for everybody: that I have instructed my office today to open an investigation into Gov. Murphy, to open an investigation into Attorney General Platkin, who has also instructed the State Police not to assist any of our federal … agencies that are under my direction.…
>
> [U.S. Attorney General] Pam Bondi has made it clear and so has our president that we are to take all criminal[s] - violent criminals and criminals – out of this country and to completely enforce federal law. And anybody who does get in that way, in the way of what we are doing, which is not political, it is simply against crime, will be charged in the state of New Jersey for obstruction, for concealment, and I will come after them hard.

This investigation appears to be part of the Trump administration's political response to those who oppose the administration's devastatingly lawless assault on immigrants and citizens, in violation of constitutional protections of due process of law.

On April 8, State Police Superintendent Col. Patrick Callahan issued a memo that reminded New Jersey law enforcement that the state's 2018 Immigrant Trust Directive limits state and local law enforcement cooperation with federal immigration authorities. Under the directive, state and local police cannot participate in federal immigration enforcement operations or keep someone detained only to comply with a civil immigration detainer request. The directive includes exemptions if the immigrant is charged with or convicted of a "violent or serious offense" or subject to a final order of removal by a judge.

New Jersey Attorney General Platkin has made clear that the Immigrant Trust Directive is "settled law" and has been "upheld by judges appointed by President Trump." In 2021, the Third U.S. Circuit Court of Appeals upheld a lower court's decision that the directive was not preempted by federal law.

On May 1, GEO Group began housing ICE detainees at Delaney Hall.

Newark Mayor Pressures ICE on Permits

On May 4 and May 5, the Newark mayor showed up at Delaney Hall with city fire officials to enforce city permits. The mayor has no legal authority to access the site without permission. ICE agents refused to let the city officials in, claiming they were violating protocols. On each visit, city fire officials issued tickets for code violations. GEO Group claims it has valid permits, but the issue remained in court, unresolved.

On May 5, NorthJersey.com reported that ICE had reopened Delaney Hall "and is holding detainees, despite a pending suit about compliance with permits, certificate of occupancy, and inspection."

Mayor Baraka slammed the GEO Group, saying it had put detainees in the facility in recent days, despite the city's suit saying the company has failed to file required permits for construction and continued occupancy and has not allowed inspectors into the facility: "They are following the pattern of the president of the United States, who believes that he can just do what he wants to do and obscure the laws – national and constitutional laws – and they think they can do the same thing in the state of New Jersey and in Newark."

GEO Group spokesperson Christopher Ferreira said Delaney Hall has a valid certificate of occupancy issued by Newark and complies with health and safety requirements. He added that the attempt by the mayor's office to stop the facility from opening was a political campaign to keep the federal government from arresting, detaining, and deporting criminal immigrants. His claim of legality was offered with no supporting evidence.

According to Ferreira:

> Delaney Hall's reactivation as a federal immigration processing center has created hundreds of unionized jobs, with an average annual salary of $105,000, and is expected to contribute $50 million to the local Newark economy. The politicized actions of local and state officials put these benefits, as well as the safety of the community, in jeopardy and are a disservice to their constituents who live in the local community and work at the facility.

Feds Arrest Mayor for 'Trespassing'

On May 9, Mayor Baraka showed up at Delaney Hall. ICE agents denied him entry, and he left to take one of his children to school. Hours later, Baraka returned to take part in a news conference planned with three members of Congress after they had toured Delancy Hall. A security guard opened Delaney Hall's locked front gate and allowed Baraka to enter, but barred him from joining the congressional representatives inside. He and several aides waited for more than an hour inside the perimeter of the detention center before he was asked to leave. By then, he had been joined by three members of Congress from New Jersey: Rep. LaMonica McIver (D-NJ), Rep. Rob Menendez Jr. (D-NJ), and Rep. Bonnie Watson Coleman (D-NJ).

Earlier, Watson Coleman had posted on X from the front gate of Delaney Hall: "We're at Delaney Hall, an ICE prison in Newark that opened without permission from the city & in violation of local ordinances. We've heard stories of what it's like in other ICE prisons. We're exercising our oversight authority to see for ourselves."

Members of Congress are entitled to inspect federal facilities without prior notice, as part of their oversight responsibility. The representatives were eventually allowed inside, but only after a chaotic scrum initiated by ICE. As video shows, they were met by a disorganized, armed horde of presumed ICE agents, some of them masked. None can be seen showing identification or behaving in a calm or mannerly way.

ICE agents asked Baraka to leave. Video shows him leaving peacefully, going outside the gate, no longer trespassing. More than a dozen ICE agents followed Baraka through the gate, intending to arrest him. "It's not entirely clear from the publicly released footage what happened next, and the government has consistently lied about it," according to legal journalist Liz Dye on Substack.

Feds Lie About May 9 Events From the Start

Even as events were unfolding at Delaney Hall, DHS Assistant Secretary Tricia McLaughlin put out an utterly false press release claiming imaginary events:

> Today, as a bus of detainees was entering the security gate of Delaney Hall Detention Center, a group of protesters, including two members of the U.S. House of Representatives, stormed the gate and broke into the detention facility. Representatives Robert Menendez, Jr. and Bonnie Watson Coleman and multiple protesters are holed up in a guard shack, the first security check point.
>
> Members of Congress storming into a detention facility goes beyond a bizarre political stunt and puts the safety of our law enforcement agents and detainees at risk. Members of Congress are not above the law and cannot illegally break into detention facilities. Had these members requested a tour, we would have facilitated a tour of the facility. This is an evolving situation.

The available video does not support the DHS claims. There is no evidence of any bus or any other vehicle. There is no evidence of any Congress members who "stormed the gate" or of any guard shack.

Video shows Baraka being freely let in through the gate, and then let out again. Once outside, Rep. Menendez warned Baraka that ICE agents were coming out to arrest him. Video shows Baraka responding, "I'm not on their property. They can't come out on the street and arrest me."

Then, ICE agents swarmed him, trying to arrest him, even though he was outside the gate. At first, he was protected by a circle of people around him, including Congress members. Rep. Watson Coleman told MSNBC: "We weren't trying to start anything. We weren't trying to do anything. We were trying to protect the mayor from what we thought was an unlawful arrest." ICE agents aggressively manhandled Rep. McIver, Rep. Watson Coleman, and others. Masked ICE agents wearing military fatigues eventually arrested Baraka for trespassing, handcuffed him, and led him away.

At a news conference shortly after the arrest, Rep. Menendez criticized ICE agents: "They feel no restraint on what they should be doing, and that was shown in broad daylight today."

Video supports that as well as what Rep. Watson Coleman said on CNN: "Nothing happened other than the chaos that they created themselves. If anything, we were pushed and shoved, and found in a very vulnerable situation, for the three of us."

Congress Members Reject ICE Version of Events

Rep. Watson Coleman commented that, "What we see here is despicable, and we should all be angry." Later, in a post on X, she uploaded a video showing the congressional delegation peacefully entering the facility, guided by ICE, after the arrest of the mayor, and said:

> Since DHS has been lying about this, allow me to correct the record. This scuffle, during which an ICE agent physically shoved me, occurred after we had entered the Delaney Hall premises. We entered the facility, came back out to speak to the mayor, and then ICE agents began shoving us. This is not how we entered the facility. We were escorted in by guards, because we have lawful oversight authority to be there.
>
> The scuffle at the gate happened after, when we came back out, and ICE moved to arrest the mayor on public property. How did we "break in" when we were already allowed inside? The idea we "stormed" a heavily guarded federal detention

center is absurd – just more lies from the most dishonest administration in history.

Rep. Menendez posted on X: "No matter what this administration tells the American people, the law is very clear: members of Congress have a legal right to enter any DHS detention facility to conduct oversight without prior notice – something I've done twice this year without issue."

He also posted the law, Public Law 118-47, which says in part:

> None of the funds appropriated or otherwise made available to the Department of Homeland Security by this Act may be used to prevent any of the following persons from entering, for the purpose of conducting oversight, any facility operated by or for the Department of Homeland Security used to detain or otherwise house aliens....
>
> A Member of Congress.... Nothing in this section may be construed to require a Member of Congress to provide prior notice of the intent to enter a facility described in subsection (a) for the purpose of conducting oversight.

After arresting Baraka on public property, ICE agents took him to a separate federal ICE facility in Newark. The DOJ filed a criminal complaint charging Baraka with trespassing. He was fingerprinted and had his mug shot taken. He was held for about five hours, until a federal magistrate judge ordered him released in a virtual proceeding. He pleaded not guilty. Baraka was greeted by a crowd that had grown throughout the afternoon to more than 200 supporters, including candidates for New York City mayor and prominent labor leaders.

On his release, Baraka told supporters, "What's happening now in this country, everybody should be scared of. They're using the courts. They're using everything else to justify what they're doing."

New Jersey's interim U.S. attorney, Alina Habba, falsely stated that Baraka had been arrested because he had "ignored multiple warnings from Homeland Security Investigations (HSI) to remove himself" and had chosen "to disregard the law." Video contradicts this assertion. Video shows ICE agents manhandling Baraka, who doesn't resist. Video shows Baraka in a public area, outside the ICE facility fence.

Feds Threaten to Arrest Congress Members

On May 10, the day after the Delaney Hall fracas, DHS threatened to arrest the three Congress members – Representatives Bonnie Watson Coleman, Rob Menendez, and LaMonica McIver of New Jersey – on assault charges for their actions during the arrest of Mayor Baraka.

As described by The New York Times, in somewhat absurdly measured language:

> Baraka was arrested by the head of Homeland Security Investigations in a brief but volatile clash that involved a team of masked federal agents wearing military fatigues and the three lawmakers…. Precisely what led to Baraka's arrest on federal trespassing charges, in a public area outside a facility that is owned by a private prison company, remains unclear. But much of what unfolded was recorded by journalists, as well as by cameras worn by law enforcement officials and videos taken by activists protesting nearby…. But videos the Trump administration released to Fox News appeared to be far from conclusive, and accounts of the confrontation from witnesses and the members of Congress differ in significant ways from the government narrative.

At a news conference, Baraka continued to push back against the government's version of events the day before: "This is all fabrication. They get on the media and they lie and lie and lie and lie."

On May 14, Homeland Security continued to lie about the events of May 9. DHS Secretary Noem testified with calm dishonesty and demagoguery. She claimed, in part, echoing an earlier DHS press release, that:

> What happened on May 9 at Delaney Hall was not oversight. It was a political stunt that put the safety of our law enforcement agents, our staff, and our detainees at risk. Here are the facts. As a vehicle approached the security [inaudible] at Delaney Hall detention center, a mob of protesters including three members of Congress stormed the gates and they trespassed into the detention facility….

On May 15, Mayor Baraka appeared in federal court on his trespassing charge. Once again, he was fingerprinted and had his mug shot taken. The hearing was brief, setting a schedule that would lead to a trial in July. Interim U.S. Attorney for New Jersey Alina Habba attended the hearing but did not speak. On leaving the courthouse, Habba was jeered by dozens of Baraka supporters.

On May 16, Newark officials came to Delaney Hall for an inspection. Three were admitted, but the inspection was cancelled when ICE refused to let three other officials in because ICE hadn't received their names in advance.

On May 19, ICE again allowed some Newark city inspectors into Delaney Hall. But ICE denied access to the city's fire official and deputy public safety director, without offering an explanation, even though they had received permission on May 16.

As reported by NJ.com, city officials declined to say what the inspectors found during their hour-long tour. City officials said four construction code officers and two health inspectors entered the facility just after 7 a.m. on Monday. Monday's walk-through of the building was a follow-up on a previous inspection, in which the city said it found various violations, including a lack of an evacuation plan. The city claims GEO Group is operating without a valid certificate of occupancy and failing to apply for a city business license. ICE continues to claim that it is in full compliance with all permit requirements.

DOJ Charges Rep. McIver With Assault

On May 19, interim U.S. Attorney Habba tweeted on X, sharing a press release from her office that said, in part:

> After extensive consideration, we have agreed to dismiss Mayor Baraka's misdemeanor charge of trespass for the sake of going forward. In the spirit of public interest, I have invited the mayor to tour Delaney Hall. The government has nothing to hide at this facility, and I will personally accompany the mayor so he can see that firsthand.... The dismissal against the mayor does not end this matter....

Hubba's May 19 tweet on X also presented a surprise announcement:

"Today my office has charged Congresswoman McIver with violation of Title 18, United States Code, Section 111(a)(1) for assaulting, impeding and interfering with law enforcement." This tweet served as Rep. McIver's first notice of the charges. Hubba's press release in the tweet stated:

> Congressional oversight is an important constitutional function and one that I fully support. However, that is not the issue in this case.
>
> Representative LaMonica McIver assaulted, impeded, and interfered with law enforcement in violation of Title 18, United States Code, Section 111(a)(1). That conduct cannot be overlooked by the chief federal law enforcement official in the State of New Jersey, and it is my Constitutional obligation to ensure that our federal law enforcement is protected when executing their duties. I have personally made efforts to address these issues without bringing criminal charges and have given Representative McIver every opportunity to come to a resolution, but she had unfortunately declined.
>
> No one is above the law – politicians or otherwise. It is the job of this office to uphold justice impartially, regardless of who you are. Now we will let the justice system work.

DOJ Pile-On Follows ICE Pile-on

Legal journalist Liz Dye on Substack had a jaundiced view of this process:

> Normal prosecutors are not in the business of "addressing issues" through extra-legal remedies. But a normal prosecutor who was serving in an interim capacity and hadn't even been nominated for Senate confirmation wouldn't scream out a press release touting herself as "the chief federal law enforcement official in the State of New Jersey...."
>
> Like every other lawyer in Trumpland, Habba is a caricature of incompetence. She came to the president's attention by making a sexual harassment suit disappear at the president's New Jersey golf club. But the way she did it was by sidling up to a 21-year-old waitress at the breakfast bar and convincing her

to fire her lawyer and then sign away her rights for $15,000 in a wildly illegal settlement agreement.

Habba quickly became Trump's go-to lawyer. Habba represented Trump in a civil fraud suit, where he and his company were ordered to disgorge $354 million in ill-gotten gains. Habba also represented Trump in both defamation cases brought by advice columnist E. Jean Carroll, where juries found him liable for $88 million in damages. Along the way she made time to sue Hillary Clinton, James Comey, and half of DC on Trump's behalf, racking up another $1 million in fines and legal fees for filing such a frivolous piece of garbage.

Also on May 19, the DOJ filed a criminal complaint against McIver, charging her with two counts of assaulting, resisting, and impeding federal officers.

The complaint consists of a declaration by DHS Special Agent Robert Tansey attesting that the congresswoman "slammed her forearm into the body" of an ICE agent, "forcibly grabbing him," and "used each of her forearms to forcibly strike" another agent. But even this sworn declaration contains obvious false statements, clearly disproven by the bodycam footage ICE released to the media. The offense can be either a misdemeanor or a felony, depending on the severity of the behavior, but the complaint does not specify what it is.

McIver is represented by former U.S. Attorney for New Jersey Paul Fishman (2009-2017), who called the decision to charge her "spectacularly inappropriate." He told NBC News:

> She went to Delaney Hall to do her job. As a member of Congress, she has the right and responsibility to see how ICE is treating detainees. Rather than facilitating that inspection, ICE agents chose to escalate what should have been a peaceful situation into chaos. This prosecution is an attempt to shift the blame for ICE's behavior to Congresswoman McIver.

This echoed McIver's statement on the charges:

> Earlier this month, I joined my colleagues to inspect the treatment of ICE detainees at Delaney Hall in my district. We were

fulfilling our lawful oversight responsibilities, as members of Congress have done many times before, and our visit should have been peaceful and short. Instead, ICE agents created an unnecessary and unsafe confrontation when they chose to arrest Mayor Baraka. The charges against me are purely political – they mischaracterize and distort my actions, and are meant to criminalize and deter legislative oversight. This administration will never stop me from working for the people in our district and standing up for what is right. I am thankful for the outpouring of support I have received, and I look forward to the truth being laid out clearly in court.

Habba's Professional Ethics Challenged

Habba's assertive use of press releases and online postings appears to be a form of trial by media. It also appears to violate professional conduct rules of the Justice Department, which state that:

> DOJ personnel shall not make any statement or disclose any information that reasonably could have a substantial likelihood of materially prejudicing an adjudicative proceeding... [including] statements concerning anticipated evidence or argument in the case."

Habba's public posturing also appears to violate New Jersey's Rules of Professional Conduct for lawyers, which bar attorneys from:

> [offering] any opinion as to the guilt or innocence of a defendant or suspect in a criminal case or proceeding that could result in incarceration... [or even] the fact that a defendant has been charged with a crime, unless there is included therein a statement explaining that the charge is merely an accusation and that the defendant is presumed innocent until and unless proven guilty.

The rules also impose an additional obligation on prosecutors to "refrain from making extrajudicial comments that have a substantial likelihood of heightening public condemnation of the accused."

The House Democratic Leadership responded immediately on May 19 with a statement of support for Rep. McIver that said in part:

> The criminal charge against Congresswoman LaMonica McIver is extreme, morally bankrupt and lacks any basis in law or fact. Members of Congress have a constitutional responsibility to conduct oversight of the executive branch wherever and whenever it is needed. We are lawfully permitted to show up at any federal facility unannounced to conduct an inspection on behalf of the American people. By visiting the detention center in Newark, Rep. McIver and two other Members of Congress were upholding their oath of office. They didn't assault anyone, but were themselves aggressively mistreated by illegally masked individuals.
>
> Shortly after the alleged altercation took place, administration officials escorted Congressmembers LaMonica McIver, Bonnie Watson Coleman and Rob Menendez on a tour of the detention center that lasted approximately an hour. There is no credible evidence that Rep. McIver engaged in any criminal activity, and she would not have been permitted to tour the facility had she done anything wrong.
>
> The proceeding initiated by the so-called U.S. Attorney in New Jersey is a blatant attempt by the Trump administration to intimidate Congress…. Everyone responsible for this illegitimate abuse of power is going to be held accountable for their actions. An attack on one of us is an attack on the American people. House Democrats will respond vigorously in the days to come at a time, place and manner of our choosing.

On May 21, Rep. McIver appeared virtually from Washington for a hearing before a federal court in Newark. She was read her rights and released on her own recognizance. She was allowed to travel domestically and internationally if needed for her congressional duties, the judge said.

In a separate hearing on May 21, the U.S. Attorney's office formally dropped trespassing charges against Baraka, nearly two weeks after he was charged. Prosecutors said they recommended dropping the charges this week after reviewing the facts of the case, saying the move is in the best interest of justice. Magistrate Judge Andre Espinosa scolded the U.S. Attorney's Office for hastily charging Baraka to begin with. The judge called the change of course an embarrassing retraction:

> The apparent rush in this case, culminating today in the embarrassing retraction of charges, suggests a failure to adequately investigate, to carefully gather facts and to thoughtfully consider the implications of your actions before wielding your immense power. Your office must operate with a higher standard than that.

Rep. McIver May Go to Trial in Summer

We don't yet know how serious these events will become. Attorney Joyce Vance, a former U.S. attorney for the Northern District of Alabama, voiced serious concerns on May 22 on Substack:

> It's hard to imagine a conviction here. The Congresswoman was engaged in statutorily and constitutionally protected congressional oversight work. The agents were in the wrong for interfering with her. In fact, given her federal status, they could just as easily have been charged for assaulting her under the statute (although they would enjoy qualified immunity). The case is likely to be dismissed by a judge in the preliminary stages.
>
> Even if the case were to go to trial, it's hard to imagine a unanimous jury verdict on these facts. The government bears the burden of proof beyond a reasonable doubt. But this sort of prosecution by the federal government achieves an entirely different goal, one reminiscent of the charges against Wisconsin Judge Hannah Dugan. This is how autocrats discourage people from getting out of line. It's how they chill dissent. It's another step on the path toward autocracy.
>
> The Trump Justice Department is breaking down norms at record speed, trying to normalize political prosecutions. They are the ones weaponizing the criminal justice system…. The Nazis used tactics like this to quiet dissent, as, of course, have many other dictators in varying degrees. Attack the judges,

attack the legislature, silence the opposition. We are on a dangerous path.... It's going to take all of us to keep the Republic.

It's not subtle. The Trump administration is approaching the republic with wrecking balls across the board. One of Trump's willing co-conspirators is Attorney General Pam Bondi, who poses as Trump's lawyer and whose commitment to the rule of law is invisible. Working in the DOJ is attorney Ed Martin, who was too toxic even for Republicans to succeed with his nomination to be U.S. attorney for the District of Columbia. That job went to Jeanine Pirro. As a consolation, Bondi named Martin assistant deputy attorney general with two positions in the DOJ: pardon attorney and head of the Weaponization Working Group. The politicization of pardons is well established. The Weaponization Group is tasked with investigating alleged weaponization of the Justice Department under Biden. Ed Martin calls himself the "Weaponization Czar." The way he describes his work, it sounds like everything that happened in Newark in May:

> There are some really bad actors, some people that did some really bad things to the American people. And if they can be charged, we'll charge them. But if they can't be charged, we will name them. And we will name them, and in a culture that respects shame, they should be people that are ashamed. And that's a fact. That's the way things work. And so that's, that's how I believe the job operates.

This is not good. And we don't know where it ends, or how it ends. For those of us old enough to remember how bleak it seemed in 1968, particularly during the Chicago police riot at the Democratic convention, it's so much bleaker now. At least then we had Chicago Mayor Richard Daley telling us, with a truthful malapropism: "The police are not here to create disorder, the police are here to preserve disorder." Back then, it seemed funny.

On June 10, acting U.S. Attorney Habba announced the indictment of the Congress member she had already charged on May 19. Habba posted on X:

> Today a federal grand jury seated in Newark, New Jersey, returned a three-count indictment charging U.S. Representative LaMonica McIver with forcibly impeding and interfering with

federal law enforcement officers. This indictment has a maximum penalty of 8 years for Count One, an additional maximum penalty of 8 years for Count Two, and a maximum penalty of 1 year in prison for Count Three.

There is nothing new about the indictment except that it lists three charges instead of the original two. The facts remain the same. On May 9, ICE agents initiated a pushing and shoving scrum to arrest the Newark mayor on public property. Rep. McIver and others surrounded the mayor to protect him. After more ICE-driven pushing and shoving, the mayor surrendered peacefully. McIver was on the scene in her official capacity, exercising her legal authority to inspect an ICE facility. Trump officials started lying about the event while it was still in progress, and have lied about it ever since. It took Habba 10 days to decide on the first charges, based on ambiguous and inconclusive video evidence taken from several angles. The evidence hasn't improved. Who needs evidence for a political trial? The point is the intimidation.

As Trump commented dishonestly to ABC News on May 20, after the initial charges were brought: "I have no idea who she is. That woman was out of control. She was shoving federal agents. She was out of control. The days of that crap are over in this country. We're going to have law and order."

ICE has issued new "regulations" requiring Congress members to schedule oversight visits in advance. This is not supported by law or the Constitution.

Rep. McIver has pleaded not guilty. Her trial was set for November 2025.

Mayor Baraka has filed a lawsuit against interim U.S. Attorney Habba for malicious prosecution and false arrest stemming from the events of May 9. Baraka also sued Habba for defamation over falsehoods she posted online. Baraka, who is Black, commented on the role of race in his arrest:

> To arrest me, to handcuff me, to drag me away, to take my fingerprints and a picture and mugshots for a class-C misdemeanor is egregious. For me to appear in a hearing and after the hearing, for the U.S. Marshals to rush in and basically to take my picture again is egregious and malicious in my mind It's easy for people to believe that a mayor being arrested,

especially a mayor that looks like me, has been arrested for something other than what just happened ... When people see me in cuffs, they automatically believe I did something wrong, I was guilty. The reality is, I didn't do anything.

Health and Human Services Suffer Under Kennedy

On January 29 and 30, 2025, Robert F. Kennedy, Jr., faced contentious Senate hearings before being confirmed as secretary of the Department of Health and Human Services (HHS) by a 52-48 vote on February 13. He was opposed by all Democrats and Republican Mitch McConnell, a childhood polio survivor and strong supporter of vaccines. McConnel wrote that:

> [HHS] deserves a leader who is willing to acknowledge without qualification the efficacy of life-saving vaccines and who can demonstrate an understanding of basic elements of the U.S. healthcare system. Mr. Kennedy failed to prove he is the best possible person to lead America's largest health agency. As he takes office, I sincerely hope Mr. Kennedy will choose not to sow further doubt and division but to restore trust in our public health institutions.

Sen. Ron Wyden (D-OR) expressed concern over Kennedy's inexperience with government healthcare programs:

> During his confirmation hearing on everything from abortion to vaccines to Medicare and Medicaid, Mr. Kennedy was given ample opportunity to go on the record about how he would improve these programs, bring down costs, save taxpayers money and improve care. Instead, he showed a complete lack of understanding of the basics on Medicaid and how it functions. I personally believe it shouldn't be too much to ask for the future CEO of Medicaid to understand how important it is to provide affordable coverage to millions of families. Republicans, with Donald Trump at the helm, are steering our country toward a healthcare cliff. Their ultimate objective is to take away Medicaid from as many people as they can.

On February 14, Kennedy took office as the 26th secretary of HHS, which was created in 1953. When Kennedy took over, it had 28 divisions and 82,000 employees. Its budget for fiscal year 2024 was $1.72 trillion (almost a quarter of federal spending). The HHS budget for 2025 is $1.8 trillion. In May, HHS proposed a 2026 budget reduced to $94.7 billion. On February 28, Kennedy streamlined decision-making at HHS by eliminating rules that required public notice and allowed for public comment.

On March 11, Kennedy falsely claimed that the measles vaccine "does cause deaths every year...." According to the Infectious Diseases Society of America, no deaths have been found to be related to the measles, mumps, and rubella vaccine among healthy people.

Cuts in HHS Programs Threaten Nation's Health

On March 25, HHS announced that the Centers for Disease Control was pulling back $11.4 billion in grants previously allocated to state and community health departments, nongovernmental organizations, and foreign recipients. The grants had been made in response to the COVID-19 pandemic, which HHS says is now over.

On March 27, in a press release, HHS announced a 25% reduction in staff, cutting 20,000 workers, reducing the agency's workforce to 62,000. HHS also announced plans to reduce its 28 divisions to 15 and to eliminate 5 of its 10 regional offices. HHS announced some specific reductions:

- Food and Drug Administration (FDA) will lose 3,500 employees;
- Centers for Disease Control (CDC) will lose 2,400 employees;
- National Institutes of Health (NIH) will lose 1,200 employees;
- Centers for Medicare and Medicaid Services (CMS) will lose 300 employees.

Dr. Georges Benjamin, head of the American Public Health Association, objected to HHS restructuring, saying it would not improve health in the country: "This is a nonsensical rearrangement of the agencies under their charge and an excuse to devastate the workforce for financial reasons. It will increase the morbidity and mortality of our population, increase health costs and undermine our economy."

On March 28, Dr. Peter Marks – the Food and Drug Administration's top vaccine official and head of the Center for Biologics Evaluation and

Research at the FDA – submitted his resignation after being forced to either resign or be fired after 13 years, according to the Wall Street Journal. In his two-page resignation letter, Marks attacked Kennedy's intellectual integrity, writing:

> Undermining confidence in well-established vaccines that have met the high standards for quality, safety, and effectiveness that have been in place for decades at FDA is irresponsible, detrimental to public health, and a clear danger to our nation's health, safety, and security....
>
> As you are aware, I was willing to work to address the Secretary's concerns regarding vaccine safety and transparency by hearing from the public and implementing a variety of different public meetings and engagements with the National Academy of Sciences, Engineering, and Medicine. However, it has become clear that truth and transparency are not desired by the Secretary, but rather he wishes subservient confirmation of his misinformation and lies
>
> My hope is that during the coming years, the unprecedented assault on scientific truth that has adversely impacted public health in our nation comes to an end so that the citizens of our country can fully benefit from the breadth of advances in medical science.

Sixteen States Sue HHS in Federal Court

On April 4, Massachusetts and 15 other states joined in a federal lawsuit (#1:25-cv-10814) against Kennedy, HHS, and its sub-agencies, challenging Kennedy's treatment of the National Institutes of Health (NIH) in an 82-page filing arguing in part:

> The National Institutes of Health (NIH) is a federal agency responsible for conducting and supporting biomedical research. Widely acknowledged as a "crown jewel" of America's scientific institutions – a characterization the agency's director recently reiterated – NIH is the largest public funder of medical research in the world.

NIH has "a long and illustrious history [of] supporting breakthroughs in biology and medicine." NIH scientists pioneered the rubella vaccine, eradicating a disease that, in the 1960s, killed thousands of babies and left thousands more with lifelong disabilities. NIH studies led to the discovery of the BRCA mutation, helping countless Americans reduce their risk of breast and ovarian cancer. NIH research fueled the development of treatments for HIV and AIDS, transforming what used to be a fatal disease into one with a nearly normal life expectancy. These are just a few of many, many examples: over the years, NIH-supported research has had a profound impact on the health and wellbeing of the American people. Indeed, it is hard to find a medical breakthrough in recent years that has not been assisted – whether directly or indirectly – by NIH's pioneering work.

NIH's activities have also contributed to our Nation's economic security and prosperity. Today, the United States is a global leader in the health and life sciences – thanks, in no small part, to NIH. The agency's grants have allowed America to train the next generation of doctors, researchers, and biomedical entrepreneurs. And they have ensured that crucial innovations take place in American institutions – allowing the United States to reap the economic benefits of those discoveries. The numbers speak for themselves: in Fiscal Year 2024 alone, NIH's more than $36 billion in awards spurred more than $94 billion in new economic activity – a return of $2.56 for every $1 invested. These investments supported more than 407,000 jobs across every State and the District of Columbia

That critical work is now in jeopardy. By law, NIH provides much of its support for scientific research and training in the form of grants to outside institutions. Since January, however, the current Administration has engaged in a concerted, and multi-pronged effort to disrupt NIH's grants. These efforts are unlawful, and plaintiffs bring this lawsuit to seek relief for the immediate harms they are causing state research institutions. [The Administration's] destructive efforts have taken the form of across-the-board delays in the review and approval of otherwise-fundable grant applications and widespread terminations of already-issued grants. Plaintiffs challenge both....

... [P]laintiffs seek swift relief from this Court. The Court should order NIH to undertake the grant-application review process as the law requires. And it should set aside the NIH's unlawful termination of plaintiffs' already-issued grants.

This lawsuit was later joined with another that raised related issues, *American Public Health Association v. National Institutes of Health et al.* (#1:25-cv-10787). Both cases are before District Judge William G. Young in Massachusetts.

On April 30, CNBC reported that Kennedy had cut jobs at all eight of HHS's minority health offices, laying off all or most workers. These offices help protect and improve the health of minority and underserved populations and help eliminate health disparities in the U.S.

HHS Attacks Vaccine Programs

On May 29, according to Ars Technica:

[T]he Department of Health and Human Services – under the control of anti-vaccine advocate Robert F. Kennedy Jr. – has canceled millions of dollars in federal funding awarded to Moderna to produce an mRNA vaccine against influenza viruses with pandemic potential, including the H5N1 bird flu currently sweeping US poultry and dairy cows.

The article said that HHS justified the cancellation of $766 million in Moderna funding by stating that "mRNA technology remains under-tested."

Ars Technica further reported:

Kennedy, a staunch anti-vaccine advocate, has unflaggingly made false claims about the safety and efficacy of mRNA COVID-19 vaccines. In 2021, Kennedy petitioned the FDA to revoke authorization for COVID-19 vaccines and refrain from issuing future approvals. In recent days, Kennedy has also restricted access to COVID-19 vaccines and unilaterally revoked recommendations for healthy children and pregnant people to get the vaccines.

The federal funding for pandemic influenza vaccines was awarded as health officials around the country, including federal officials, were closely monitoring the swift and unprecedented spread of H5N1 bird flu through US dairy cows, which also spread to 70 people and killed one. Under the Trump administration, regular updates on the outbreak have ceased, and experts fear that cases are going undocumented.

HHS Attacks Search for H.I.V/AIDS Vaccine

On May 30, 2025, HHS terminated a $258 million program that was instrumental in the search for an H.I.V./AIDS vaccine. The program was a consortium of medical agencies, based at Duke University and the Scripps Research Institute. This was the latest in a series of HHS cuts to H.I.V./AIDS initiatives, particularly those aimed at prevention. HHS also paused funding for a clinical trial of an H.I.V. vaccine made by Moderna and shut down the H.I.V. prevention division of the Centers for Disease Control and Prevention. (In January, Trump cut the President's Emergency Plan for AIDS Relief, known as PEPFAR, a $7.5 billion program that supplied most of the treatment for H.I.V. in Africa and developing countries worldwide.)

H.I.V. infections have been declining since 2010, but the World Health Organization reported 1.3 million new cases in 2023, 10% of them children. There was no support for HHS cuts in the medical community. As John Moore, an H.I.V. researcher at Weill Cornell Medical in New York, put it, "H.I.V. pandemic will never be ended without a vaccine, so killing research on one will end up killing people. The N.I.H.'s multiyear investment in advanced vaccine technologies shouldn't be abandoned on a whim like this."

On June 3, fired HHS employees filed a class action suit in federal court in Washington, D.C. (#1:25-cv-01750), against HHS, DOGE, and others. The employees claimed their firings were based on records "riddled with errors" in violation of the Privacy Act. They seek actual damages of not less than $1,000 per person. The case is ongoing before Judge Beryl A. Howell.

On June 9, Kennedy dismissed all 17 members of the Advisory Committee in Immunization Practices (ACIP) at HHS. This committee helps determine which vaccines children and adults receive, what gets covered by insurance, and which shots are made available free of charge to millions of low-income children. The move was widely criticized by medical groups, including the American Medical Association.

Kennedy has falsely claimed that ACIP members had conflicts of interest. This is contradicted by a government report. Kennedy defended his action in a statement rife with falsehoods: "A clean sweep is necessary to reestablish public confidence in vaccine science. ACIP new members will prioritize public health and evidence-based medicine. The Committee will no longer function as a rubber stamp for industry profit-taking agendas."

Kennedy has been prominent for years in undermining public confidence in vaccine science with such false comments as "autism comes from vaccines." Kennedy has also opposed fluoride, which is in 63% of the country's drinking water, claiming falsely that fluoride is "associated with arthritis, bone fractures, bone cancer, IQ loss, neurodevelopmental disorders, and thyroid disease." In 2024, Kennedy falsely told a press conference, "COVID-19 is targeted to attack Caucasians and black people. The people who are most immune are Ashkenazi Jews and Chinese."

On June 11, Kennedy named eight replacement members for ACIP, including vaccine skeptic Vicky Pebsworth.

More Than 100 Kennedy Lies Documented

On June 13, 2025, NewsGuard reported that HHS submitted a memo to Congress that reinforced Kennedy's anti-vaccine views by lying about a study. Kennedy's memo claimed that the study showed COVID-19 vaccines were a cause of miscarriages, which was not true. Kennedy used this "information" to support his agency's decision to stop recommending COVID-19 vaccines for pregnant women. NewsGuard's "RFK Jr. Healthcare Claims Depository" has documented 106 provably false health claims advanced by Kennedy and the anti-vaccine nonprofit he founded. These include claims that the vaccines have increased infant mortality rates and that they cause miscarriages.

On June 16, federal district judge William G. Young ruled from the bench on two cases against HHS filed in April, alleging that the National Institutes of Health (NIH) terminated or denied hundreds of grants solely because they reflected government-banned terms such as "gender identity" or "diversity, equity, and inclusion." The lawsuits argued that these decisions were violations of the Administrative Procedure Act, the Fifth Amendment, and the separation of powers principle. The judge agreed, after an evidentiary hearing, and issued restraining orders that blocked the NIH from cutting hundreds of grant programs to universities, hospitals, and other organizations.

In issuing his ruling, Judge Young minced no words: "The court finds and rules that [NIH's] explanations are bereft of reasoning, virtually in their entirety." He said that NIH actions "are of no force and effect. They are void and illegal." He ordered that nearly $3.87 billion across 367 grants be restored, pending appeal. He noted that in his 40 years on the bench, he had never seen such "palpable" racial and LGBTQ discrimination by the government.

During the hearing, Judge Young constantly pressed the government for public information about its process and decision-making. He did not get satisfactory answers. The judge expressed deep skepticism that the Trump administration had followed normal, dispassionate processes. He also expressed dismay that much of the publicly available information about the cancellations was provided by Grant Watch, an independent database compiled by a small team of academics that documented the Trump cuts through crowdsourcing.

Justice Department lawyer Thomas Ports argued that the director of NIH had the sole authority to decide that research in fields such as gender identity was "not worth pursuing," ignoring the agency's two-level peer review process. Judge Young repeatedly questioned the government's good faith, sharply rejecting its arguments:

> I understand that the extirpation of affirmative action is today a valid government position. I understand that. Affirmative action had various invidious calculus based upon race. I understand that. That's not a license to discriminate....

This [government behavior] represents racial discrimination and discrimination against America's LGBTQ community. That's what this is. I would be blind not to call it out. My duty is to call it out....

It is palpably clear these directives and the set of terminated grants here also are designed to frustrate, to stop research that may bear on the health – we are talking about health here – the health of Americans, of our LGBTQ community. That's appalling.

Point me just anywhere in this record where it's pointed out that any particular grant or group of grants is being used to support unlawful discrimination on the basis of race. From what I can see, it's the reverse.

How have we fallen so low? Have we no shame?

On June 24, after Judge Young refused to stay his order, NIH set about to reinstate about 900 grants affected by the court's judgment. This is less than half the roughly 2,300 grants cancelled by NIH since January. But NIH officials decided not to terminate any further grants and to reinstate the 900 grants "as soon as practicable."

Los Angeles, Invaded by U.S. Government, Resists

During the 2024 presidential campaign, Trump wrote: "Order will be restored, the Illegals will be expelled, and Los Angeles will be set free."

On June 6, the 81st anniversary of the Allied invasion of France, the U.S. Department of Homeland Security (DHS) sent waves of ICE and other federal agents in a fierce surprise attack of disorganized brutality into sections of Los Angeles presumed to harbor vulnerable immigrants. The attack came without warning, in multiple locations, as heavily armed, masked agents surged from unmarked cars, grabbing anyone who looked "wrong." DHS made no effort to coordinate with any local authorities. The Trump administration had launched what amounted to an illegal, race-based war against Los Angeles County.

Heavily armed agents in tactical gear from ICE, DHS, FBI, and DEA carried out coordinated, military-style raids across greater Los Angeles.

Agents blocked off streets, used drone surveillance, and herded people into indiscriminate groups. As has become common with ICE and the other agencies, their raids were illegal and brutal: men in masks, with no identification, no judicial warrant, just seizing anyone who looked like an "illegal" and taking him or her into custody with no due process of law – supposedly targeting undocumented individuals but indiscriminately sweeping up legal migrants and citizens as well. ICE reported 118 detainees, almost none of them "criminal" beyond a misdemeanor.

In swift reaction to these illegal assaults, Los Angelenos took to the streets, both in the neighborhoods that were raided and in downtown L.A. The disrupted communities massively resisted the invasive tactics that took away mostly innocent, harmless, law-abiding people, including long-time neighbors and family members. The response was overwhelmingly a non-violent protest.

As news of the ICE raids spread, crowds gathered in downtown L.A., focusing mass protests outside the Roybal Federal Building, where ICE detainees were being held incommunicado, in deplorable conditions. Protesters blocked entrances and clashed with law enforcement. LAPD declared the gathering an unlawful assembly. Some protesters threw bricks, put up roadblocks, or sprayed graffiti on public buildings. Police responded with billy clubs, rubber bullets, and flash-bang grenades. By evening, police in full riot gear covered downtown Los Angeles, clashing with protesters during a tense standoff. The area of disturbance was limited to a few city blocks, kept under control by LAPD (L.A. Police Department) and LASD (L.A. Sheriff's Department). LAPD Chief Jim McDonnell stated that before ICE started its raids, "federal officials did not brief his department, which made it difficult to respond to the mobs of people who began to protest."

Trump posted falsely on Truth Social that a "once great American City, Los Angeles, has been invaded and occupied by Illegal Aliens and Criminals [and overrun by] violent, insurrectionist mobs." He called for administration officials to "take all such action necessary to liberate Los Angeles from the [imaginary] Migrant Invasion, and put an end to these [imaginary] Migrant riots."

Popular L.A. Labor Leader Arrested for Observing

Earlier on June 6, federal agents arrested David Huerta, 58, the well-known president of the Service Employees International Union (SEIU) California – the state's largest public-sector union. Huerta was observing a business that ICE was raiding. He was reportedly pepper-sprayed and physically subdued by federal agents. They tased him, pushed him to the ground, and pinned him while they handcuffed him, injuring his shoulder. He was hospitalized for treatment and later transferred to custody in the Metropolitan Detention Center. News of his arrest spread through the community, heightening local resistance. Huerta said in a statement: "What happened to me is not about me, this is about something much bigger. This is about how we as a community stand together and resist the injustice that's happening. Hardworking people, and members of our family and our community, are being treated like criminals."

The government promptly lied about Huerta's arrest. U.S. Attorney Bill Essayli, posting on X with the usual government disregard for the rights of the accused, gave a different version of Huerta's arrest:

> Federal agents were executing a lawful judicial warrant at a LA worksite this morning when David Huerta deliberately obstructed their access by blocking their vehicle. He was arrested for interfering with federal officers and will face arraignment in federal court on [June 9].

Essayli attached video to his post that showed a van working its way through a crowd of protesters to get inside an ICE compound gate. The video did not show Huerta blocking the van or getting arrested. It did show one woman blocking the van and an ICE agent picking her up bodily and moving her out of the way, without arresting her.

Second Day of Massive ICE Raids, Protests Grow

On June 7, protests against the illegal ICE raids continued throughout the day, especially around a Home Depot in Paramount, attempting to disrupt an ICE raid there. Protests also continued around the downtown detention center. Protesters blocked the 101 Freeway and set fire to driverless taxis there. Local law enforcement held protesters at bay with tear gas, flash-bang grenades, and less-than-lethal bullets. They shot at least three reporters at close range. They made several dozen arrests. Rights groups alleged that detainees, including children, were held overnight without adequate food, water, or bedding in the Federal Building in downtown Los Angeles. ICE denied mistreatment, but refused to allow independent confirmation. Many detainees remained in custody with limited information about their status or whereabouts. They were not allowed to communicate with family or attorneys.

In the early evening of June 7 in Washington, without consulting with California's governor as required by law, Trump ordered some 2,000 California National Guard members to Los Angeles. His memo was titled "Department of Defense Security for the Protection of Department of Homeland Security Functions." It did not mention Los Angeles but spoke more generally to rebellion against the nation as a whole, a false representation of reality with ominous overtones:

> Numerous incidents of violence and disorder have recently occurred and threaten to continue in response to the enforcement of Federal law by U.S. Immigration and Customs Enforcement (ICE) and other United States Government personnel who are performing Federal functions and supporting the faithful execution of Federal immigration laws. In addition, violent protests threaten the security of and significant damage to Federal immigration detention facilities and other Federal property. To the extent that protests or acts of violence directly inhibit the execution of the laws, they constitute a form of rebellion against the authority of the Government of the United States....
>
> I hereby call into Federal service members and units of the National Guard under 10 U.S.C. 12406 to temporarily protect ICE and other United States Government personnel who are performing Federal functions, including the enforcement of Federal law, and to protect Federal property, at locations where protests against these functions are occurring or are likely to occur based on current threat assessments and planned operations....

In response to Trump's plan to federalize the National Guard, Governor Newsom objected "unequivocally and publicly" to the order. At 5:13 p.m. on June 7, Newsom posted on social media:

The federal government is moving to take over the California National Guard and deploy 2,000 soldiers. That move is purposefully inflammatory and will only escalate tensions.

LA authorities are able to access law enforcement assistance at a moment's notice. We are in close coordination with the city and county, and there is currently no unmet need.

The Guard has been admirably serving LA throughout recovery [from the wildfires]. This is the wrong mission and will erode public trust.

According to the New York Times on June 7, "California Democrats have braced for months for the possibility that President Trump would seek to deploy U.S. troops on American soil in this way, particularly in Democratic-run jurisdictions. Privately, they have acknowledged that such a move, absent the state's agreement, would have profound implications."

National Guard Arrives, Can't Find Invasion

On June 8, shortly after 2 a.m., the National Guard started to arrive in Los Angeles. By that time, the streets were quiet. Trump praised them for doing a good job. LA Mayor Karen Bass objected to the National Guard's presence, calling it a provocation. Other local officials pointed out that the National Guard had made absolutely no difference.

The White House press secretary issued a dishonest statement that misrepresented reality on the ground and claimed an "invasion" that doesn't exist:

In recent days, violent mobs have attacked ICE Officers and Federal Law Enforcement Agents carrying out basic deportation operations in Los Angeles, California. These operations are essential to halting and reversing the invasion of illegal criminals into the United States. In the wake of this violence, California's feckless Democrat leaders have completely abdicated their responsibility to protect their citizens.... The Trump

Administration has a zero tolerance policy for criminal behavior and violence…. The Commander-in-Chief will ensure the laws of the United States are executed fully and completely.

This is a big lie based on a fabric of lesser lies. The "invasion" is a lie. The "illegal criminals" is a lie. The attack on Democrats is a lie. The Trump administration's "zero tolerance" for criminal behavior is a lie that begins with ICE but runs through the administration to Yemen and Iran. Executing the law "fully and completely" is a lie, as more than a hundred judges have found. It's all a lie that, if allowed to stand, expands the power of the president/felon to deploy troops in the U.S. anywhere, anytime, on any bogus pretense.

Reality Isn't Necessarily What You Say It Is

On June 8, protests continued, especially in downtown LA. The National Guard was deployed to protect federal buildings, but took no active role in responding to protests. The LAPD used tear gas for the first time in decades. ABC News reported:

In contrast to the clashes seen in the cities of Paramount and Compton, demonstrations in L.A. "remained peaceful," police said in a statement….

Despite the national picture, the protests were confined to a very small area of a couple of blocks in Paramount and downtown L.A. Most of the city is operating as per normal with no signs of unrest….

Gov. Gavin Newsom's office told ABC News Sunday that about 300 National Guard troops are on the ground, contrary to the 2,000 the Trump administration says have been activated.

The Los Angeles Police Department and the L.A. County Sheriff's Department say they have come in to help clear the streets and protect lives, but will not take part in immigration enforcement. Chief Jim McDonnell and Sheriff Robert Luna have repeatedly said they will not enforce federal immigration law, but will protect the lives of federal agents and protesters.

Their lack of willingness to engage has led to federal leaders criticizing local police as being unhelpful and leading to the need for National Guard.

On June 8, DHS issued a press release suggesting that the protests weren't the real target of Trump's actions – the DHS headline: "California politicians and rioters are defending heinous illegal alien criminals at the expense of Americans' safety."

Assistant Secretary of Homeland Security Tricia McLaughlin baldly lied in the press release, posing an astonishingly dishonest question based on a false hypothesis. Then she answered her own question with an even more dishonest answer that described a fiction:

> Why do Governor Newsom and Los Angeles Mayor Karen Bass care more about violent murderers and sex offenders than they do about protecting their own citizens? These rioters in Los Angeles are fighting to keep rapists, murderers, and other violent criminals loose on Los Angeles streets. Instead of rioting, they should be thanking ICE officers every single day who wake up and make our communities safer.

That last sentence is a particularly shameful denial of reality. It was ICE, with its heavy-handed, illegal, and often violent assaults on random gatherings, that made communities around Los Angeles unsafe.

On June 9, nationwide protests against ICE activity included a large gathering in New York City in solidarity with Los Angeles. Governor Newsom expressed concern about the National Guard's presence and requested their removal. Mayor Bass stated the deployment was not about public safety. Trump maintained the National Guard was necessary and authorized another 2,000 Guardsmen, who had not yet been deployed. The Pentagon ordered the deployment of 700 Marines to LA.

SEIU president David Huerta was released on $50,000 bond. He was charged with felony conspiracy to impede an officer. Video of his arrest did not support that charge.

Governor Gavin Newsom and Attorney General Ron Bonta filed a 22-page complaint (3:25-cv-04870) in the federal district court of Northern California seeking an injunction against Trump's federalizing the California National Guard, calling it unwarranted, illegal, and unconstitutional. The basis of Trump's action, his assertion that local law enforcement had lost control of the situation, is disputed in Newsom's lawsuit:

> LASD's [L.A. Sheriff's Department] standard practice is to call in assistance from other local agencies, such as sheriff's departments from neighboring counties, and then for direct aid from state agencies when LASD determines that it cannot handle a situation. These two steps would be done before a request for federal assistance would be made. But LASD did not need and did not request the assistance of other agencies to gain control of the protests.
>
> Governor Newsom has also taken steps to ensure that the State itself is actively providing support, in close coordination with the City and County, and there are no unmet needs from local law enforcement. Local law enforcement agencies have not requested any assistance, but if they were to do so, the State is more than prepared to meet any needs that may arise. As an example, on June 6 and June 7, the State deployed additional California Highway Patrol.

Trump Officials Keep Lying About Reality

DHS Assistant Secretary McLaughlin issued another fraudulent email:

> As rioters have escalated their assaults on our DHS law enforcement, and activists' behavior on the streets has become increasingly dangerous, Secretary Noem requested [Defense] Secretary Hegseth direct the military on the ground in Los Angeles to arrest rioters to help restore law and order....

This was too much even for DHS, as an unnamed official walked it back, saying the posture of the "troops has not changed." The unnamed official added: "Please disregard the previously sent statement, and instead use this one. THANK YOU!" [emphasis in original]

For context on the ground, The Intercept reported:

> [W]hile National Guard troops mostly stood around outside federal buildings, it was the Los Angeles Police Department whose members brutalized protesters with batons, tear gas, and

so-called "less-lethal" munitions, drawing blood and bruising people who turned out to protest U.S. Immigration and Customs Enforcement raids.

At the federal detention center, most of the recent detainees had yet to speak with an attorney, family members and attorneys told The Intercept. Federal officials illegally denied entry to members of Congress, including California Democratic Reps. Jimmy Gomez and Maxine Waters. Attorneys seeking access to their clients told The Intercept that some women being detained had to sleep outside, in tents without blankets, due to overcrowding....

Video recordings from throughout the weekend showed other aggressive tactics. One video from [June 8] showed a man getting beaten by mounted LAPD officers charging at him and swinging batons. Another recording showed one protester trampled by officers on horseback. In a live broadcast from near a federal courthouse, an LAPD officer pointed their weapon in an Australian reporter's direction before firing and striking her in the leg [the bullet, imbedded, had to be removed by surgery]. Agents with [DHS] and some National Guard troops fired pepper-ball bullets and tear gas on smaller groups of protesters and journalists outside the downtown federal detention facility throughout the weekend....

Local Authorities Restored Order in Three Days

On June 10, National Guard members reportedly began accompanying ICE agents on some raids. Seven hundred Marines also arrived. Mayor Bass declared a local state of emergency and implemented an 8 p.m. curfew in part of downtown due to concerns about vandalism and looting. The National Guard and Marines remained on the sidelines.

Trump posted falsely on Truth Social: If I didn't "SEND IN THE TROOPS" to Los Angeles the last three nights, that once beautiful and great City would be burning to the ground right now, much like 25,000 houses burned to the ground in LA due to an incompetent Governor and

Mayor....

On the same day, during a visit to Fort Bragg, one of several military bases recently re-renamed for a Confederate traitor, Trump had some more harsh and dishonest demagoguery for Los Angeles:

> We will not allow an American city to be invaded and conquered by a foreign enemy. That's what they are.... generations of Army heroes did not shed their blood on distant shores only to watch our country be destroyed by invasion and third-world lawlessness.... what you're witnessing in California is a full-blown assault on peace, on public order, and on national sovereignty, carried out by rioters bearing foreign flags. We will liberate Los Angeles and make it free, clean and safe again.

As of June 11, according to the Los Angeles Times, ICE had detained an estimated 330 people, of whom roughly 33 have any significant criminal record (being undocumented is a civil offense, the equivalent of a speeding ticket). Greater Los Angeles has an estimated one million undocumented immigrants, some of them having lived there for decades.

Also on June 12, the Marines were deployed on the street for the first time since their arrival, guarding an unthreatened federal building on Wilshire Avenue, several miles from the area of protest.

DHS Press Conference Traps U.S. Senator

On June 12, DHS Secretary Kristi Noem held a press conference in the secure federal building in LA. She began by thanking her audience of law enforcement officials for "working every single day to bring law and order and peace back to the citizens of Los Angeles and to the state of California." She promoted the standard administration lie about "... operations that have been working to bring in criminals that have been on our streets for far too long. We are making sure these criminals, bad actors, rapists, traffickers are brought to justice finally under this administration...."

She went on to thank the various participants in these operations, in this order: ICE officers, HSI (Homeland Security Investigations), federal protective services and border patrol agents, the Army, the Marines, the National Guard, the U.S. Attorney, the Department of Justice, the DEA

(Drug Enforcement Administration), the FBI, the IRS (Internal Revenue Service), and the U.S. Marshalls. With bald demagoguery, Noem said, offering no evidence, that the IRS "is helping us track how these violent protests are funded, what NGO's out there, what unions, what individuals may be funding these violent perpetrators...."

Also in the federal building at the same time was U.S. Senator Alex Padilla (D-CA). He was accompanied, as required by protocol, by a National Guardsman and an FBI agent. When he learned of Noem's press conference, he decided to attend to see if he could learn more. He arrived with his security guards about eight minutes after the press conference began, as Noem was saying:

> The Department of Homeland Security and people that are working on this operation will continue to sustain and increase our operations in this city. We are not going away. We are staying here to liberate the city from the socialist and burdensome leadership that this governor and this mayor have placed on this country and what they have tried to insert into the city....

This was news to Senator Padilla, who interrupted, identified himself, and tried to ask a question. Several plainclothes security officers swarmed the senator and pushed him out of the room with little resistance. His security guards did nothing. One of his staff members filmed the episode. In the hallway, three uniformed FBI agents forced the senator to the floor and handcuffed his hands behind his back. Inside, Noem continued her statement, hardly missing a beat.

Later, on social media, DHS posted several lies about the event. DHS falsely claimed the senator didn't identify himself. Video clearly shows him identifying himself. DHS falsely claimed he "lunged" at Noem. Video shows he didn't lunge at anyone. Security agents swarmed the senator almost as soon as he started to speak. DHS claimed the secret service thought he was an attacker, even though he was accompanied by two security agents. Video shows no effort by any agent to proceed calmly, to find out who Padilla was. Is it too cynical to assume he was taken down for asking a question while being Latino?

On the evening of June 12, Federal District Judge Charles Breyer ruled that the administration had unlawfully federalized the National Guard, thereby returning control of the Guard to the California Governor. The Trump administration immediately appealed the decision. The Ninth Circuit Court of Appeals promptly entered an administrative stay, which restored control of the Guard to Trump.

Assault on Colleague Stirs Few Senators

On the floor of the Senate, Senator Elizabeth Warren (D-MA) responded to the treatment of Senator Padilla at the hands of DHS security guards earlier in the day:

> This a horrifying moment in our nation's history. Today, United States Senator Alex Padilla was violently removed from a public briefing for asking questions on behalf of the people he represents….
>
> He was put in handcuffs for asking a simple question. He was put in handcuffs for doing his job as a United States Senator. If you are not yet convinced that President Trump and his administration are trying to undermine the foundations of our democracy. Watch the video….
>
> And here is the really chilling part…. Every day Donald Trump is making this nation look more and more like a fascist state….
>
> I know my Republican colleagues can see what happened today was wrong. But will any Republican senator speak up for our democracy?
>
> They know Senator Padilla's character. They know that Senator Padilla is a kind man. A man who is concerned for his children. A man who is concerned for his home. A man who has dedicated his life to public service. A man who is a patriot….
>
> This is not a drill. This is an assault on our democracy. I am calling on my Republican colleagues to join us in demanding a bipartisan investigation into this incident.

Warren's call was met by an outpouring of bipartisan silence, except for those Republicans who blamed Padilla for being "inappropriate" and "orchestrating a political stunt." Watch the video.

On June 14, "No Kings Day" in Los Angeles, an estimated 200,000 people rallied peacefully for hours in downtown. At mid-afternoon, an LAPD social media post confirmed: "Demonstration is in the thousands and is taking up all lanes of traffic.... March is peaceful."

Lawless Police Confront Lawless Protesters, Cops Win

Later in the day, violence erupted, with each side blaming the other. According to eyewitness Justin Glawe on Public Notice:

> It was the presence of the Marines in front of the federal building on Saturday that enraged the crowd on its steps, prompting minor pushing and shoving and a lot of name-calling toward the young men in uniform. It wasn't long after these dust-ups that the LAPD, in conjunction with the county sheriff's office and California Highway Patrol, took care of the protesters so the Marines wouldn't have to.
>
> Just after 4 pm Saturday, the officers on horseback lurched into the crowd. Their horses nosed protesters along as some of the officers swung their batons downward, causing the crowd to scatter and flee south on Los Angeles Street....
>
> The 4pm cavalry charge and ensuing launch of less-lethal munitions came as a surprise to those of who were on Los Angeles Street near the 101. There, I didn't see anyone throwing anything at police, and heard no orders to disperse. Instead, the cops on horseback just went for it.
>
> Over the next four hours, police chased crowds of protesters in every direction throughout downtown LA. It was extremely intense. Police fired thousands – and probably more like tens of thousands – of foam munitions and other projectiles, including what looked like old-school pepper balls. Tear gas and flash grenades added to the chaotic atmosphere, providing Fox News and right-wing media the shocking images for their context-free coverage.
>
> Police say the official cause of the unrest was "outside

agitators" who threw debris, rocks, and "commercial-grade fireworks at officers," according to the LAPD and the LA County Sheriff's Office.

But on Los Angeles Street where it meets the 101 freeway, I didn't see anyone attacking police, nor did I hear orders to disperse. Like all riots, the matter of who started it remains, at best, an open question. But the police at the very least escalated the situation...

What I saw was a crackdown on protesters who were largely peaceful, followed by a voluminous use of force by local police that included indiscriminately firing on protesters regardless of whether they were attacking police or simply walking on the streets. This included cops swinging batons at an elderly man, firing on a man at point-blank range who appeared to be doing nothing but filming them, kneeling on the back and neck of a petite young woman as she was arrested, and launching thousands of rounds of non-lethal weapons for hours as protesters mostly walked away or tried to hold their ground.

Police have claimed they were attacked, but haven't provided much evidence to back it up despite the surveillance drones flying overhead and the officers filming protesters.... Saturday's unrest led to 10 injuries to law enforcement, police have said. At least two protesters were seriously injured.

One man was struck in the eye by a foam bullet fired by police, bloodying his face and swelling the eye shut. After a five-hour surgery and being told he could lose vision in his right eye, Marshall Woodruff spoke from a hospital bed, explaining that he didn't hear any orders to disperse from law enforcement. "Nobody on any megaphones, nobody, you know, shouting clear orders," Woodruff told KTLA. "It was just, you know, chaos."

An LAPD social post at 7:13 p.m. said "people in the crowd are throwing rocks, bricks, bottles and other objects" when the march passed by the Edward R. Roybal Building, guarded by Marines and National Guard, who remained disengaged. The same post said that dispersal orders had been issued in two areas. The police and sheriff's deputies responded to rock-throwing with smoke bombs and flash-bangs to move the crowd away from the federal building. The curfew began at 8 p.m.

CBS News quoted an unnamed protester saying the police escalated the violence: "They came in super, super hard and aggressive, and that's what created all of this. No warning. They just masked up.... It's upsetting because how are people supposed to feel like their voices are being heard when they're being violently put down by the state itself."

Another LAPD social media post at 9 p.m. warned: "Traffic Advisory! Outside agitators have blocked Spring St south of Temple and set up fencing and other blocking materials." At 10 p.m., LAPD posted: "Agitators are throwing rocks and other objects at the Officers."

What Were Trump's Long-Term Plans for Los Angeles?

Late in the day, Mayor Karen Bass told CB News: "You know, we're not against protests. We want people to exercise their First Amendment rights. That is part of our American tradition and system. But it is not a part, nor is it acceptable, for that to deteriorate to violence, and when that happens, people will be held accountable."

Bass also wondered what the Trump administration planned to do, since its communications with California officials were at best limited. Bass expressed the hope that DHS would dial down the ICE raids that had antagonized Los Angeles since June 6, so that the city could get back to normal.

On June 15, Trump demagogued on Truth Social, that cities targeted by the immigration raids, like Los Angeles, Chicago and New York, "are the core of the Democrat Power Center, where they use Illegal Aliens to expand their Voter Base, cheat in Elections, and grow the Welfare State, robbing good paying Jobs and Benefits from Hardworking American Citizens."

On June 16, The Intercept reported that, since Trump deployed nearly 5,000 federal troops to LA on June 7, they had done almost nothing. According to a military spokesman, the 5,000 National Guard and Marines operating in Southern California had carried out exactly one temporary detainment (a citizen and veteran who made a wrong turn on June 13). This massive deployment has already cost taxpayers well over $100 million. Rep. Ro Khanna (D-CA) told The Intercept: "It's a complete waste of resources, but it's also the unnecessary militarization of the United States using U.S. forces on U.S. soil against U.S. citizens. There was no reason for this to be done when local law enforcement and the state were capable of addressing the issue."

Marcos Leao, 27, the unresisting man detained on June 13 by six Marines in combat gear, with automatic weapons, and two security officers, was not involved in any protest. Leao was wearing shorts, a t-shirt, and sunglasses. Marines took him down and zip-tied him. Leao is a former Army combat engineer who gained U.S. citizenship through his military service. He told Reuters that he was rushing to an appointment in the Veterans Affairs office in the building the Marines were guarding. He crossed a strand of caution tape, and an armed Marine came sprinting toward him. He was soon released with no charges. Leao, of Angolan and Portuguese descent, said he was treated "very fairly…. They're just doing their job."

This was the high point of action for the Marines, who were withdrawn in late July after a mission accomplishing essentially nothing.

From June 8 to June 16, according to the LAPD, it had made 561 arrests related to the protests, 203 of them on June 10 for "failure to disperse." Most of the arrests in this period were for failure to disperse or curfew violations. Most of the arrests – 370 – occurred during the three-day period of June 9-11. There were five arrests for assault with a deadly weapon (one of them a Molotov cocktail). A dozen LAPD officers were injured during the protests. The police offered no accounting of protesters, bystanders, or reporters who were injured. LAPD had no comment about Martin Santoyo, who was shot in the groin at close range with a rubber bullet that shattered one of his testicles. He was hospitalized but not charged.

Los Angeles Dodgers Caught Up in Struggle

On June 17, the Ninth U.S. Circuit Court of Appeals held a hearing on the Trump administration's appeal of the lower court ruling that federalizing the National Guard had been illegal. That ruling was stayed pending this appeal.

After the court hearing, the U.S. Northern Command announced the deployment of 2,000 more California National Guardsmen to Los Angeles, bringing the reported total deployment to 4,100. Even though the troops were barred from taking part in civilian policing, a military press release said: "The soldiers are completing training on de-escalation, crowd control, and use of the standing rules for the use of force in advance of joining the federal protection mission."

Governor Newsom called the new deployment "Reckless. Pointless. And disrespectful to our troops." Mayor Bass called it a "chaotic escalation."

On the morning of June 18, what looked like agents in plainclothes driving unmarked vehicles showed up outside a locked gate at Dodgers Stadium. Word spread quickly on social media. Twenty or so protesters showed up. The Dodgers called the LAPD because of the protesters. Before the police arrived, the unidentified agents left to boos and taunts from the crowd. The Dodgers took credit for not letting them into the parking lot, posting on social media: "ICE agents came to Dodger Stadium and requested permission to access the parking lots. They were denied entry to the grounds by the organization."

Meanwhile, ICE took to social media to say they hadn't been at Dodger Stadium. The Department of Homeland Security (DHS) said, no, it wasn't ICE, it was CBP (Customs and Border Protection). CPB said nothing.

The Dodger fanbase is estimated to be more than 40% Latino. There had been talk of boycotting the Dodgers because of the team's failure to oppose ICE's Gestapo tactics. Two days earlier, against the team's wishes, Latina singer Nezza sang the national anthem in Spanish. This set off right-wing protests on Fox News. On June 17, the Dodgers announced plans to figure out a way to support local communities impacted by ICE raids. Three days after that, the Dodgers announced the team would provide $1 million in direct aid to immigrant families suffering from Trump's assaults.

On June 18, Mayor Bass told MSNBC: "It's felt in LA like we're part of a grand experiment. How far will the public tolerate the federal government intervening and seizing power from a governor? I think it's being tried out here."

In a congressional hearing in Washington, former CIA officer Rep. Elissa

Slotkin (D-MI) asked Defense Secretary Hegseth: "Have you given the order [to the Guard] to be able to shoot at unarmed protesters in any way?" Hegseth wouldn't answer the question.

Rankin Seeks Investigation into Padilla Assault

On June 18, Rep. Jamie Rankin (D-MD) wrote a long, detailed letter to the head of the FBI demanding an investigation of the federal officers' June 12 assault on U.S. Senator Alex Padilla (D-CA). Raskin's letter began:

> Last week, Alex Padilla, the senior Senator from California, attempted to ask Department of Homeland Security (DHS) Secretary Kristi Noem a question during a public press conference in a federal building in Los Angeles, California. He was dragged out of the room, tackled to the ground, and handcuffed by multiple armed federal agents, including agents of the Federal Bureau of Investigation (FBI). Can you explain why asking government officials to answer basic questions is such a threat to this Administration that it would resort to such tactics against a United States Senator?

> This Administration has much to answer for. It has sent masked agents in unmarked vans to disappear people from American streets, it has violated the rights of the people of the United States to free speech and due process, it has spirited people away to the torture prisons of foreign dictators, and it has defied the orders of judges. This assault on Senator Padilla, captured on video and broadcast worldwide, is another vivid episode of authoritarian tactics and brute force being used to crush oversight and critical questioning – including from sitting Members of Congress exercising their constitutional duty. I write to demand that you immediately provide answers and conduct an investigation into the FBI's role in this disgraceful and indefensible assault of a Member of Congress.

On June 19, White House Press Secretary Leavitt warned on FOX News: "President Trump has directed all of our ICE officers to do everything in their power to carry out the single largest mass deportation operation in history. Illegal criminals who are hiding in America's so-called 'sanctuary cities' will be increasingly targeted for removal."

Appeals Court Rules for Trump on Sending Guard

Late on June 19, the Ninth Circuit Court of Appeals ruled that Trump had likely acted lawfully when he ordered 2,000 National Guard troops to Los Angeles over the objections of California officials. The court's unsigned ruling did not decide the actual question of constitutional legality but held only "that it is likely that the President lawfully exercised his statutory authority." A roll of the legal dice.

To reach that conclusion, the court concluded – falsely – that LA lacked the ability to control its streets even though the governor, mayor, chief of police, and sheriff all asserted they had everything under control. Federal District Judge Charles Breyer had agreed with California officials, ruling that Trump's actions were illegal and returning control of the guard to the state.

The Appeals court's ruling put a stay on Judge Breyer's ruling while the matter was being litigated. The ruling also left Trump in control of the 4,000 National Guard troops in Los Angeles. But the appeals court unanimously rejected Trump's assertion that the courts had no authority to review the president's decision.

Protesters Caught Between Violent Gangs of ICE and LAPD

Looking back to June 6, the Los Angeles Times reported:

> For two weeks in June, protesters across L.A. made front page news. In groups large and small, they showed up to oppose immigration raids, marched on the federal building downtown and rallied to cry out "no kings" in the United States.
>
> They faced a downtown curfew, an onslaught of insults from the president, dissension in their own ranks, violent or messy compatriots, and whack-a-mole attempts to try to keep up with the federal immigration enforcement agents crisscrossing the region.
>
> They also faced the Los Angeles Police Department.

The LAPD's protest response, which left many protesters injured, has once again triggered lawsuits and outrage.

Despite years of costly lawsuits, oversight measures and promises by leaders to rein in indiscriminate use of force during protests, the LAPD faces sharp criticism, fresh litigation, and questions about tactics used by officers over the past two weeks.

On June 20, CounterPunch writer Maga Miranda assessed the state of play in Los Angeles after two weeks of federal intervention despite the objections of California'a duly-elected leaders. Chicana scholar Maga Miranda is a postdoctoral fellow in Chicana/o-Latina/o Studies at Pomona College in Claremont, CA. She is a native of Los Angeles – America's second largest metropolitan area of some 13 million people– more than a third of whom are Hispanic.

While rejecting the politically motivated violence of the Trump regime, Miranda had no kind words for "the absurdity and impotence of elected Democrats" whose priorities were "optics" and "tone-deaf condemnations of 'riots and looting,'" even though most of the violence on the streets came from local and federal law enforcement officers. She wrote defiantly:

> Donald Trump's agenda will never win Los Angeles – at least not in the traditional sense, and certainly not through votes or on the ideological terrain. But the campaign of terror being unleashed upon the city is not about a conventional victory. Instead, Trump intends to terrorize Los Angeles into submission, creating a spectacle and inflicting chaos in an attempt to break the political and moral backbone of a city that refuses to submit to authoritarian ethnonationalism. Faced with extreme federal overreach, which has taken the form of ICE abductions and the deployment of militarized forces, Los Angeles now finds itself at a crossroads....
>
> To be more precise, what is taking place now is a retaliatory campaign – a punishment for Los Angeles' defiance and a message to every city that dares to resist Trump's ethnonationalist agenda.... I argue that we are seeing the righteous resistance to defend the sovereignty – and the soul – of Los Angeles....

The reality is that Los Angeles has never been – and will never be – a white-majority city, much to the dismay of figures like Stephen Miller, Donald Trump, and the current regime. From its founding in 1781 by the original Pobladores – a group of Black, Indigenous, mestizo, and Spanish settlers – Los Angeles has always been a multicultural city. By 1850, roughly 75 percent of its population was of Mexican descent. Even after the so-called Mexican Repatriation of the 1930s, when close to one million people (including thousands of U.S. birthright citizens) were forcibly removed and deported, Los Angeles has continued to be a majority minority city....

Los Angeles is currently under siege. Federal agencies including ICE, CBP, DHS, Border Patrol, HSI, FBI and even the DEA have descended upon the city in an unprecedented show of force. Two [four] thousand National Guard troops and seven hundred marines have been deployed.... Undercover agents operate in civilian clothes and unmarked vehicles, snatching people off the streets, at their workplaces and their homes. At the time of this writing, more troops are stationed in Los Angeles than in Iraq and Syria combined. This is hardly "enforcement." It's quite literally an occupation....

Los Angeles today is what it looks like when a city refuses to surrender its sovereignty and its soul. Rapid response networks have mobilized to confront federal agencies and local police directly, with the aim of disrupting and preventing the execution of this campaign of terror. These networks represent the city's urgent commitment to protecting its undocumented residents who, at nearly 10 percent of the population, are our neighbors, coworkers, family members, classmates, and in some cases, even our adversaries – immigrants who are part of the social fabric of Los Angeles....

Armed with the sense that no one is coming to rescue us, it has become a moral imperative for many Angelenos to show up for one another however they can.... [After the raids of June 6]

[t]housands took to the streets, with rapid response networks swelling in size. Frontline defenders mobilized in person while secondary and tertiary networks offered remote support organizing legal aid, supplies distributions, and sharing real-time updates. The resistance was decentralized, strategic, and deeply rooted in the spirit of mutual care.... what is emerging is an even deeper, city-wide commitment to community self-defense. Angelenos are acting decisively, collectively, and with the clear understanding that only the people will save the people....

Like a Dog With a Bone

On July 7, unannounced and for no apparent reason, a heavily-armed, masked force of more than a hundred U.S. personnel, including a line on horseback crossing a soccer field, supported by armored vehicles and helicopters, invaded MacArthur Park, 35 acres of hills and waterways in the middle of Los Angeles. The park was mostly empty. The lines of dozens of ICE agents and 80 National Guard marched through the park in waves, damaging the landscape. They scared off 20 children at a summer camp. They interrupted doctors giving medical care to homeless people. They made no arrests.

Soon after the military force appeared, Mayor Karen Bass showed up, calling the show of force "unacceptable." She demanded to know why they were there. No reason. She spoke to the man in charge of the operation, Gregory Bovino, a Customs and Border Protection "section chief" in Southern California. She told him to remove the troops. The troops were removed. At a press conference that afternoon, Bass excoriated the federal intimidation as "outrageous and un-American":

> What I saw in the park today looked like a city under siege, under armed occupation.... It's the way a city looks before a coup.... To me, this is another example of the administration ratcheting up chaos by deploying what looked like a military operation in an American city. It's a political agenda of provoking fear and terror.... Home Depot one day, a carwash the next, armed vehicles and what looked like mounted military units in

a park the next day.... There is no plan other than fear, chaos, and politics.

The response of the Trump administration pretty much confirmed Bass's darkest thoughts. A DHS spokesperson responded to inquiries with an email that said only: "The operation is ongoing. So that should be a message in of itself." Driving that attitude home, CBP section chief and unelected bureaucrat Bovino told Fox News, "We will go anywhere, anytime we want in Los Angeles." He also texted: The federal government is not leaving LA. I don't work for Karen Bass. The federal government doesn't work for Karen Bass. We're going to be here until that mission's accomplished, as I said, and better get used to us now because this is going to be normal very soon.

In the month since the Trump administration invasion of Los Angeles began on June 6, more than 2,300 Angelenos have been "disappeared and uprooted from their homes and communities," according to Jeanette Zani Patton, director of policy and advocacy at True LA. In many cases, their whereabouts and their well-being are unknown. What is known is that the conditions in ICE detention facilities are typically sub-human and ICE refuses to allow legal oversight of their gulag by Congress or anyone else.

On July 11, U.S. District Judge Maame Ewusi-Mensah Frimpong issued two temporary restraining orders (TRO) against ICE in the case *Perdomo, et al. v. Noem, et al* (2:25-cv-05605-MEMF-SP), reigning in some of ICE's chronic, illegal practices. The first TRO requires ICE to allow all detainees to meet with their legal representatives seven days a week. ICE must also allow detainees to call their legal representatives at no cost, and ICE must not screen, record, or otherwise monitor such calls. And ICE must show cause as to why the court should not enjoin ICE from making any further violations of the Fifth Amendment of the Constitution.

The second TRO requires ICE to follow the Fourth Amendment's duty to have probable cause in any seizure. The TRO bars ICE agents from using any (or any combination) of the following criteria when detaining a subject: apparent race or ethnicity; speaking Spanish or English with an accent; presence at a particular location (bus stop, carwash, agricultural site, etc.); or the type of work a subject does.

The second TRO further orders ICE to show cause why it should not also be ordered to maintain and provide documentation of detentive stops, develop guidance for agents to know when they have "reasonable suspicion" under the law, and train their agents to follow the law.

According to a press release from the California attorney general, California and 17 other states filed an amicus brief supporting the plaintiffs "seeking a temporary restraining order to enjoin the United States Immigration and Customs Enforcement (ICE) and Customs and Border Protection (CBP) from engaging in unconstitutional and unlawful stops of Los Angeles residents during immigration sweeps. The lawsuit comes amid the Trump Administration conducting aggressive, militaristic immigration raids in Los Angeles that have terrified immigrant and non-immigrant residents alike, chilled community members' participation in civic society, and impeded law enforcement and public safety."

On July 13, the U.S. Attorney appealed on behalf of ICE, opposing the restraining orders. The appeal agreed as to the legal and constitutional arguments, that the alleged behavior was illegal but argued that "none of this is actually happening."

Decades of Fear-Mongering About Iran's 'Nuclear Weapons'

On June 13, Israel started an unprovoked, undeclared war with Iran, bombing multiple sites, both military and civilian. Israel claimed, without providing evidence, that Iran was on the verge of developing a nuclear weapon. This is a claim that has been dishonestly made for decades. It's never turned out to be true.

No one knows whether it's true or not this time. The supporting evidence is sketchy at best. In March, Director of National Intelligence Tulsi Gabbard testified before Congress that a consensus of U.S. intelligence agencies agreed that Iran did not appear to be building a nuclear weapon. Gabbard said that the intelligence community "continues to assess that Iran is not building a nuclear weapon, and Supreme Leader Khamenei has not authorized the nuclear weapons program that he suspended in 2003." She continued:

> In the past year, we've seen an erosion of a decades-long taboo in Iran on discussing nuclear weapons in public, likely

emboldening nuclear weapons advocates within Iran's decision-making apparatus. Iran's enriched uranium stockpile is at its highest levels and is unprecedented for a state without nuclear weapons.

That assessment had not changed by June 17, when Trump said of U.S. intelligence, "I don't care. I think they were very close to having one." Gabbard told reporters that Trump was just saying what she had told Congress. Trump was still hinting at taking the U.S. into the war, while also coyly saying no one knew what his plans were.

In March, Trump had written to Iran's Supreme Leader Ayatollah Ali Khamenei proposing bilateral talks about limiting Iran's nuclear program. That program is real, at least to the extent that it involves enriching uranium, which can be used for nuclear reactors or enriched to bomb-grade quality. There is intelligence uncertainty as to whether Iran has bomb-grade uranium. There is intelligence consensus that Iran has no reliable means of delivering a nuclear weapon if it had one but that its missile capability is improving. The Iranian nuclear "threat" has been a cry of wolf for decades.

In response to the call for talks, Khamenei reportedly said: "The insistence on the part of some bully states on negotiations is not to resolve issues, but to dominate and impose their own expectations."

Iran Enters Talks with U.S. over Nuclear Program

Nevertheless, Iran agreed to talks with the U.S., with Trump setting a deadline for a deal by 60 days from April 12, when the talks began. As talks continued over the next several weeks, participants called them "constructive." On May 27, Trump claimed the talks were close to a deal, with strong inspections. An Iranian spokesman was less hopeful, calling Trump's apparent desire to control Iran's nuclear program "a fantasy." At the same time, Israel was threatening a "pre-emptive" attack on Iran.

The 60-day deadline passed on June 12, with further talks still scheduled. Israel attacked on the 61st day, and further talks were canceled.

In 2015, the Iran nuclear issue had been effectively settled under the auspices of the Obama administration, which negotiated a five-power agreement with Iran. Under the agreement, the Joint Comprehensive Plan of

Action, Iran reduced its uranium enrichment program from more than 7,500 kilograms enriched uranium (below bomb-grade) to almost zero. This agreement held for five years, even after the Trump administration pulled out of it in 2018. According to the Council on Foreign Relations, Iran has increased its uranium enrichment program, including a small quantity of bomb-grade material, but overall production remains about one-third less than in 2015.

Besides pulling the U.S. out of the Joint Comprehensive Plan of Action, Trump had further chilled U.S.-Iran relations by assassinating Iranian General Qasem Soleimani with an American drone strike in Baghdad on January 3, 2020.

Trump Called for Iran's 'Unconditional Surrender'

On June 18, 2025, Trump called for Iran's "unconditional surrender" even though the U.S. was not at war with Iran. He also called for talks. He did not call for a ceasefire between Iran and Israel. But he continued to forestall U.S. participation in the war, which was widely opposed in the U.S., even among his supporters. He played word games about what he might or might not do in two weeks.

The Israeli war with Iran continued unchecked. Even if this was mostly political theatre, the casualties in Iran and Israel were all real.

Shortly after midnight on June 22, Trump initiated Operation Midnight Hammer, in which U.S. B-2 bombers flew from Missouri to bomb three nuclear installations in Iran. In his address to the nation later that night, Trump said: "Tonight, I can report to the world that the strikes were a spectacular military success. Iran's key nuclear enrichment facilities have been completely and totally obliterated. Iran, the bully of the Middle East, must now make peace. If they do not, future attacks will be far greater and a lot easier."

This was mostly posturing. He had no way of knowing what effect the bombing had had, if any. His action stirred controversy, objection, and concern about U.S. involvement in yet another Middle East war. All that was certain – and mostly left unsaid – was that the raid had been an act of aggressive war, a violation of international law, and a war crime.

On June 23, Trump announced a ceasefire, posting on Truth Social: CONGRATULATIONS TO EVERYONE! It has been fully agreed by and between Israel and Iran that there will be a Complete and Total CEASEFIRE... in approximately 6 hours from now, when Israel and Iran have wound down and completed their in-progress, final missions!

... On the assumption that everything works as it should, which it will, I would like to congratulate both Countries, Israel and Iran, on having the Stamina, Courage, and Intelligence to end, what should be called, "THE 12 DAY WAR."

The final missile exchanges between Israel and Iran carried on longer than Trump had anticipated. On his way to the NATO summit, Trump told reporters: "We basically have two countries that have been fighting so long and so hard that they don't know what the fuck they're doing."

Trump got into a snit over a Defense Intelligence Agency assessment that the bombing of the Iranian nuclear facilities may have done only limited damage, setting the program back by just a few months. The Pentagon later suggested the setback might be years. Then the IAEA (International Atomic Energy Agency) said no, more like months, and Iran said it would limit cooperation with the IAEA. Nobody knew for sure what had been accomplished. But the ceasefire was holding. And the Israelis continued their Gaza genocide.

On July 1, Trump announced that Israel had accepted terms for a 60-day ceasefire in Gaza. Israel disagreed. Israel said it will only agree to end the war if Hamas surrenders, disarms. and exiles itself. Hamas said it's willing to free the remaining 50 hostages in exchange for a complete Israeli withdrawal from Gaza and an end to the war. Both sides agreed to take part in the talks Trump suggested.

Robert Reich Finds Hope in This Moment

Robert Reich, 78, former labor secretary under President Clinton and professor of public policy at UC Berkeley, posted philosophically on Substack on May 18:

We had to come to this point. We couldn't go on as we were,

even under Democratic presidents. For 40 years, a narrow economic elite has been siphoning ever more wealth and power for themselves.

I'm old enough to remember when CEOs took home 20 times the pay of their workers, not 300 times. When members of Congress acted in the interests of their constituents rather than be bribed by campaign donations to do the bidding of big corporations and the super-wealthy. When our biggest domestic challenges were civil rights, women's rights, and gay rights – not the very survival of democracy and the rule of law.

But starting with Reagan, America went off the rails. Deregulation, privatization, free trade, wild gambling by Wall Street, union-busting, record levels of inequality, near-stagnant wages for most, staggering wealth for a few, big money taking over our politics. Stock buybacks and the well-being of investors became more important than good jobs with good wages. Corporate profits are more important than the common good.

Democratic presidents were better than Republican, to be sure, but the underlying rot continued to worsen. It was undermining the foundations of America. We couldn't go on as we were.

The Trump regime has harmed many innocent people. Its lawless cruelty is sickening – as is the cowardice of so many CEOs, Wall Street bankers, law firms, university presidents, publishers, social media titans, Republican politicians, some Democratic politicians, and other so-called "leaders" who are staying mum or obeying in advance or sucking up to Trump.

There will be a reckoning. As bad as this "fucking nightmare" gets, it will awaken the sleeping giant of America to what has happened to this country – and what we must do to get it back on the track toward social justice, democracy, and widespread prosperity. That's what I believe. That's my faith, even as we slide into deepening darkness.

Appendix

The following is an excerpt from *Trump 2.0 Survival Guide: A Snarky Weekly Planner for Fighting Back and Staying Sane While the Country Goes Bananas* by Diantha Boardman (available from **DianthaDesigns** on **etsy.com**):

12 Rules for Surviving Trump 2.0

1. Stay Human

We will not let the madness strip us of our empathy. Kindness isn't weakness; it's rebellion.

2. Protect Your Energy

No is a complete sentence. If it drains you, stresses you, or feels like an emotional leech, set a boundary and stick to it. You're no good to the fight if you're running on fumes.

3. Be Informed, Not Overwhelmed

Keep up with the news, but don't let it swallow you whole. One doomscroll session per day, max. If you're obsessing over headlines at 2 AM, you're not saving the world —you're just losing sleep.

4. Pick Your Battles

You can't fight every fight, and that's okay. Focus on one cause at a time and go all in. The rest? Trust someone else to carry that torch.

5. Invest In Community

No one survives alone. Build your tribe, whether it's your neighbors, on-line friends, or the crew at your favorite coffee shop. Resistance thrives in connection.

6. Channel Your Anger

Anger isn't bad; it's fuel. Write letters. Join protests. Donate to causes. Turn your rage into action, and suddenly, it's not just anger—it's power.

7. Laugh, Dammit

You're allowed to find joy. Humor is not just a coping mechanism; it's a survival skill. Watch cat videos. Make bad jokes. Share funny memes. Laugh until your ribs hurt.

8. Stock the Essentials

And by "essentials," I mean more than canned beans. Have a stash of good snacks, your favorite tea (or your drink of choice), cozy socks, a kick-ass playlist, guilty-pleasure shows, art supplies, or whatever else you're into. Have things on hand that can help you unwind and feel good at the end of a long day without putting you at risk of developing a substance use issue.

9. Use Your Voice

Call your representatives. Sign petitions. Post videos. Write op-eds. You have more power than you think - use it.

10. Rest Without Guilt

Rest isn't laziness; it's a strategic necessity. Sleep in. Take a break. Take a 3-day weekend. Unplug when you need to. Even Beyoncé takes naps sometimes; you can too.

11. Celebrate Your Wins, Big or Small

Did you show up for something important today? Celebrate. Did you just make it through a tough week? Celebrate. Did you resist the urge to scream at your racist relative during dinner? Celebrate. Small victories are still victories, and now more than ever, it's important to acknowledge them.

12. Refuse to Quit

The most rebellious thing you can do in a world that wants you to feel powerless is to refuse to give up. Even on the hard days, even when you're tired. Keep going. Keep fighting. No matter what.

Acknowledgments

First and foremost, thanks to my publisher and friend for almost 70 years, Ed Shiller. In early 2025, he suggested it might be a good idea to have a book about Trump's threat to America. He offered endless support as this eccentric tome emerged and helped shape its final, open-ended form.

Thanks also to Rosemary Shiller for all her time and energy formatting the book and making sure my text was polished, exhibiting only those quirks that I insisted on.

Thanks to the artist Marianne Clemons for the caricature of me at a faculty meeting so many years ago.

Thanks to my daughter Diantha for her support and for permission to excerpt her practical workbook, *Trump 2.0 Survival Guide*.

Thanks to my companion Deirdre Larson for her comfort and support, and for being a willing sounding board.

Alas, one acknowledgement can't be made, because we weren't able to turn *Circling the Drain* into an effective flotation device.

About the Author

Like anyone else paying the least bit of attention, William Boardman has seen something like our current crisis coming for half a century or more, and he can document it (coming up). In 1979, he created The Panther Program on Vermont Public Radio (and nationally syndicated briefly), a program of comedy and comment in songs and sketches. During the Iranian hostage crisis, the program reminded listeners that the Iranians had a point, given that in 1953 the U.S. had imposed one of the world's nastiest dictatorships on them. In 1981, when President Reagan was shot, the program joked that "doctors who treated Reagan revealed that the bullet had actually hit Reagan's heart, but was unable to penetrate."

As Reagan's hardheartedness became increasingly apparent, the program created the U.S. Bureau of Cruelty as a comedic vehicle for where he was taking the country. The bureau evolved in the Department of Cruelty as things grew progressively worse. Over the decades, official American cruelty became institutionalized, bipartisan, profitable for a few, and mystifyingly without much traction when its victims went to the polls. Now we're in Trump 2.0, a Government of Cruelty. We didn't vote for this. Well, yes we did, again and again (with a little help from the Supreme Court). And it's still possible for it to get worse.

William Boardman grew up in Manhattan; went to Yale; wrote for *The Week That Was*, *Captain Kangaroo*, and *Treasure Isle*; moved to Vermont in 1971, where he was a reporter and did the VPR gig (until blacklisted); then was a non-lawyer judge for 20 years. For 10 years, he wrote more warnings of American decline for Reader Supported News, the best of which were collected in his 2019 book *EXCEPTIONAL: American Exceptionalism Takes Its Toll*, published by Yorkland Publishing. None of it has made any noticeable difference; *vox clamantis in deserto*.

www.ingramcontent.com/pod-product-compliance
Lightning Source LLC
Chambersburg PA
CBHW051711020426
42333CB00014B/943